FOR REFERENCE ONLY
Do Not Remove From This Room

THE GROLIER LIBRARY
OF
NORTH AMERICAN
BIOGRAPHIES

PRODUCED BY THE PHILIP LIEF GROUP, INC.

MANAGING EDITOR
Julia Banks

EDITORS
Vida Petronis

Laura-Ann Robb

Gary Sunshine

EDITORIAL STAFF
Tanya Agathocleous

Kelli Daley

Jennifer Hirshlag

Anne Pierce

Rosemary Pitkin

Naomi Starr

WRITTEN AND RESEARCHED BY:
Kevin Osborn

Diana L. Ajjan

Gregory Galloway

Robert Hernandez

Ann Keene

Victoria Sherrow

Liz Sonneborn

Rebecca Stefoff

Karen Watts

THE GROLIER LIBRARY
OF
NORTH AMERICAN
BIOGRAPHIES

Activists

VOLUME 1

GROLIER EDUCATIONAL CORPORATION
Sherman Turnpike, Danbury, Connecticut 06816

Published 1994 by
Grolier Educational Corporation
Danbury, Connecticut 06816

Published by arrangement with
The Philip Lief Group, Inc.
6 West 20th Street
New York, New York 10011

The publisher gratefully acknowledges permission from the following sources to reproduce
photographs: page 91, courtesy of University of Michigan; page 225, courtesy of Tamiment
Institute Library; page 39, Ronald Reagan Library; pages 44, 86, 115, 133, 208, 254, copyright
Washington Post, reprinted by permission of D.C. Public Library. All other photos courtesy of
the Library of Congress and the National Archives.

ISBN 0-7172-7246-X
Library of Congress Catalog Number: 93-079222
Cataloging information to be obtained directly from Grolier Educational Corporation.
First Edition
Printed in the United States of America

Contents

Introduction

Ralph Waldo Emerson (1803–1882), American essayist, poet, and philosopher, wrote, "There is properly no history; only biography." THE GROLIER LIBRARY OF NORTH AMERICAN BIOGRAPHIES embodies this spirited idea by presenting, in ten volumes, the lives of hundreds of our continent's most enterprising and talented individuals. Students can choose among the volumes to read about the experiences and achievements of people as diverse as the Brooklyn-born Supreme Court Justice Ruth Bader Ginsberg; astronomer Carl Sagan, who has brought the immensity of the universe to readers of all ages through his books and television series; African American writer, singer, actor, and civil rights activist Maya Angelou, who recited a poem about our nation's multicultural diverseness at President Clinton's inauguration; Canada's first woman Prime Minister Kim Campbell; South Dakota-born Native American Russell Means, who led the Native American protest at Wounded Knee and advocated for a peaceful settlement with the government; and popular filmmaker Spike Lee, whose controversial movies raise questions about complex urban problems and concerns.

Creating a mosaic that spans time and geography while overcoming the boundaries of gender, race, and class, THE GROLIER LIBRARY OF NORTH AMERICAN BIOGRAPHIES shows students the rich heritage of our North American culture. It also shows them just how valuable the contribution of one individual can be to family, community, and nation. American anthropologist Margaret Mead (1901–1978) said it this way, "If we are to achieve a richer culture, rich in contrasting values, we must recognize the whole gamut of human potentialities, and so weave a less arbitrary social fabric, one in which each diverse human gift will find a fitting place."

Each biographical entry describes how a subject came to be a person of historical significance—detailing how that person grew up and emphasizing important childhood events and inspirational figures, as well as deeply held values and beliefs. His or her note-worthy discoveries, inventions, and achievements are placed in a historical context to show their influence within that period in time. The impact of each subject's contribution is then explained, giving students a sense of how these North Americans have affected their lives, directly or indirectly.

Many of the challenges met by the women and men chronicled in the NORTH AMERICAN BIOGRAPHIES can inspire young readers today. As students relate to these exceptional individuals, they can begin to discover that even the most far-reaching goals and professions can be realized in their own lifetimes:

Volume 1: Activists   Inspirational and devoted advocates of social and political change;

Volume 2: Athletes   Skilled players of a variety of sports from basketball and boxing to soccer and table tennis;

Volume 3: Entrepreneurs & Inventors   Enterprising business leaders, engineers, and pioneers of discovery;

Volume 4: Explorers   Bold prospectors of land, sea, air, and space;

Volume 5: Performance Artists   Talented actors, dancers, comedians, musicians, radio, television, and filmmakers;

Volume 6: Political and Military Leaders   Influential government leaders, including presidents, judges, governors, generals, mayors, senators, and congressional representatives;

Volume 7: Scholars and Educators   Innovative thinkers of philosophy, mathematics, literature, history, economy, and the law;

Volume 8: Scientists   Tenacious discoverers and doctors exploring the social and physical sciences;

Volume 9: Visual Artists   Creative painters, photographers, sculptors, architects, and filmmakers;

Volume 10: Writers   Stirring voices of poets, prose writers, playwrights, and journalists.

The ten-volume GROLIER LIBRARY OF NORTH AMERICAN BIO-GRAPHIES reveals the range and power of our rich cultural heritage, giving students a greater knowledge of the remarkable achievements and successes of our continent's past and present, while encouraging their dreams and aspirations for its future.

Abbott, Grace

(1878–1939)

SOCIAL WORKER, GOVERNMENT OFFICIAL

Grace Abbott dedicated her life to protecting the rights of immigrants and children. Abbott became interested in public service through her father, the first lieutenant governor of Nebraska. She learned to fight for her ideals from her mother, who had participated in the movement to abolish slavery and in the struggle of American women to win the right to vote. Abbott spent her early adulthood as a high school teacher in her home town of Grand Island, Nebraska. In 1907, she moved to Chicago, where she achieved a graduate degree in political science. While there, she became a resident of Hull House, the pioneering **settlement house** founded by Jane Addams. In settlement houses, social workers, educators, lawyers, and artists would settle among the poor and attempt to improve living and working conditions, thereby bringing social reform to a neighborhood level.

While living at Hull House, Abbott in 1908 became the first director of the Immigrants' Protective League. Abbott wrote a weekly newspaper column, focusing the attention of the press and public on the plight of immigrants. Phony employment agencies, savings banks, travel agents, and many others preyed upon newcomers to the United States. Abbott also pushed for the passage of new laws protecting immigrants and punishing those who took advantage of them. In 1917, a series of articles Abbott had written on the abuse of immigrants was published as a book: *The Immigrant and the Community.*

That same year, Julia Lathrop asked Abbott to join the staff of the federal Children's Bureau. Abbott's job was to administer newly passed child labor laws. After those laws were declared unconstitutional in 1918, Abbott tried to win popular support for adding a child-labor amendment to the U.S. Constitution. In 1921, President Warren G. Harding asked Abbott to succeed Lathrop as head of the Children's Bureau, a position she would hold until 1934. Under Abbott's direction, the bureau administered grants to states to help them develop programs to advance the health care offered to mothers and infants. These grants led to the opening of more than three thousand child health clinics and prenatal care centers in forty-five of the forty-eight states. After leaving the Children's Bureau, Abbott helped write the laws on child welfare contained in the Social Security Act as a member of President Franklin D. Roosevelt's Council on Economic Security. *See* ADDAMS, JANE; LATHROP, JULIA

Abernathy, Ralph

(1926–1990)

CIVIL RIGHTS MOVEMENT LEADER

You can kill the dreamer but you cannot kill the dream.

—Abernathy, *The New York Times* (18 April 1990)

Abernathy meets with members of Congress at the Capitol.

With these words, Ralph David Abernathy vowed to carry on the work of his friend, slain civil-rights leader Martin Luther King Jr. A Baptist minister, Abernathy in 1968 took over the leadership of the **civil rights movement**: the struggle to win equality for the nation's African Americans and other racial minorities.

The grandson of a slave, Ralph Abernathy was the tenth of twelve children born on his parents' farm in Linden, Alabama. His parents were devout Christians, an influence that would later lead to his choice of a career in the ministry. Young Ralph's life was centered around his church, his family, and his studies. "All that we knew was home, church, and school," he once told an interviewer.

After serving briefly in the Army near the end of World War II, Abernathy studied for both the ministry and mathematics. Ordained as a Baptist minister in 1948, he received a degree in mathematics from Alabama College two years later. While studying at Atlanta University for a graduate degree in sociology (the study of society and its institutions), Abernathy attended the Ebenezer Baptist Church. There, he met the minister's son, Martin Luther King Jr. The two quickly became friends. After receiving his degree in 1951, Abernathy became pastor of a Baptist church in Montgomery, Alabama. Three years later, King became pastor of another Baptist church in the city. The two civil rights leaders would work closely together until King's death in 1968.

Abernathy and King achieved their first victory in the struggle for justice in Montgomery from 1955 to 1956. In 1955, Rosa Parks, an African American, refused to give up her seat on a bus to a white person. She objected to the policy of **segregation** (unequal treatment of people due to race or color) on the city's buses. After Parks was arrested for her protest, Abernathy suggested a citywide bus **boycott**, a refusal by African Americans to ride on the city buses. Abernathy hoped that if the bus companies lost enough riders and enough money, they would have to change their policy. King and Abernathy formed the Montgomery Improvement Association to run the bus boycott. For more than a year, thousands of African Americans walked miles to and from work every day. In 1956, the boycotters achieved their goal. A court order forced the bus companies to stop practicing segregation.

Inspired by their success in Montgomery, King and Abernathy decided to use the same tactics throughout the South. The following year, King and Abernathy met with other African American leaders and created a group called the Southern Christian Leadership Conference (SCLC), which would lead the peaceful struggle for equal rights. King was elected the SCLC's president and Abernathy its secretary-treasurer.

The struggle of African Americans for equal rights angered many whites, and that anger sometimes turned violent. Despite a bomb attack that destroyed the church building, Abernathy did not waver in the fight for equal rights. The SCLC vowed to use all peaceful means to end segregation. Abernathy and King led protest marches, they staged sit-ins, and organized campaigns to register African-American voters in the South. Many of their protests involved **civil disobedience**, refusing to obey laws they regarded as unjust. Abernathy and King were jailed together seventeen times for their acts of civil disobedience. Many times, the protesters were beaten by police or attacked by angry whites. Yet throughout their struggle, Abernathy and King maintained the SCLC's commitment to nonviolence. "Violence is the weapon of the weak," Abernathy insisted, "and nonviolence is the weapon of the strong." Slowly, step by step, their efforts helped end segregation in the South.

In 1968, a sniper in Memphis, Tennessee shot and killed Dr. King. Abernathy quickly showed that the struggle for justice would not die with King. Abernathy and King's widow, Coretta Scott King, led a march supporting Memphis garbage haulers who were striking for better wages—a march King had planned to lead. Abernathy, King's closest friend and ally, was named the new president of the SCLC. Abernathy's first major act was leading the "Poor People's Campaign" in 1968. He led several thousand poor people in a demonstration in Washington, D.C. African Americans, Native Americans, Puerto Ricans, Mexican Americans, and whites came from all over the country. They built plywood shacks in a Washington park to bring poverty to the attention of the nation's lawmakers. They called for more jobs and increased government aid for those who could not find jobs. A month after the protestors began camping out, fifty-thousand supporters joined them for a rally at the Lincoln Memorial. After six weeks, the shacks were torn down and Abernathy was arrested and sentenced to twenty days in jail.

Abernathy did not draw praise in his nine years as leader of the SCLC. Many African Americans regarded him as overly conservative. Others criticized him for failing to inspire African Americans as Dr. King had. Under Abernathy's leadership, the SCLC plunged into debt. Finally, in 1977, the organization forced Abernathy to resign and named Reverend Joseph Lowery as the new president. Abernathy returned to Atlanta, where he ran unsuccessfully for the House of Representatives. He remained a Baptist minister until his death. *See* KING, MARTIN LUTHER, JR.; LOWERY, JOSEPH; PARKS, ROSA

Addams, Jane

(1860–1935)

PIONEER SOCIAL REFORMER

> I gradually became convinced that it would be a good thing to rent a house in a part of the city where many primitive and actual needs are found, in which young women who have been given over too exclusively to study, might restore a balance of activity along traditional lines and learn of life from life itself; where they might try out some of the things they had been taught.

—Addams *Twenty Years at Hull-House,* (1910)

Jane Addams wrote these words in 1910, twenty-one years after bringing her idea to life. Addams founded Hull House, only the second **settlement house** in the United States. The settlement house fulfilled two purposes: It brought much-needed social services directly to the working-class neighborhood surrounding the house, and it gave educated young women an opportunity to put their ideals into practice.

Addams, the youngest of four surviving children, was born in Cedarville, Illinois. Addams' mother died when Jane was only two. Her father impressed young Jane with his honesty and his stand against slavery. A friend of President Abraham Lincoln, John Addams served eight terms as a member of the Illinois State Senate.

In 1877, she began studying at the nearby Rockford Female Seminary, where her sisters had gone before her. Addams longed to become a college graduate, a rare accomplishment for women in her era, yet Rockford did not offer college degrees. As a result of her efforts, however, the school started a degree program. Addams was a member of the first graduating class. A popular student leader, Addams admired the idealism of her fellow students. After graduating at the head of her class in 1881, Addams studied medicine at the Women's Medical College of Pennsylvania for a year. However, illness forced her to drop out of medical school.

A trip to Europe from 1883 to 1885 first awakened Addams to the hardships of the poor who live in city slums. Returning to the United States, She worked among poor African Americans in Baltimore, Maryland for two years. A second trip to Europe from 1887 to 1888 provided Addams with the seed for Hull House. In London, she visited Toynbee Hall, founded four years earlier in the city's slums. Young graduates of Oxford University lived in the slum settlement, working to lessen some of the miseries brought on by factory work. This inspired Addams to create a similar settlement in Chicago.

In 1889, Addams and her friend Ellen Gate Starr moved into an abandoned mansion in Chicago called Hull House. They immediately invited their neighbors—mostly working-class Greek, Italian, Russian, German, Sicilian, and other immigrants—to visit them often and take advantage of the services they provided. The pioneering settlement house offered English language classes, health-care advice, and cultural activities. Addams also invited other young women to live at Hull House and volunteer their services to the community. Through

Hull House, Addams offered young women a chance to learn by doing: to recognize the needs of the community and then respond to those needs. The opportunity to put their schooling and skills to good use attracted such talented women as Julia Lathrop and Grace Abbott. Artists, lawyers, teachers, social workers, and business people also volunteered at Hull House.

Addams enriched the lives of thousands of the neighborhood's poor immigrants through Hull House, which would remain her home for the rest of her life. By 1893, Hull House had become the community's social, medical, and cultural center. Every week, two thousand people visited and received services. The variety and quality of services made Hull House a model for settlement houses throughout the nation.

In 1895, Addams and her staff published *Hull-House Maps and Papers*. The book examined slum housing, sweatshop factories, child labor, and other conditions in their community. The authors recognized that it would take more than social clubs and community services to correct the problems of the poor. Hull House began to serve as the voice of the community, appealing to the government to meet its needs. In 1893, Addams and her staff helped win passage of an Illinois law to monitor working conditions in the state's factories. By the end of the century, Hull House had also worked to obtain laws limiting child labor, requiring children to attend school, and establishing an eight-hour working day for women. Hull House also called for reforms in slum housing and welfare and the recognition of labor unions. Addams also worked for the creation of the nation's first juvenile court in Chicago.

In the first two decades of the twentieth century, Addams devoted herself not only to her settlement work, but also to the causes of world peace and to the women's **suffrage movement**: the right to vote. In *Newer Ideals of Peace*, published in 1907, Addams suggested that the sense of community that Hull House had helped build on a small scale might serve as a model for world peace. Just as the various immigrants in her community had learned to live together, so might the nations of the world coexist peacefully. During the same year, she joined in the drive to win the vote for women in the city of Chicago. Addams became the first woman elected president of the National Conference of Charities and Correction—the nation's leading group of social workers—in 1909. The following year, she published the most famous of her twelve books, *Twenty Years at Hull-House*, which sold eighty-thousand copies during her lifetime. From 1911 to 1935, Addams served as the first president of the National Federation of Settlements. She was also a vice president of the National American Woman Suffrage Association from 1911 to 1914. Her work for women's suffrage grew out of her desire for social reform and greater social justice. Addams believed that if women had the power to vote, they could help correct the ills of society.

As World War I raged in Europe, Addams was elected chair of the Woman's Peace Party in 1915. She was also appointed president of the International Congress of Women, which urged the warring nations to allow neutral countries to negotiate a peaceful end to the conflict. When the U.S. entered the war, Addams worked in the government's Food Administration from 1917 to 1918. She urged the nation's people to increase food production in order to provide aid to the victims of the war. After the war ended, Addams became the first president of the Women's International League for Peace and Freedom, holding the post from 1919 until her death in 1935.

During the war and its aftermath, many Americans became intolerant of radical ideas. Criticizing the government or the society bordered on treason in the eyes of many. The attempts to place limits on "allowable" speech and thought disturbed Addams. In 1920, she helped found the American Civil Liberties Union, an organization dedicated to defending freedom of expression. In recognition of a lifetime of work for social justice and world peace, Addams received the Nobel Peace Prize in 1931. In an act that typified her wholehearted, unselfish commitment to the causes of peace and justice, Addams donated the $16,000 prize to the Women's International League for Peace and Freedom. *See* ABBOTT, GRACE; LATHROP, JULIA

Alinsky, Saul David

(1909–1972)

ACTIVIST FOR IMPROVED WORKING CONDITIONS,
BETTER HOUSING, AND EQUAL EDUCATION

Saul David Alinsky, who called himself a "professional radical," organized poor people, blue-collar workers, and minorities to fight for improved living and working conditions. Alinsky, the son of Russian–Jewish immigrants, grew up in the slums of Chicago. After obtaining a degree in archeology, Alinsky worked with children charged with crimes at Chicago's Institute for Juvenile Research in 1931. In the 1930s, Alinsky began working as an organizer for the Congress of Industrial Organizations, the nation's leading labor group. In 1938, he joined Chicago's Back of the Yards movement, a group of mostly Irish-American laborers in an impoverished neighborhood located behind the city's meat-packing yards. Alinsky and the movement used picketing, rent strikes, sit-down strikes, and **boycotts** to pressure landlords, meat packers, local businesses, and the city government to provide better jobs and improvements in housing.

Alinsky's success at the local grass-roots level in Chicago inspired him to introduce his organizing skills to other neighborhoods. Alinsky founded the Industrial Areas Foundation (IAF) in 1939. The IAF trained its staff to organize groups on a local level throughout the country. Alinsky believed that the people in poor communities needed to band together to create a force powerful enough to compete with the established power centers of big business and the government. His goal was to create communities powerful enough to secure for themselves the right to decent housing, jobs, and equality in education. Alinsky's foundation strictly observed two conditions: It would only send organizers to the communities that asked for IAF's help, and the professional organizers would leave the management of the movement to local leaders after two to three years.

Despite frequent jailings, Alinsky persisted in his efforts to organize local protest movements for more than three decades. In the 1940s and 1950s, Alinsky organized local movements primarily among poor communities and blue-collar workers. In the 1960s, however, Alinsky turned his attention to minority communities. Alinsky organized in African-American ghettos in the Northeast and Midwest, in Mexican-American slums in the Southwest, and on Indian reservations in Canada. Yet the aim of his work remained the same as it had always been: motivating people to demand improved working conditions, better housing, and equal education.

Andrews, Fannie Fern Phillips

(1867–1950)

EDUCATIONAL REFORMER

Fannie Fern Phillips Andrews promoted peace through the education of the nation's children. After teaching children in her home town of Lynn, Massachusetts for six years, Andrews obtained a degree in education and psychology from Radcliffe College in 1902. Although she participated in many of Boston's social reform movements—including the struggle to secure women's right to vote—she devoted most of her energies toward educational reform. In 1907, she helped create the Boston Home and School Association, which she presided over from 1914 to 1918. Andrews founded the American School Peace League, in 1908, which established branches in forty states by 1915. The league urged the teaching of international justice in American schools as a means of promoting peace. Andrews served as the league's most prominent lecturer, writer, organizer, and spokesperson. She also helped create the educational materials introduced in classrooms across the country. These materials included descriptions of peace work, the words of diplomats and soldiers who deplored war, and poetry that spoke to the ideal of international kinship. Andrews also advocated the creation of an international bureau of education to foster this same ideal.

During World War I, Andrews joined the League to Enforce Peace and the Central Organization for Durable Peace. As a member of these organizations, she urged an end to the war and the establishment of an agency that would bring the world's nations together to promote peace and mutual cooperation. In 1918, President Woodrow Wilson chose Andrews to attend the Paris Peace Conference, where she actively campaigned for the creation of the League of Nations. After obtaining a doctorate in international law and diplomacy from Radcliffe in 1923, Andrews became a renowned scholar in international relations, one of very few women prominent in that field. In 1934 and 1936, President Franklin D. Roosevelt chose Andrews as a delegate at meetings of the agency she had promoted for almost twenty years: the new International Bureau of Education.

Anthony, Susan B.

(1820–1906)

ACTIVIST FOR WOMEN'S
SUFFRAGE

> It was we, the people, not we, the white male citizens, nor yet we, the male citizens, but we, the whole people, who formed this Union.
>
> —Anthony, from a speech (1873)

Susan Brownwell Anthony quoted the first words of the United States Constitution to drive home the point that women deserved an equal voice in the affairs of the nation. A **feminist**, Anthony supported equal rights for women in marriage and in the workplace. But she concentrated most of her activist efforts on achieving the single goal of the women's **suffrage movement**: the right to vote.

Born in Adams, Massachusetts, Susan Anthony was reared according to her father's Quaker faith. Quaker prayer meetings helped instill in Susan a belief in the equality of men and women. Both sexes speak as equals before God in gatherings of "Friends." In her teens, Susan began teaching at the school her father ran for his children and the young workers in his cotton mill, then at a local school, and finally at a Quaker girls' school in New Rochelle, New York. While heading a girls' school in upstate New York from 1846 to 1849, Anthony left behind the Quaker church. She abandoned the Quakers' plain style of dress and formal patterns of speech. To protest the increasing opposition to the antislavery movement among some Quakers, Anthony began attending the Unitarian church.

Returning to the family farm in Rochester, New York in 1849, Anthony became active in the **temperance movement,** which encouraged a ban on liquor. As president of the local Daughters of Temperance, she gave her first public speech that year. In 1851, Amelia Bloomer, a fellow temperance worker, introduced Anthony to Elizabeth Cady Stanton. Anthony and Stanton quickly became friends and joined in the cause of women's rights. In 1852, the Sons of Temperance refused to allow Anthony to speak at one of its meetings. Outraged, Anthony and Stanton founded the Woman's State Temperance Society. After the World's Temperance Convention in New York City denied women the right to speak, Anthony helped organize the "Whole World's Temperance Convention."

Anthony's experience in the temperance movement made her an ardent feminist. After attending her first women's rights convention in 1852, she organized conventions throughout New York state for the rest of the decade. Beginning in 1854, Anthony and Stanton campaigned for a state law (passed in 1860) that gave married women control over their own earnings.

Anthony also became active in the antislavery movement. From 1856 to 1861, she organized statewide lecture tours and often spoke on behalf of the American Anti-Slavery Society. Anthony wanted more than simply to prevent the expansion of slavery into new states. During the presidential campaign of 1860, she called for the immediate freeing of all slaves. This stand prompted violent attacks by proslavery mobs the following year. With Stanton, Anthony founded the Women's Loyal National League in 1863. Anthony gathered hundreds of thousands of signatures on petitions to free the slaves.

When the Civil War ended in 1865, Anthony returned to the cause of women's rights. Her efforts soon focused on the single issue of suffrage. In 1866, she helped form the American Equal Rights Association to promote suffrage for both women and African Americans. Although she supported the rights of African Americans, Anthony felt that because women were better educated, they deserved the right to vote first. She was also concerned that male African-American voters might only increase the numbers of voters opposed to women's suffrage. Anthony organized petitions to Congress for national women's suffrage and unsuccessfully tried to win support for women's suffrage in both Kansas and New York.

From 1868 to 1870, Anthony was publisher of *The Revolution*, a radical newspaper. She used the paper to speak out against the Fourteenth and Fifteenth Amendments to the U.S. Constitution, which ignored women in giving citizenship rights and the vote to African-American men. Anthony's paper also called for equal pay for men and women for equal work and an equal chance for women to enter any occupation. With Stanton and the paper's typesetter, Augusta Lewis (later Troup) Anthony founded the Working Women's Association. The association supported the creation of unions to seek higher wages and shorter hours for working women.

In 1869, Anthony organized the first women's suffrage convention since the Civil War. When the American Equal Rights Association supported the Fifteenth Amendment later that year, Anthony and Stanton founded the National Woman Suffrage Association (NWSA). Stanton served as president, while Anthony sat on the executive committee. Anthony would serve as NWSA's chief lecturer and organizer for the rest of her life. She campaigned for women's suffrage in frontier towns throughout the far West in 1871. Anthony led a small group of women who voted in the 1872 presidential election in Rochester. Anthony contended that the Constitution did not prohibit women from voting. A year later, she was found guilty of voting illegally and fined $100. When Anthony refused to pay the fine, however, no further action was taken. Anthony tried to win support for state suffrage laws in both Michigan and Colorado in the 1870s. Unlike the rival American Woman Suffrage Association (AWSA), however, NWSA focused on the issue of national women's suffrage. In 1878, NWSA proposed women's suffrage as the Sixteenth Amendment to the Constitution. Two years later, Anthony gave up her lecture tours and settled for over a decade in Washington, D.C., where she urged members of Congress to enact the proposed amendment. Anthony, Stanton, and Matilda Joslyn Gage worked together on the three-volume *History of Woman Suffrage* from 1881 to 1886. Anthony and Stanton also organized the first meeting of an international committee for women's rights in 1888. At this meeting, delegates from fifty-three American groups and forty-nine foreign countries created the International Council of Women.

When NWSA and AWSA merged to form the National American Woman Suffrage Association (NAWSA) in 1890, Anthony was named vice president at large. Two years later, she was elected president of NAWSA. Throughout the decade, Anthony campaigned ceaselessly for women's suffrage on both national and state levels. Her efforts helped win the support of the American Federation of Labor, a network of skilled workers' unions, for the proposed women's suffrage amendment in 1899. After resigning from the NAWSA presidency in 1900, Anthony continued to work for women's rights. That year, she helped pressure the University of Rochester to admit female students. Attending the International Council of Women meeting in Berlin, Germany in 1904, Anthony founded the International Woman Suffrage Alliance. In appreciation of the thirty-five years she had worked for the cause, the group chose Anthony as its honorary president. *See* BLOOMER, AMELIA; STANTON, ELIZABETH CADY; TROUP, AUGUSTA

Baker, Sara Josephine

(1873–1945)

PUBLIC HEALTH ADMINISTRATOR, CHILD HEALTH REFORMER

Dr. Sara Josephine Baker saved the lives of more than ten-thousand babies in New York and set an example that allowed others to save hundreds of thousands more. Baker decided to become a doctor at age sixteen, when both her father and brother died. Baker hoped to support her family. In 1898, Baker received her medical degree from the Women's Medical College of the New York Infirmary for Women and Children. While serving as an intern at the New England Hospital for Women and Children in Boston, Baker worked part-time in a slum clinic, treating the city's poor.

As a female doctor in private practice in New York, Baker did not make as much money as she had hoped. So in 1901, she accepted a part-time appointment as a medical inspector for the city health department. In 1907, Baker was appointed assistant to the city health commissioner. Baker instituted a policy of sending sick children home from school to prevent them from infecting other children. She also gained a little fame by helping to track down "Typhoid Mary" (Mary Mallon), a restaurant worker who unwittingly infected thousands of customers with typhoid fever.

Baker began devoting her energies to reducing the death rate of city infants—which climbed to 1,500 a week during the summer months. She introduced the practice of making preventive care an essential part of public health policy. She emphasized keeping healthy babies healthy, rather than waiting for them to get sick before providing medical care. In 1908, Baker led a team of thirty trained nurses who taught the basics of child care to residents of an Italian immigrant slum where the infant death rate was high. Baker's nurses instructed mothers in proper ventilation and clothing, frequent bathing, and the health benefits provided by breastfeeding. As a result, the infant death rate dropped 1,200 in a single year.

Baker's success led to her appointment as first director of the health department's Division of Child Hygiene. This division was the first government-sponsored agency in the world intended to improve the health of children. Baker pioneered public health education: teaching non-professionals about health and hygiene. She established "baby health stations" that offered advice, medical referrals, tests for diseases, and pure milk throughout the city. She introduced hygiene into New York's classrooms. Baker trained and licensed midwives, non-professional women who help deliver babies. She lowered the death rate of orphans by removing them from hospitals and placing them with loving foster mothers. Baker also established "Little Mothers' Leagues" to train the daughters of working mothers in the proper care of younger siblings.

In 1909, Baker helped found the American Child Hygiene Association, which she presided over from 1917 to 1918. She also served as the first president of the Babies Welfare Association (later called the Children's Welfare Federation of New York) from 1911 to 1914, and as the chair of its executive committee from 1914 to 1917. In 1916, Baker began offering annual lectures on child hygiene at the New York University-Bellevue Hospital Medical School and she also enrolled in the university's new School of Public Health. A year later, she became the first woman to earn a doctorate in public health.

By the time Baker retired from the Bureau of Child Hygiene in 1923, the death rate of New York's children was the lowest of any city in the United States or Europe. Baker continued to use her recognition as an authority on children's health to spread the word about proper health care for women and children. She lectured extensively and wrote five books on the health of mothers and children as well as an autobiography published in 1939.

Balch, Emily Greene

(1867–1961)

SOCIAL REFORMER AND ACTIVIST FOR PEACE

Balch, third from bottom left, with other suffragists.

A member of the first graduating class at Bryn Mawr College in 1889, Emily Greene Balch would become a renowned peace advocate and social reformer. Balch chose to study economics as a means of addressing social questions about class differences and poverty. As the first recipient of the Bryn Mawr European Fellowship, Balch studied government programs for the poor in Paris, France from 1890 to 1891. After a year's apprenticeship in the Boston Children's Aid Society, she founded Boston's Denison House, a **settlement house** intended to improve the living conditions of the poor among whom she settled. But Balch ultimately rejected social work. She believed she could have an even greater impact as a teacher, inspiring young women to work toward social justice.

Balch began working at Wellesley College in 1896. Her classes focused on immigration, women's role in the economy, and **socialism**: a system of government that outlaws private property and attempts to distribute goods and services on an equal basis to all individuals. She hoped these courses would arouse her students' sense of social responsibility. While teaching, Balch ardently joined in the struggle of laborers for justice:

advocating minimum wages for women, supporting local labor strikes, and in 1902 co-founding the Boston Women's Trade Union League.

Beginning in 1904, Balch took a two-year leave from Wellesley to study U.S. immigrants from southeastern Europe. She lived in both immigrant communities in the U.S. and in Europe. *Our Slavic Fellow Citizens*, published in 1910, offered a first-hand perspective of immigrants' conditions and denounced racist views of these new immigrants.

Balch accepted a five-year appointment as a full professor at Wellesley and head of the economics and sociology departments in 1913. Two years later, she participated in the International Congress of Women, which met to develop peaceful ways to end World War I. She later met with Scandinavian, Russian, and British leaders and President Woodrow Wilson to convey the congress's message of **pacifism**: the opposition to war or violence as a means of settling disputes. Balch continued to write, speak, and organize protests against the war and the **draft** (the selection of men to become soldiers) even after the U.S. joined in the conflict in 1917. She strongly defended the rights of immigrants and those who refused to fight in the war because they believed it to be morally wrong.

In 1917 Balch helped found the Emergency Peace Federation. Her support for the People's Council of America, which called for a radical new social order, led to the loss of her job in 1918. Fearing her association with socialist causes would damage the college's reputation, Wellesley decided not to extend her contract in 1918. Three years later, Balch joined the Quakers, a sect of pacifist Christians supportive of individualism and cooperation.

Balch became an active member of the newly formed Women's International League for Peace and Freedom (WILPF) in 1919. As its international secretary-treasurer until 1922, Balch helped determine the group's guidelines and its direction: understanding and eliminating the causes of war. In 1922, she resigned her paid position and became WILPF's voluntary leader. She cochaired the league's executive committee from 1929 to 1931, presided over the American section in 1931, and was named honorary international president in 1937. She helped organize sections of WILPF in more than fifty countries and promoted the education of children in the ways of peace. The success of WILPF under Balch's direction showed how effective women could be in working for social reform.

Despite her commitment to pacifism, Balch supported the entry of the United States into World War II in 1941, because she deplored the torture and murder of millions of Jews under Germany's leader Adolf Hitler. Throughout the war, she worked on behalf of Japanese Americans, who were unjustly placed in prison camps to prevent the possibility of spying for the enemy. In recognition of a lifetime of work for peace, Balch in 1946 became only the second American woman to be honored with the Nobel Peace Prize.

Barrett, Kate Harwood Waller

(1857–1925)

FOUNDER OF RESCUE HOMES FOR SINGLE MOTHERS

An unwed mother, carrying her baby, approached Kate Harwood Waller Barrett, wife of an Episcopal reverend in Richmond, Virginia, and asked for her help. Barrett had always considered single mothers "fallen women." Yet through this personal contact, she began to see them as women struggling to survive and she resolved to help them. From 1880 to 1886, she joined her husband and worked among prostitutes in Henderson, Kentucky. In 1892, Barrett earned an M.D. from the Women's Medical College of Georgia. The next year, she opened her first "rescue home" for single mothers in Atlanta, but was forced to move four times by outraged communities who disapproved of the women. Barrett secured a $5,000 contribution from Charles N. Crittenton, who operated several rescue homes for single mothers and former prostitutes in New York and California. Barrett's home thus became the fifth Florence Crittenton home (named after Crittenton's daughter, who had died in 1882).

In 1896, Barrett began working for the National Florence Crittenton Mission, which then operated fifty rescue homes throughout the country. As vice president and general superintendent of the mission, Barrett offered local homes financial support, advice, and encouragement. In time, she stopped trying to convert prostitutes to Christianity and instead focused on the needs of pregnant, single mothers. The mission offered them shelter, maternity care, training in baby care, and job counseling. Barrett and the mission acted in the firm belief that these newborns should remain with their mothers rather than being put up for adoption or placed in an orphans' home. After Crittenton's death in 1909, Barrett continued as general superintendent and also assumed presidency of the mission until her death in 1925.

Barton, Clara

(1821–1912)

HEALTH CARE PIONEER,
ORGANIZER OF THE AMERICAN
RED CROSS

On March 1, 1882, President Chester Arthur finally agreed to charter the American Red Cross. Clara Barton, a nurse and health care pioneer, had for years urged the American government to join the international organization.

Clara's parents were a well-to-do couple who had a sawmill in North Oxford, Massachusetts. Clara was born ten years after the youngest of her older siblings—because of this she felt a bit like an only child growing up. But her older siblings taught her many things: reading and mathematics; how to ride a horse, swim, handle tools and throw a ball. Yet she was also very shy as a girl, and her mother was advised that she needed responsibility and should become a teacher.

Although she was just fifteen, Clara threw herself into the project, and set up a school near her father's mill for the children of the workers. The school was a success, and she was well liked by her young pupils. After several years, in 1851, Clara Barton decided to improve her own education. At the age of 30, she attended a school in Clinton, New York before accepting a teaching position in Bordentown, New Jersey. Once again, she was highly successful in her role. What began as a six pupil school in a run-down old building became, in two years, a six-hundred pupil school housed in a brand new building. The school was so successful that the local school board decided it couldn't be run by a woman, and hired a male principal to supervise her. Barton was so angry that she resigned at once and put teaching behind her for good.

In 1861, the Civil War between the Northern and Southern States began and Clara Barton was involved from the start. When Northern soldiers arrived in Washington wounded, bleeding and without their baggage, Barton placed an advertisement in a local newspaper asking for contributions of supplies and clothing. She used her own small rooms to house what gifts she received. After the battle of Bull Run, Washington was once again flooded with wounded soldiers. Barton again placed an ad asking for bandages, medicine, food and tobacco. As donations came pouring in, she rented a warehouse to store them. But this time, she wanted to deliver the supplies to the battlefield personally. The War Department objected; at that time, it was unheard of for a woman to visit the battlefield. But Barton wouldn't give up, and finally the War Department agreed to give her a general pass, extending to any battle situation. Eventually, she was even given carts and teams of mules which she used to distribute the bandages and medicine to the sick and wounded soldiers.

When she arrived at the front, she distributed the wagon

loads of supplies she had brought with her. She arranged for bread, soup and coffee to be served to the hungry soldiers.

Then she turned to nursing the sick. Concerned that the men would lose too much blood if they were transported from the battlefield to the hospital, she had the then-revolutionary idea to bring medical care right to the front. She set up nursing stations in tents and wagons. She also insisted that she be allowed to treat the soldiers from the enemy's army, though this too was an unheard of idea at the time. Because of her tireless activities, the Civil War soldiers nicknamed her the "Angel of the Battlefield."

Throughout her life, Barton had periodically suffered from nervous disorders and she finally suffered a nervous breakdown. In August 1869 she went to Switzerland to regain her strength. In Geneva, she learned about the International Red Cross, a ten-year old organization set up to help sick and wounded soldiers in wartime situations. The United States did not wish to join the organization because of its policy—called the Monroe Doctrine—of staying out of foreign affairs.

Barton went to Strasbourg to join the Red Cross in helping victims of the Franco-Prussian War. When she returned to the United States, she continued to campaign for United States participation in the Red Cross. Because she wanted to appeal to Americans, many of whom wished to believe there would never be a war in their country again, she added the "American Amendment" to the constitution of the Red Cross. This amendment outlined a peacetime role for the organization: helping the victims of floods, fires, earthquakes, hurricanes, droughts and epidemics. Finally, her efforts paid off and in 1882, the United States agreed to establish the American Red Cross with Clara Barton as the first president.

Barton continued to work for relief efforts in the U.S. and abroad. But Red Cross workers complained that she did not handle money or administrative responsibility very well. The organization began to suffer from internal problems and when Clara Barton voted herself president for life in 1902, things did not improve. Instead, contributions and membership dropped off and in 1903 President Theodore Roosevelt withdrew the federal government's support.

Clara Barton retired to Glen Echo, Maryland but she remained active and her fame continued to grow, with medals and honors coming from Germany, Russia, Turkey and Serbia. She spent her time writing in her diary and studying religions until her death at the age of 91. *See* ANTHONY, SUSAN B.

Bellanca, Dorothy Jacobs

(1894–1946)

TRADE UNION ORGANIZER

Dorothy Bellanca's career began in Baltimore, Maryland at age thirteen. An immigrant from Latvia, Dorothy Jacobs began sewing buttonholes by hand in a men's overcoat factory. After four weeks of "training," in which she earned no pay, Dorothy earned just $3 a week doing painful work that permanently misshaped her index fingers. Although the factory owners at first paid little attention to the protests of such a young girl, Dorothy had within two years organized other young, female immigrant workers to form Local 170 of the United Garment Workers of America (UGWA), a trade union.

In 1914, Jacobs left UGWA and joined the newly formed Amalgamated Clothing Workers of America (ACWA), a union of unskilled workers. She negotiated contracts, organized locals, especially among immigrant women, and in 1916, became the only woman elected to ACWA's executive board. Two years later, Jacobs resigned from the board to marry another ACWA organizer, August Bellanca.

In the 1920s, the Bellancas both organized workers in New Jersey, Connecticut, Pennsylvania and upstate New York. They targeted factories that had moved out of New York City to escape labor unions and thereby lower labor costs. In 1924, Dorothy Bellanca was appointed head of the newly formed Women's Bureau of ACWA, which lasted only two years. Bellanca continued her organizing activities among textile and clothing workers in the mid-Atlantic states in the 1930s. Her organizing efforts between 1932 and 1934 led to thirty-thousand shirt workers—most of them women and girls who had worked for very low wages—joining ACWA. From 1934 until her death, Bellanca again served on ACWA's executive board.

In addition to her labor-organizing activities, Bellanca also accepted a number of political appointments. One of the founders of the American Labor party in 1936, Bellanca was elected New York State vice chair in 1940 and 1944. In 1938, she served on the Labor Department's Committee on Maternal and Child Welfare. She attended conferences of the International Labor Organization in 1939 and 1941 as a labor adviser. As a member of the Women's Policy Committee of the War Manpower Commission, Bellanca helped insure safe working conditions for the great number of women entering industry during World War II.

Berrigan, Daniel

(1921–   )

JESUIT PRIEST AND ACTIVIST FOR PACIFISM AND CIVIL RIGHTS

A Jesuit priest, poet, and teacher, Daniel Berrigan was one of the first two Roman Catholic priests sentenced to U.S. federal prison for protesting against war. The other was his brother Philip Berrigan. Daniel was reared by a father who was a **socialist** and labor organizer and a mother who often welcomed the poor into her home, offering them food and shelter. In 1939, Berrigan began a thirteen-year course of spiritual and intellectual training from the Society of Jesus. Ordained as a Jesuit priest in 1952, Berrigan studied for a year with activist priests in France. Upon returning to New York in 1954, he led groups of students who worked among Puerto Rican immigrants in Brooklyn and Manhattan.

From 1957 to 1963, Berrigan taught courses in the New Testament at the Jesuits' Le Moyne College. While there, he attracted a large following of Catholic activist students deeply committed to the causes of pacifism, civil rights, and radical social work. His following apparently disturbed his Jesuit superiors, who sent Berrigan on a year's study to Europe.

When he returned to the U.S. in 1964, Berrigan began protesting against American military action in Vietnam. Berrigan led fasts, pickets, and sit-ins: peaceful protests in which demonstrators would sit in a government or academic office in order to disrupt normal operations. In 1965, Berrigan founded Clergy and Laymen Concerned about Vietnam, a group that brought together people of various religions who opposed the war. Two years later, Berrigan accepted a job with the Office of Economic Opportunity, working with poor Mexican Americans in Pueblo, Colorado.

In 1968, Berrigan became the first Roman Catholic priest on the Cornell University faculty when he accepted the position of director of its United Religious Work. Later that year, Berrigan, his brother, and seven other radical Catholics entered a draft board office in Catonsville, Maryland. There, they emptied hundreds of draft records from filing cabinets into trash cans, took them outside, and burned them. Berrigan explained that they had chosen this symbolic act, burning paper, to protest against the burning of children in Vietnam. The "Catonsville Nine" were tried and convicted of conspiracy and destruction of government property.

In 1970, Daniel Berrigan, his brother Philip, and two others from the group went into hiding to avoid serving their prison sentences. Berrigan saw becoming a fugitive as a continuation of his resistance activities. He believed that in submitting to the laws and punishments of a government he viewed as mired in evil, he would be supporting its injustices. After four months, however, Berrigan was captured and began serving out his three-year prison term in Danbury, Connecticut.

A prominent poet and writer, Berrigan has published several books of poetry, collections of essays, and a 1970 play, *The Trial of the Catonsville Nine*. He has written countless articles opposing the death penalty, abortion, nuclear power, the Persian Gulf War of 1991, and the notion that any war could be considered "just." *See* BERRIGAN, PHILIP

Berrigan, Philip

(1923–   )

CATHOLIC PRIEST AND ACTIVIST FOR PEACE

The first Roman Catholic member of the clergy to be sentenced to jail for political activism in the U.S., Philip Berrigan is an author, former priest, and a peace activist. Berrigan's mother fed and sheltered the poor in her home, while his father actively participated in **socialist** party activity and labor organizing. After serving as an infantryman in World War II, Berrigan earned an undergraduate degree in English from Holy Cross College. In 1950, Berrigan entered the Society of St. Joseph Seminary, where he studied for the priesthood. After being ordained in 1955, he was assigned to New Orleans, Louisiana, where he continued his education. Berrigan received a degree in secondary education from Loyola University in 1957, and a graduate degree from Xavier University in 1960. At Xavier, Berrigan began teaching English and religion and counseling students in an African-American ghetto high school run by the Josephites. His work with the urban poor of New Orleans led to Berrigan's involvement in the **civil-rights** movement: the struggle of African Americans to win the same rights as white Americans. Berrigan worked with such prominent civil-rights organizations as the Congress of Racial Equality, the Student Nonviolent Coordinating Committee, and the Urban League.

Berrigan continued his activism after being transferred to the faculty of a Josephite seminary in Newburgh, New York. He organized protests on behalf of the poor and began delivering the first of many speeches and sermons against war and the arms race between the United States and the Soviet Union. Berrigan believed that the United States' war against the Vietnamese, like its racial and economic oppression at home, was both brutal and immoral. In 1964, he helped found the Emergency Citizens' Group Concerned About Vietnam in Newburgh and the Catholic Peace Fellowship in New York. Transferred to an African-American ghetto in Baltimore,

Maryland, Berrigan founded the Baltimore Interfaith Peace Mission. While in Baltimore, he regularly led protests for peace and urged members of Congress and federal officials in nearby Washington, D.C. to end the war. Yet Berrigan grew increasingly frustrated at the ineffectiveness of these "tame" protests against the war.

In 1967, Berrigan led a four-person raid on a draft-board office in Baltimore. The four activists opened file cabinets and poured duck blood on draft files as a symbolic protest against the waste of American and Vietnamese blood. Berrigan was convicted of defacing government property and interfering with functioning of the Selective Service (draft-board) system. While awaiting sentencing, Berrigan persuaded his brother Daniel and seven other Catholic activists to stage another demonstration against what they viewed as a sickness of the spirit. Berrigan targeted the draft board in Catonsville, Maryland because its offices were located in a hall owned by the Knights of Columbus, a society of Roman Catholic men. To Berrigan, this demonstrated the church's approval of the government's immoral warfare. The Berrigans and their fellow protesters removed draft records from the office, burned them, and awaited arrest. Berrigan was sentenced to six years in prison for the Baltimore protest and a concurrent sentence of three-and-one-half years for the Catonsville demonstration. Like his brother, Philip went underground in 1970 to avoid prison, but was captured by FBI agents within two weeks.

While in prison in Lewisburg, Pennsylvania, Berrigan got a fellow inmate to carry letters to Elizabeth McAlister, a nun and fellow peace activist whom he had secretly married in 1969. The inmate turned copies of the letters over to the FBI, which led to the capture of Daniel Berrigan and the arrest of draft resisters in Rochester, New York. Berrigan and McAlister were convicted of smuggling letters in 1972. But the conviction was overturned by an appeals court that ruled that since the FBI had cooperated in delivering the letters, no smuggling had occurred.

Berrigan has written several books promoting activism. These include a book on racism, *No More Strangers* (1965); *Punishment for Peace* (1965), written in a Baltimore jail; and *Prison Journals of a Priest Revolutionary* (1970). After spending more than three years in prison, Berrigan continued his anti-war protests. In 1975, Berrigan and twenty-one others threw a red liquid on military planes on display at Pratt & Whitney Aircraft in East Hartford, Connecticut. Charges of criminal mischief, criminal trespass, and disorderly conduct were later dropped. Berrigan has protested against equipping the U.S. Navy with nuclear weapons, the Persian Gulf War of 1991, and conditions in the nation's prisons. In 1992, Berrigan was jailed once again for his role in nuclear protests. *See* BERRIGAN, DANIEL

Birney, James

(1792–1857)

ABOLITIONIST

Reared after his mother's death by an aunt who owned many slaves, lawyer and writer James Gillespie Birney became a leading voice against the institution of slavery. After graduating from the College of New Jersey (later called Princeton University) in 1810, Birney returned to his hometown of Danville, Kentucky in 1814 to practice law. After serving briefly on both the Kentucky and Alabama state legislatures, Birney drank and gambled himself into debt. After selling his plantation and most of his own slaves, he established a successful law practice in Huntsville, Alabama.

Birney's growing opposition to slavery led him to give up his law practice and work for the end of slavery. In 1832, he joined the American Colonization Society, which supported the resettlement of freed slaves in Africa. Two years later, however, convinced that this course served white interests more than the interests of the African Americans it claimed to serve, Birney resigned. In 1835, after freeing his last two slaves, Birney helped establish the Kentucky Anti-Slavery Society. A year later, he moved to Cincinnati, Ohio to avoid threats of violence. He founded the *Philanthropist*, an antislavery newspaper, but within a year, a mob had destroyed his press.

After being tried for harboring a fugitive slave, Birney in 1837 accepted the position of executive secretary of the American Anti-Slavery Society in New York. Birney became a prominent spokesperson for the organization. In 1840, he helped found the antislavery Liberty party and ran as its candidate for president in both 1840 and 1844. Birney also served as vice president of the World Anti-Slavery Convention in 1840. In *The American Churches, the Bulwarks of American Slavery*, published in England in 1840, Birney attacked U.S. religious leaders for accepting and supporting the immoral institution of slavery.

Blackwell, Elizabeth

(1821–1910) and

Blackwell, Emily

(1826–1910)

TWO OF THE FIRST WOMEN TO RECEIVE MEDICAL
DEGREES IN THE U.S.

> The idea of winning a doctor's degree gradually assumed the aspect of a great moral struggle, and the moral fight possessed immense attraction for me.
>
> —From Elizabeth Blackwell's
> autobiography, *Pioneer Work in Opening
> the Medical Profession to Women* (1895).

Born in Bristol, England, Elizabeth and Emily were the third and sixth of nine surviving children. In 1832, the Blackwells moved to New York. Both were strongly influenced by their father: a social reformer who supported women's rights, the end of slavery, and **temperance**: giving up liquor. In New York, Samuel Blackwell opened a sugar refinery, but refused to use cane sugar grown on southern slave plantations. By 1838, his unsuccessful attempts to refine beet sugar had forced a move to Cincinnati, Ohio, where Samuel Blackwell's death left his family close to poverty. To help make ends meet, Elizabeth Blackwell, her two older sisters, and her mother founded a private boarding school for girls. During this period, young Emily was especially impressed with her older sister Elizabeth. Following in Elizabeth's footsteps, Emily would become a teacher and then a doctor. Like all of their sisters, both Elizabeth and Emily remained single throughout their lives.

Although teaching bored her, Elizabeth Blackwell supported herself by teaching for several years. The notion of women's rights, especially regarding the equality of education, began to draw her interest. In 1843, a dying friend deplored the lack of women doctors and urged Blackwell to study medicine. Overcoming her disgust for the human body, Blackwell soon welcomed the idea as an alternative to marriage and economic dependence on a man. From 1845 to 1847, Elizabeth Blackwell raised money through teaching while privately studying medicine in North and South Carolina. Although every medical school in Philadelphia and New York turned down her application, Geneva Medical College in upstate New York accepted her. Blackwell experienced isolation and loneliness in her studies. One professor attempted to keep her out of his lectures on the reproductive system, because he considered them inappropriate for a woman to attend. While working at the Philadelphia Hospital the following summer, she encountered further hostility, this time at the hands of male residents. The sight of women hospitalized for sexually transmitted diseases made a powerful impression on Blackwell. The experience inspired her later lectures on the need for women to emphasize morality in their sexual relations.

In 1848, Emily Blackwell decided to become a doctor as well. Like her sister, she privately studied medicine while raising money for her education through teaching, which she also disliked. The following year, Elizabeth Blackwell graduated at the head of her class, becoming the first woman ever to receive a degree from an American medical school. From 1849 to 1851, she went to Europe to gain practical experience. The only job she could get in Paris, France, however, was as a student midwife. An eye disease contracted from one of her young patients left her blind in one eye, destroying her hope of becoming a surgeon. Returning to the United States, Blackwell found job opportunities no better for a woman doctor in New York than they had been in Paris. She found herself unable to rent office space because at that time, the term "female physician" referred solely to practioners of abortion. To make money, she began lecturing on good hygiene, women's sexual morality, and the need for young women to exercise.

Emily Blackwell, rejected by eleven medical schools including Geneva Medical College, was accepted by Rush Medical College in Chicago in 1852. The following year, however, under pressure from the Illinois State Medical Society, the school refused to allow her to resume her studies. After working for the summer in her sister's newly opened charity clinic in New York, Emily Blackwell was admitted to the medical college of Western Reserve University in Cleveland. After graduating with honors in 1854, she too spent two years in Europe for further study and practical experience.

After returning to the U.S., Emily Blackwell joined her sister in enlarging the small clinic into a sixteen-bed hospital: the New York Infirmary for Women and Children, founded in 1857. Directed by women and staffed by women doctors, the infirmary offered a rare opportunity for both female patients and female physicians seeking clinical experience. While performing surgery, Emily Blackwell also had to take care of nursing and housekeeping duties and to raise funds. Except for one year, in which Elizabeth Blackwell traveled to England to promote the cause of women in medicine, the sisters worked together in the infirmary for the next twelve years. The infirmary established a training program for nurses, obtained financial assistance from the state of New York, and grew rapidly. The number of patients the Blackwells treated rose from two hundred in 1853 to over 3,600 in 1860.

During the Civil War (1861–65), Elizabeth Blackwell helped form the Woman's Central Association of Relief, which provided aid to troops on the front lines. Both sisters also selected and trained nurses to treat wounded soldiers. In 1866, after the war had ended, the Blackwells established the first medical social service in the United States. The infirmary appointed a "sanitary visitor," who visited the poor in their homes, offering care and training in proper hygiene. Two years later, Elizabeth Blackwell established the Woman's Medical College of the New York Infirmary. Although not the first medical college for women, it raised the standards of medical training for women. The college introduced entrance exams and, through the infirmary, provided clinical experience in addition to academic training. The college also set the standard for all medical schools by increasing the course of training from two years to three years in 1873, and then to four years in 1893.

Elizabeth Blackwell moved to England permanently in 1869. Emily Blackwell took charge of both the infirmary and the medical college, becoming the school's dean and professor of **obstetrics** (delivering babies) and women's diseases for the next thirty years. In England, Elizabeth Blackwell continued her work for improved hygiene and the advancement of women in medicine. In 1871, she founded the National Health Society in London, which promoted hygiene as a means of preventing illness and maintaining good health. Four years later, she helped found the New Hospital and London School of Medicine for Women. In 1876, poor health forced her to retire from medicine, but Elizabeth Blackwell then turned to moral reform through her lectures, essays, articles, and books. Her books include *Counsel to Parents on the Moral Education of Their Children* (1878) and *The Human Element in Sex* (1884). In addition to stressing hygiene and preventive medicine, her writings called for the same moral standards to be applied to the actions of both men and women.

In 1899, when the new Cornell University Medical College began accepting women, Emily Blackwell arranged for her remaining students to transfer to Cornell and closed the Women's Medical College. The college had trained 364 female doctors in thirty-one years. Through the college and the infirmary, the Blackwells, pioneering women doctors, had set high standards for women doctors in medicine.

Bloomer, Amelia J.

(1818–1894)

ACTIVIST FOR WOMEN'S RIGHTS, JOURNALIST, AND INVENTOR OF THE BLOOMER

> It is the fault of education that she [woman] is now intellectually inferior. . . . Throw open the door of our colleges and schools of science and bid her enter, teach her that she was created for a higher purpose than to be a parlor ornament or mere plaything for man, show her that you regard her as an equal . . . , in short, treat her as an intelligent, accountable being, and . . . if she prove herself not man's equal in intellect I will yield the point and admit her inferiority.
>
> —Bloomer in D.C. Bloomer, *Life and Writings of Amelia Bloomer* (1895)

For many, Amelia Jenks Bloomer became known only for the style of dress that bears her name: full-length trousers under a short skirt. But Bloomer was much more than a trendsetter. Through her newspaper, *The Lily*, and her public speaking, Bloomer promoted such social reforms as women's rights and **temperance**: giving up liquor.

Born in Homer, New York, Amelia Jenks had little formal schooling, but was educated by her mother at home. After teaching for one term in Clyde, New York, Jenks moved to Waterloo, New York. There, she served as a governess and private tutor from 1837 to 1840. She married Dexter Bloomer, a law student, newspaper editor, and antislavery reformer, in 1840. In her first public act in support of women's rights, Bloomer omitted the word "obey" from the traditional bride's vow "to love, honor, and obey" her husband.

The couple settled in Seneca Falls, where Amelia Bloomer began writing articles for her husband's newspaper, *The Seneca County Courier*. Her articles, written under a **pseudonym**, addressed the social, moral and political issues of the day. She also began writing short articles for *The Water Bucket*, a local journal that promoted temperance, and *The Temperance Star*, published in Rochester, New York. In 1848, Bloomer helped organize the Ladies' Temperance Society and served as one of its officers.

Bloomer met Elizabeth Cady Stanton the following year in a women's reading and discussion group Bloomer had established. Under the name "Sunflower," Stanton began writing articles on women's rights for Bloomer's newspaper, *The Lily*, which began publishing in 1849. *The Lily*, the official newspaper of the Ladies' Temperance Society, was the nation's first newspaper entirely owned, published, and edited by a woman. Although it remained dedicated to the cause of temperance, *The Lily* expanded its interest in social reforms to embrace the cause of women's rights. Bloomer herself began writing articles and editorials on women's rights in 1850. Her activist stand came in response to the Tennessee legislature, which had ruled that women could not own property because they had no souls. Through Bloomer's direction, *The Lily* became the first newspaper in the country to focus on women's concerns, including legal status, education, and marriage laws. By the early 1850s, Bloomer had added a banner to the front page of the newspaper that read: "The Emancipation of Woman from Intemperance, Injustice, Prejudice, and Bigotry."

The Lily became nationally known in 1851. Stanton had begun wearing trousers covered by a short skirt that winter. The new style, a protest against traditional clothing that restricted women, allowed women more freedom and a more active life. Bloomer's editorial defense of this "dress reform" in *The Lily* was reprinted in newspapers throughout the country. The "Bloomer costume" became a symbol of women's new freedom. Bloomer herself wore the style for most of the decade. The demand for information and patterns for the costume rapidly increased *The Lily*'s circulation, which rose from five hundred in 1849 to more than six thousand in 1853.

Elected an officer of the recently founded New York State Woman's Temperance Society in 1852, Bloomer began speaking out in support of a woman's right to divorce her husband for drunkenness. The following year, she joined Susan B. Anthony and other **feminists** (supporters of women's rights) in a statewide lecture tour promoting both temperance and women's rights. After attending the National Woman's Rights Convention in Cleveland that year, she remained in the Midwest, where she continued to speak out for women's rights and temperance. Later that year, the World's Temperance Convention in New York refused to allow women to participate. Bloomer helped Anthony organize the "Whole World's Temperance Convention," which recognized the rights of women to take part in social reform.

From 1853 to 1855, while continuing to edit and publish *The Lily*, Bloomer became assistant editor of her husband's *The Western Home Visitor*, a weekly reform newspaper published in Mount Vernon, Ohio. The Bloomers supported women's rights not only in the pages of this newspaper, but behind the scenes as well. They hired women as typesetters and, despite a threatened strike by their male coworkers, refused to fire the women. When the Bloomers moved to the frontier town of Council Bluffs, Iowa, in 1855, Amelia Bloomer sold *The Lily* due to the impracticality of publishing it from the frontier.

The remoteness of the frontier forced Bloomer to abandon national reform issues and instead focus on state and local reforms. She worked to found churches and local temperance organizations. And she promoted women's rights, especially the cause of women's **suffrage**. Although she obtained support for a women's suffrage law in the House of the Nebraska Territory in 1856, the Senate rejected the bill. During the Civil War, (1861–65), Bloomer organized a local group to provide relief and aid to northern soldiers. In 1869, she served as an Iowa delegate to a meeting of the American Equal Rights Association. This group supported the right to vote for both women and African Americans. Two years later, the Iowa Woman Suffrage Society elected Bloomer as its president. In this office, she helped secure property rights for married women in Iowa that were almost equal to those for married men. *See* ANTHONY, SUSAN B.; MOTT, LUCRETIA; STANTON, ELIZABETH CADY

Bonney, Mary L.

(1816–1900)

ACTIVIST FOR NATIVE AMERICAN'S RIGHTS

Mary Lucinda Bonney, whose mother had been a teacher, taught school herself from 1835 to 1850. In 1850, she founded the Chestnut Street Female Seminary in Philadelphia, Pennsylvania. She served as senior principal of the school, renamed the Ogontz School for Young Ladies in 1883, until 1888. In the 1860s, Bonney actively participated in the Women's Union Missionary Society of America, which sent female missionaries to minister to women in Asia.

In 1879, Bonney took up the cause of Native American reform. Gold miners had already invaded Sioux territory in the Black Hills of the Dakotas. Congress had just introduced a bill permitting white settlement in the Oklahoma Territory, which had been reserved for Native Americans by treaty. Outraged, Mary Bonney called on the United States government to honor its treaties. With the help of Amelia Quinton, Bonney resolved to arouse the conscience of Congress and the American people. Bonney and Quinton gathered more than thirteen-thousand signatures on petitions to President Rutherford B. Hayes and the Congress. The petitions urged the U.S. to honor its treaties and end white settlements in territories reserved for Native Americans. The following year, Bonney's second petition, signed by fifty-thousand people, called on Congress to protect Native American lands.

In 1881, Bonney and Quinton formed the Indian Treaty-

Keeping and Protective Association. Bonney was named first president of the women's organization. A year later, a third petition, with one-hundred-thousand signatures, was presented to Congress. This document called on the government to allot tribal lands to individual Native Americans. This strategy was intended to absorb Native Americans into U.S. society and citizenship and end the reservation system. In 1887, Congress enacted this program. It broke up tribal reservations into individually owned parcels of land, and unfortunately, proved a disaster for Native Americans. The actual result was destruction of tribal life and white ownership of Native American lands.

In 1883, Bonney and Quinton changed the name of their organization to the Women's National Indian Association (WNIA). Although she resigned as the WNIA's president shortly thereafter, Bonney remained executive board member and honorary president—and personally financed the WNIA for five years. In addition to pressuring Congress on Native American policies, the WNIA introduced programs to educate Native American women in child care and domestic skills. WNIA missionaries also provided religious instruction, job training, and classes in the English language. By 1886, the WNIA had established eighty-three branches in twenty-seven states.

Bonnin, Gertrude

(1876–1938)

ACTIVIST FOR NATIVE AMERICAN'S RIGHTS

Unlike many Native Americans in the nineteenth century, Gertrude Simmons Bonnin was educated by whites, first at a Quaker mission school in Wabash, Indiana and later at Earlham College in Richmond, Indiana. Simmons was half-Sioux and, although she had distanced herself from tribal life, she did not find herself welcomed by the white society that had schooled her in its culture.

Simmons taught other Native Americans at a school in Carlisle, Pennsylvania, from 1897 to 1899. In 1900, she began writing autobiographical essays and Native American legends under her Sioux name, Zit-kala-sha, for popular magazines. At this time, Simmons took a job with the federal government's Bureau of Indian Affairs (BIA). Working as a clerk on the Sioux Reservation at Standing Rock, she met and married a Sioux coworker, Raymond Bonnin, in 1902. For the next fourteen years, the Bonnins worked on the Uintah and Ouray Reservation in Utah, where Gertrude Bonnin held positions as a clerk and later a teacher.

In the early 1910s, she joined the Society of American Indians (SAI), the first Native American reform group not managed by white reformers. The SAI wanted to secure political equality, preserve Native American history and culture, and improve the quality of life for Native Americans. Toward these ends, Bonnin ran an SAI community center in Fort Duchesne, Utah and corresponded with the federal BIA. In 1916, Bonnin moved to Washington, D.C. as the new secretary of SAI. She edited the society's *American Indian Magazine* from 1918 to 1919 and lectured on behalf of Native American rights.

When the Society of American Indians collapsed in 1920, Bonnin began working with the General Federation of Women's Clubs. After establishing its Indian Welfare Committee in 1921, Bonnin helped investigate the government's treatment of various Native American tribes. She also spoke out for improvements in their schools and hospitals. In 1924, she traveled from reservation to reservation, urging Native Americans to support a bill granting them citizenship—and to exercise their new right to vote. In 1926, Bonnin helped found the National Council of American Indians. Serving as the council's president until her death, Bonnin exposed the horrifying conditions of life on Native American reservations and urged Congress to adopt laws improving Native American conditions and protecting their rights.

Brady, James S.

(1940–   )

REPUBLICAN POLITICIAN AND
ACTIVIST FOR GUN CONTROL

After surviving a gunshot wound in March, 1981, that left him partly paralyzed, James Scott Brady worked to reform laws regulating the purchase of handguns. Brady earned an undergraduate degree in communications and political science from the University of Illinois at Champaign-Urbana in 1962. As a student, he served as president of the campus chapter of Young Republicans. This began his long involvement with Republican politics. In the 1960s, Brady worked for Republican senatorial and congressional candidates in several Illinois election campaigns. In 1973, Brady left the Chicago public relations firm where he had risen to executive vice president to accept an appointment by President Richard Nixon. After serving two years as special assistant to the secretary of Housing and Urban Development, Brady was named by Nixon's successor, President Gerald Ford, as assistant to the director of the Office of Management and Budget. Brady also served briefly as the assistant to the secretary of defense in 1976.

In 1979, Republican presidential candidate John Connally, the former governor of Texas, asked Brady to act as his campaign press secretary. When Connally later dropped out of the race, Brady joined the campaign of Ronald Reagan. Brady's success in arranging media coverage to Reagan's liking led to his appointment as White House press secretary in 1981.

In March, 1981, Brady was shot in the head in an unsuccessful attempt to assassinate President Reagan. The shots wounded four men, one of them the president. Brady endured a five-hour operation on his brain, where four or five bullet fragments had lodged. Complications led to further surgery on his brain and lungs. His brain injuries left Brady's left arm and leg paralyzed, slightly slurred his speech, and impaired his short-term memory. Although Brady remained the White House press secretary until the end of Reagan's presidency in 1989, deputies assumed most of his duties.

Brady and his wife Sarah did not immediately take up the cause of gun control. But in 1984, Brady's five-year-old son played with a pistol he had found in a family friend's pickup truck. Although the incident did not lead to tragedy, Sarah changed her stance and became a prominent volunteer with Handgun Control, Inc. Until 1988, Brady remained loyal to the positions of the Reagan White House, which opposed gun control of any kind. In the closing days of the administration, however, he actively opposed the National Rifle Association (NRA), the gun lobby and supporter of President Reagan. Brady helped build support for a Maryland law banning the manufacture and sale of handguns known as "Saturday-Night Specials." Brady had been shot with one of these pistols, the most common gun used in urban crimes.

In 1989, Brady became chair of the National Organization on Disability, a group seeking improved living conditions and expanded opportunities for the physically challenged. Brady himself is for the most part confined to a wheelchair, although he can walk with difficulty using a cane.

Brady also began lobbying actively for gun control. He has testified before a congressional committee, urging passage of the Brady Handgun Violence Prevention Act (the "Brady Bill"). This "crime control" bill calls for a seven-day waiting period in order to purchase a handgun. This week allows police, if they choose, to investigate the background of the buyer. In 1991, the bill received unexpected support from former President and longtime NRA member Ronald Reagan and overwhelmingly passed House and Senate votes as part of separate crime law packages. The bill has not yet become law because of unresolved House and Senate differences.

Brown, John

(1800–1859)

ABOLITIONIST

> I believe that to have interfered as I have done in behalf of
> His despised poor, is no wrong, but right. Now, if it is
> deemed necessary that I should forfeit my life for the fur-
> therance of the ends of justice, and mingle my blood with
> the blood of millions in this slave country whose rights are
> disregarded by wicked, cruel, and unjust enactments, I say
> let it be done.
>
> —Brown, final statement to court, (1859)

John Brown, a militant **abolitionist** (an activist dedicated to
the end of slavery) uttered these words before sacrificing his
life to the cause of abolition. Hanged for leading a violent raid
on the slave-holding town of Harpers Ferry, Virginia in 1859,
Brown became a **martyr** to the abolitionist cause. His attack
and hanging heightened the tensions between northern abolitionists and southern slaveowners that helped lead to the Civil
War two years later.

Born in Torrington, Connecticut, Brown was taught to fear
God and obey God's commandments by his parents, who were
Puritan Calvinists. Owen Brown, who helped escaped slaves
find freedom in the North, also reared his son John to oppose
slavery. The Browns moved to Hudson, a town on the Ohio
frontier, in 1805. John received little education, although his
father taught him the trade of tanning: turning animal skins
into leather. During the War of 1812, young John drove cattle
to supply the American troops. As a boy, the sight of a master
brutally beating a young slave made a profound impression on
him. In his teens, John helped at least one escaped slave reach
the safety of Canada.

During the 1820s, Brown settled in Richmond, Pennsylvania.
His neighbors soon learned that Brown judged others solely
by their stand on slavery. In Richmond, he fathered seven children—five of whom survived childhood—with his first wife.

After his first wife died in 1932, Brown remarried the following year. With his second wife, he had thirteen more children. A stern father, Brown beat his children for breaking God's commandments. He also taught his children to oppose slavery by any and all means. Brown regarded slavery as the world's greatest evil, and urged his children to fight against evil with their lives. Three of his sons would later join him in giving their lives for the cause of abolition.

John Brown was not a successful businessperson. His tannery business failed in 1835, causing him to resettle in Franklin Mills, Ohio. By 1842, a bankruptcy court had seized virtually everything Brown owned. His financial troubles did not interfere with his activism, however. In 1839, the Congregational church expelled him for his protest against **segregation** (separation of the races) in the church. Twice, Brown had led African Americans from their seats in the rear of the church and invited them to join him in his pew. As Brown offered more and more help to escaped slaves, he became convinced that the end of slavery was a cause worth dying for.

His involvement in the abolitionist movement deepened when he moved his family to Springfield, Massachusetts in 1846. Brown rejected all political solutions that would allow slavery in some parts of the country while outlawing it in others. He also regarded appeals to the morality of slaveowners as futile. In his 1848 essay, *Sambo's Mistakes*, Brown called upon slaves to wage war on their masters, killing them in order to win their freedom. He criticized African Americans for submitting to slavery instead of fighting it to their deaths. At this time, Brown began considering the possibility of waging a guerrilla war (irregular warfare through harrassment and sabotage) to terrorize Southern plantation owners and free their slaves.

Brown put this idea aside to settle in North Elba, New York from 1849 to 1851. There, on land donated by abolitionist Gerrit Smith, he taught free African Americans how to farm. While he was their teacher, Brown treated African Americans as his equals. In 1850, Congress passed the Fugitive Slave Act, which increased the powers of federal marshals to return escaped slaves to their former masters. The act prohibited African Americans from speaking in their own defense and denied them the right to a trial by jury. Brown saw the new law as an attempt not only to recapture escaped slaves, but also to enslave free African Americans. In Springfield, he organized the United States League of Gileadites in 1851. The league instructed free African Americans in ways to prevent federal marshals from recapturing fugitive slaves.

In 1855, Brown moved to the Kansas Territory, where he joined five of his sons in the fight against the introduction of slavery in the region. From 1854 to 1859, "Bleeding Kansas" was the site of a territorial civil war that anticipated the national Civil War that began in 1861. Abolitionists and those favoring slavery struggled for control of the territory's future. Proslavery mobs crossed the border from Missouri, only to clash with antislavery activists from the Northeast. In 1856, a proslavery mob attacked and burned Lawrence, Kansas, a center of antislavery activity. The mob killed five abolitionists. Three days later, Brown led seven others in an attack on proslavery activists in Pottawatomie Creek. Seeking revenge for the five killed in Lawrence, Brown's gang murdered five men with their swords. Kansas thus became the main battleground for Brown's three-year war against slavery. He led several raids on proslavery settlers that summer, sometimes stealing their cattle. Late that summer, four-hundred Missourians raided and burned Brown's camp in Osawatomie, wounding Brown and killing one of his sons. After obtaining a supply of money, rifles, and revolvers from Boston abolitionists in 1857, Brown returned to Kansas. There, he led several raids to free slaves on Missouri plantations, killing at least one slave owner. In 1858, Brown met with white and African-American supporters in Ontario, Canada. He told them of his plans to establish a free nation centered around a military base in the Appalachian Mountains. The meeting approved its own constitution and elected Brown commander-in-chief.

By 1859, Brown's efforts to sneak freed slaves to Canada had led President James Buchanan to offer a $250 reward for his capture. After raising more money from New England abolitionists, Brown staged his famous raid on Harpers Ferry. Brown and twenty-one others—including five African Americans—captured the town, freed its slaves, took sixty hostages, and took control of the town's federal armory. Brown hoped that the slaves he freed would join in his rebellion, forming an army to free other slaves. But his plans were thwarted when a marines unit led by Robert E. Lee, who would later command southern troops in the Civil War, recaptured the town. In the battle, seven members of the government's troops were killed. Among Brown's band, five escaped and ten died, including one of Brown's sons. The other seven, including Brown, were tried and convicted of murder, inciting slaves to rebellion, and treason. Sentenced to hang, Brown and the others became willing martyrs. To the end, Brown insisted that he was right to wage war on slavery and slaveowners.

Brownmiller, Susan

(1935–)

FEMINIST AND WRITER

> Rape is nothing more or less than a conscious process of intimidation by which all men keep all women in a state of fear.

—From Brownmiller's *Against Our Will: Men, Women, and Rape* (1975)

Writer Susan Brownmiller staked out new ground for the **feminist movement** with her book, *Against Our Will: Men, Women, and Rape.* Brownmiller saw rape as a "political" crime—an act used by one group to demonstrate their power over another group. She urged women to fight back against the fear that she believed men deliberately created.

The only child of two Jewish working parents, Susan was born in Brooklyn. In 1952, she enrolled in Cornell University, where she planned to take pre-law courses. As a student, she demonstrated a political activism unusual in the 1950s. She joined the campus chapter of the National Association for the Advancement of Colored People (NAACP). The NAACP played a leading role in that decade's **civil rights movement**, which sought equality under the law for African Americans. Against the objections of her parents, she also joined Students for Peace, a small group of campus radicals. In the anti-communist hysteria of the 1950s, peace groups were often suspected of communist leanings.

A year short of graduating, she left Cornell in 1955 to pursue an acting career in New York. Although she appeared in two off-Broadway shows, Brownmiller decided after many years of effort to abandon the stage. During the mid-1960s, she resumed her activism. She spent two summers in Mississippi, working for civil rights. She also began taking part in protests against U.S. involvement in the Vietnam War.

At this time, Brownmiller began her career as a writer. After doing research for *Newsweek* magazine and writing for *Coronet* magazine, she spent a year as a television reporter in Philadelphia in 1965. She then worked as a newswriter for the ABC-TV network before joining the writing staff of the *Village Voice* in New York in 1967. In an article written for *Esquire* in 1968, Brownmiller questioned the fairness of the trial and conviction of three African-American men in Maryland accused of raping a white girl. She suspected that racial prejudice lay behind the trial. Although the rape charges were later dropped and the convictions overturned, within several years Brownmiller came to believe that the young girl had told the truth about her rape.

In 1968, Brownmiller helped found New York Radical Feminists, a group dedicated to achieving equal rights for women. That fall, she led the group in picketing the Miss America Pageant in Atlantic City. Beauty pageants, Brownmiller argued, insulted and degraded not only the contestants, but all women. In 1969, she wrote a profile of Shirley Chisholm, an activist member of Congress, for *The New York Times Magazine*. The article led to her first book, *Shirley Chisholm*, a biography for young readers published the following year.

In March, 1970, Brownmiller wrote an article on the women's liberation movement for *The New York Times Magazine*. That same month, she led a **sit-in** at the offices of the *Ladies Home Journal*. More than one hundred feminists joined her in protesting the magazine's presentation of women as little more than homemakers, cooks, and mothers. The protesters called on *Ladies Home Journal* to publish an issue that reflected women's liberation from these roles and to stop printing advertising that degraded women.

The following year, Brownmiller organized a conference on rape, encouraging victims to speak out about the crime. The conference changed her views on rape. What she once saw as an insane sex crime, she now viewed as an attempt to oppress and shame women. For the next four years, she researched rape and conducted interviews with rape victims. The result of her work was *Against Our Will: Men, Women and Rape*, published in 1975. In exploring in detail the history of rape, Brownmiller tied the crime to the concerns of the feminist movement: the domination of women by men. Although she recognized that not all men committed rape, she charged men as a group with tolerating the crime. Brownmiller called for reforms in police procedures and the court system to address the rapidly increasing crime of rape. Brownmiller also urged women to learn the art of self-defense, which she had begun learning in 1973.

Brownmiller has also condemned pornography (sexually explicit magazines, movies, books, and videos) because it turns women into objects. People who accept this view of women, she argued, become less sensitive to rape. Brownmiller spoke out against prostitution on similar grounds. In 1977, she headed a group of feminists committed to educating Americans about the increasing brutality of pornography. *See* CHISHOLM, SHIRLEY

Carmichael, Stokely

(1941–   )

CIVIL RIGHTS ACTIVIST AND LEADER OF BLACK PANTHERS

Born in Trinidad in the British West Indies, Stokely Carmichael later became a leading figure in the call for black liberation in the United States. Carmichael first encountered racism in a British boys school, where he was taught that blacks did not exist until a white man had discovered them. In 1952, Stokely rejoined his parents, who had immigrated nine years earlier, in Harlem, New York. Harlem presented quite a contrast to Trinidad, where blacks held most positions of power. Although Harlem was an African-American community, whites occupied most positions of authority. The owners of the buildings where African Americans lived and of the stores where they shopped were white—as were the police. When the Carmichaels moved to a white neighborhood in the Bronx, Stokely became the only African American in an otherwise white gang. But he left the gang to devote himself to his studies at the Bronx High School of Science.

In 1960, Carmichael joined the **civil rights movement**, participating in protests for equal treatment of African Americans staged by the Congress of Racial Equality (CORE). As a student at Howard University in Washington D.C., Carmichael took part in CORE's "Freedom Rides." On the Freedom Rides, whites and African Americans sat together on bus rides through the South to protest against **segregation** (the separation of people based on race) in interstate bus terminals.

After earning an undergraduate degree in philosophy in 1964, Carmichael became an organizer for the Student Nonviolent Coordinating Committee (SNCC). SNCC volunteers taught reading and writing to African Americans in the South, helped them register to vote, and established health clinics. Carmichael, leading a SNCC task force into Mississippi's Lowndes County, increased the number of registered African-American voters from seventy to 2,600, surpassing white registration in the county. He also organized the Lowndes County Freedom Organization, which adopted the black panther as its symbol. Like many other civil rights organizations, SNCC became increasingly militant in the mid-1960s. Whites were asked to leave SNCC, which now abandoned nonviolence and called for black liberation rather than an end to segregation.

Carmichael helped lead SNCC in this shift. In 1966, he was elected chair of SNCC, which now stood for the Student National Coordinating Committee. Carmichael popularized the slogan "Black Power," which many in the white media attacked as reverse racism. Carmichael, however, explained the slogan as a call not to overthrow the country, but to fight for liberation and to win political and economic power. Carmichael wanted to see the money spent by African Americans stay in their communities. He called for African-American control of the institutions—banks, businesses, stores, and governments—in their own communities. Carmichael lectured extensively on college campuses and wrote *Black Power*, published in 1967.

That same year, Carmichael left SNCC to head the more militant Black Panther Party. The Black Panthers, an African-American liberation movement popular in Northern cities, had been founded a year earlier in Oakland, California by activists Huey P. Newton and Bobby Seale. Originally created as an African-American self-defense force, the Black Panthers patrolled urban ghettos to prevent police brutality directed against African Americans. Chapters also introduced positive reforms into African-American communities: creating children's lunch programs and founding anti-drug clinics. By 1969, most U.S. cities had chapters of the Black Panthers.

In 1969, Carmichael resigned from the Black Panthers to protest their growing alliances with white radicals, whom he feared would try to take over the party. Carmichael, who had been arrested thirty-five times for his part in the civil rights movement, left the United States for the African country of Guinea. *See* NEWTON, HUEY

Carson, Rachel

(1907–1964)

SCIENTIST, ENVIRONMENTALIST, AND AUTHOR

> We stand now where two roads diverge . . . The other fork
> in the road—the one 'less travelled by'—offers our last, our
> only chance to reach a destination that assures the preserva-
> tion of the earth.
>
> —Carson, in *Silent Spring*

In *Silent Spring*, marine zoologist and environmentalist Rachel Carson, who had achieved fame for *The Sea Around Us*, an account of life in the ocean, questioned the widespread use of pesticides—chemical poisons used to kill insects that eat or damage food crops—and their effect on all forms of life. With this book Carson brought environmental issues to the attention of policymakers and the public.

Rachel Louise Carson was born on May 27, 1907 in Springdale, Pennsylvania. There, she spent time with her mother, taking long walks in the nearby woods. Maria Carson had been a teacher before her marriage, and she taught Rachel the names of plants, birds, insects and animals they encounted. Soon, Rachel was able to identify dozens of wild things.

Maria Carson also fostered her daughter's intellectual development, and encouraged her to have high expectations of herself. Her efforts paid off: Rachel was an excellent student and although it was unusual for girls of her generation to pursue an education after high school, she received a scholarship to the Pennsylavania College for Women (later renamed Chatham College). She planned to major in English Literature, but during her second year, she took a biology course with Mary Scott Skinker, who became a good friend. By the time she graduated from college with honors, she had decided to specialize in marine biology—the study of animal life in the ocean. In 1929, she won a fill scholarship to Johns Hopkins University in Baltimore, Maryland, to continue her studies.

After obtaining her graduate degree, Carson found that jobs

in her field were difficult to find, especially for women. She took part-time jobs teaching college, and began writing newspaper articles. Then, in 1935, she landed a job writing radio scripts about ocean life for the United States Bureau of Fisheries (later renamed the United States Fish and Wildlife Service).

After about a year, her supervisor was impressed by a piece of writing he had assigned to her. At his suggestion, she submitted it to The Atlantic Monthly, a magazine which published it with the title *Undersea* in 1937. She decided to expand the article into a longer work, and her book *Under the Sea-Wind* was published in 1941. Even though the book did not become popular, Carson kept writing and in 1951, her second book, *The Sea Around Us*, became a best-seller. Two more successful books, *The Edge of the Sea* (1955) and *The Sense of Wonder* (1956) soon followed.

But Carson's interest in the natural world was not confined to the water. As far back as 1945, she had expressed concern about the use of DDI, a new pesticide developed to kill disease-carrying insects like mosquitoes. In the late 1950's, she again turned her attention to these chemical poisons, which were routinely sprayed on crops, animals, homes and farms. The problem, as she saw it, was this: while it was clear that chemical pesticides were effective against ants, mosquitoes and the like, there had been no extensive testing to discover what the onging use of such poisons might have on other forms of life, such as birds, fish, animals, and ultimately, human beings. It was Carson's belief that these chemicals were harmful when eaten, drunk, or breathed in by animals of all kinds. And because little animals are often eaten by larger animals, the build-up of poisons didn't stop—it just got passed along to the next creature in what is called the **food chain**.

Silent Spring was the result of Carson's research, and an alarm meant to warn people about the long-term effects of chemicals in the environment. When it appeared it was greeted by a storm of controversy. There were many people—including chemical company representatives and government officials—who attacked both book and author. Carson was called sinister, an alarmist, and a communist.

Yet despite these attacks, many of them personal, other

members of government responded positively to Carson's message. President John F. Kennedy established the Presidential Science Advisory Committee (PSAC), an eight month investigation into the dangers and benefits of pesticide use which confirmed what Carson had written in *Silent Spring*. Because of the PSAC's endorsement and her appearance on national television, the environmental cause started to attract attention.

Politicians who once ignored environmental issues began writing Carson for advice. By the end of 1962, more than 40 pesticide regulating bills had been introduced in state legislatures across the nation. In 1964, Congress demanded that chemical manufacturers prove the safety of products, rather than leaving it to the government to demonstrate that they were unsafe. When near the end of her life, Carson was awarded the Audubon Medal (she was the first woman to receive it), she said, "Conservation is a cause that has no end. There is no point at which we will say our work is finished."

Chavez, Cesar

(1927–1993)

LABOR UNION ACTIVIST

Cesar Chavez, left, confers with organizational members.

Cesar Chavez was born on March 31, 1927 on a farm near the town of Yuma, Arizona. Cesar's grandfather, for whom he was named, had been a poor farm worker in Mexico. He brought his family to America, settling on a 160-acre section of what is now Arizona where he grew corn, lettuce, beans and a little cotton.

But with the coming of the **Great Depression**, a time when the country's economy failed and people lost their money and their jobs, the family could no longer make a living from working the land. In 1937, they sold the farm and house for whatever the bank would offer and headed for California. The members of the Chavez family became migrant workers, who moved from farm to farm as the seasons changed. Cesar went to more than thirty elementary schools in California and Arizona. Finally, when he reached the seventh grade, he dropped out of school entirely. Although he was just a boy, Cesar had to work:

ten to twelve hours a day, six and sometimes seven days a week, he toiled in the fields with his family.

During World War II, Chavez served in the United States Navy. After the war, he continued working as a migrant laborer. He married and started a family, the work paid very poorly, and it was always a struggle to make ends meet.

One day in 1952, an organizer named Fred Ross approached Chavez and asked him to help convince other Mexican-American farm workers to start helping themselves. Chavez agreed, and spent the next ten years working with Ross and his boss, Saul Alinsky. Alinsky's group was called the Community Service Organization (CSO). As part of the CSO, Chavez helped Mexican-Americans register to vote, so they could participate in elections. He helped farm workers who were in trouble with the police or who needed money. He showed workers how to petition farm owners for toilets, clean housing and safe drinking water. While helping others, Chavez was also helping himself: he was improving his English, studying the law, and learning to become an effective public speaker.

In 1962, Chavez left the CSO to take a non-paying job with the newly formed National Farm Workers Association. Going from farm to farm, he urged workers to join the union. Many were afraid because they thought the big growers would take away their jobs. But slowly, Chavez was able to convince them to organize and the union grew. They started a credit union, a gas station, and a grocery store. The union was able to offer burial arrangements so workers would not have to go into debt to pay for the funeral of a family member, and also hired lawyers to help workers who had been cheated by their bosses.

Chavez helped organize strikes, which meant that unless conditions improved for the workers, they would refuse to work. The growers did become angry when they saw the crops rotting in the fields with no one to pick them. There were fights and beatings. Some union members were sent to jail. But Chavez believed the changes he sought could come about without violence, and he continued to work peacefully towards achieving his goals.

In 1965, Chavez and the union called for a **boycott** against the grape growers. The boycott gained national attention. In front of supermarkets all over America people carried signs that said "Don't Buy Grapes!" Donations of money poured in from all over the country. Important political leaders, like Robert F. Kennedy, Eugene McCarthy, and Hubert Humphrey gave their support to the migrant workers.

Through it all, Chavez worked to keep up the spirits of the workers. He spoke at churches, colleges and union meetings. He organized a march from Delano, California to the state capital at Sacramento—a distance of three hundred miles. Some of Chavez's followers grew impatient, and wanted the union to use violence to get their demands met. But Chavez refused. Like Martin Luther King Jr., he believed that resistance and negotiation were the best weapons of all.

Slowly, the boycott began to work. Some of the growers agreed to let Chavez and his union bargain for the migrant workers. That meant more money and better working conditions. In 1970, the grape boycott ended and Chavez called for a national boycott of lettuce that lasted until 1978.

Chavez was an active union member until his death in 1993. Along with his children and grandchildren, he continued to march, demonstrate and organize to improve working conditions for migrant farm workers throughout the United States. *See* ALINSKY, SAUL

Chisholm, Shirley

(1924–   )

FEMINIST AND ACTIVIST FOR CIVIL RIGHTS

> The argument that this amendment will not solve the problem of sex discrimination is not relevant. . . . Of course laws will not eliminate prejudice from the hearts of human beings. But that is no reason to allow prejudice to continue to be enshrined in our laws—to perpetuate injustice through inaction.
>
> —Chisolm, House of Representatives floor debate on the Equal Rights Amendment, August (1970)

The first African-American woman ever elected to Congress, Shirley Anita St. Hill Chisholm fought to change the laws to insure greater justice. She championed the cause of women's rights and promoted the rights of African Americans and Puerto Ricans, who made up 70 percent of the population in her Brooklyn congressional district. An educator and expert in child welfare, Chisholm also advocated greater attention and assistance for the nation's children.

Chisholm was born in the Bedford-Stuyvesant section of Brooklyn, New York. Both her parents were immigrants: her father from British Guiana and her mother from Barbados. At age three, Shirley St. Hill was sent to Barbados to live with her grandmother. This allowed her mother, who worked as a seamstress and domestic worker, and her father, who worked in a burlap-bag factory, to save money for their daughter's education. Her grandmother, she later recalled, taught her "pride, courage, and faith." Young Shirley, who learned to read and write by the time she was four years old, was educated in a British elementary school on the island. Returning to the U.S. in 1936, Shirley later graduated from a girls' high school in Brooklyn. Shirley St. Hill obtained an undergraduate degree in sociology from Brooklyn College, then taught in a nursery school while studying for a graduate degree in elementary education from Columbia University.

During the 1950s, Shirley Chisholm became an authority on early education. She directed the Friends Day Nursery and then the Hamilton-Madison Child Care Center, both located in New York. Recognizing her expertise, the city's Bureau of Child Welfare appointed her an educational consultant in its day-care division in 1959. Chisholm also became involved in community welfare, serving on the Board of Directors of the Brooklyn Home for Aged Colored People. She became politically active in such groups as the Democratic Women's Workshop, the League of Women Voters, and the local Bedford-Stuyvesant Political League. In 1964, Chisholm left the Child Welfare Bureau to run for the New York State Assembly. Her election made her only the second African-American woman to serve in the state legislature. Chisholm continued to promote child welfare as a legislator. She introduced a state law that funded the creation of day-care centers. She also won support for the development of a state program called SEEK (Search for Elevation, Education and Knowledge). SEEK provided poorly schooled African-American and Puerto Rican students the opportunity to enter state universities and receive remedial training.

In 1968, Chisholm ran for Congress in the poor Brooklyn ghetto known as Bedford-Stuyvesant. Chisholm called for improved education, employment, and housing for ghetto residents. The Democrat also took a stand opposing U.S. involvement in the Vietnam War. After easily winning the election, Chisholm remained outspoken as a member of the House. She urged reform of the seniority system that determines appointments to congressional committees. As a representative from a city district, she particularly objected to her assignment to a subcommittee on agriculture. Since Congress only had nine African-American members, she urged the House to use them more effectively. The House quickly reassigned her to a committee on Veterans Affairs. In her first term in Congress, she called for the creation of a national program modeled on New York's SEEK program.

Chisholm's autobiography, *Unbought and Unbossed*, was published in 1970. The following year, she joined with Betty Friedan, Gloria Steinem and fellow Congress member Bella Abzug to form the National Women's Political Caucus. The group looked for and encouraged women to run for political office. In 1972, Chisholm became the first woman ever to mount a serious campaign for the presidential nomination of a major party. Although she did not win the nomination, her run symbolized the emerging political power of both African Americans and women. For the next decade, Chisholm served as the voice of minorities, women, and children in Congress. She opposed the war in Vietnam, fought for welfare and tax reform, and helped save government programs that fought poverty in the 1970s. She also supported a woman's right to a safe and legal abortion and the Equal Rights Amendment, which would have guaranteed equal legal rights for men and women. In 1982, Chisholm left Congress and began teaching courses on politics, race, and women at Mount Holyoke College. *See* FRIEDAN, BETTY; STEINEM, GLORIA

Cleaver, Eldridge

(1935–   )

MUSLIM MINISTER AND ACTIVIST FOR BLACK
LIBERATION

Leroy Eldridge Cleaver overcame nearly twenty years in
prison to become a leading voice in the black liberation movement of the 1960s. While attending junior high school, Eldridge
was arrested for stealing a bicycle and sent to a reform school.
Shortly after his release in 1953, he was arrested for selling
marijuana and returned to reform school. Within days of his
release in 1954, he was again arrested for possession of marijuana. By then an adult, Cleaver received a two-and-one-half-
year sentence at the state prison in Soledad, California. While
in prison, Cleaver completed his high school education through
self-teaching and read constantly. Upon his release from
prison, Cleaver returned to selling marijuana. He also turned
to sexually attacking women. Tried and convicted of assault
with intent to kill in 1957, Cleaver received a sentence of two
to fourteen years in prison.

At Folsom Prison, Cleaver began writing as a means of examining—and saving—himself. He converted to the Nation of
Islam, a religion that urged African Americans to take pride
in themselves, discipline themselves, and separate themselves
from the oppression of white society. Becoming a Muslim minister, Cleaver was regularly placed in solitary confinement as
a punishment for his preaching. Yet he regarded this time
alone, with nothing but a Bible to read, as a religious retreat.

In 1966, the liberal magazine *Ramparts* began publishing
Cleaver's prison memoirs and essays, which were collected
and published in 1968 as *Soul on Ice*. The articles brought
Cleaver the promise of a job with the magazine and support
for his parole from famous writers and intellectuals. Released
from prison, Cleaver wrote for *Ramparts* and helped found
Black House, an African-American youth center in San Francisco. At Black House, he met Huey P. Newton and Bobby

Seale, the co-founders of the Black Panther party, a militant black liberation group that Cleaver joined in 1967. The Black Panthers believed that fear of the police prevented many African Americans from joining in the struggle for equality. Cleaver helped patrol Oakland's ghettos to protect African Americans from harassment by the white police. Although many Black Panthers carried guns on these patrols, Cleaver remained unarmed because he was still on parole. In April 1968, Cleaver and other Black Panthers urged young African Americans in San Francisco to forego violence in the wake of the assassination of Martin Luther King, Jr. In an exchange of gunfire between Oakland police and a group of Black Panthers, Cleaver was wounded. Although he had not violated his parole, Cleaver was sent to jail for two months until a judge ruled that he had been unlawfully imprisoned.

As minister of information for the Black Panthers, Cleaver rejected the call of Stokely Carmichael for "Black Power." Cleaver wanted all people to have equal access to power. He defined black liberation as the removal of obstructions that blocked African Americans from reaping every available economic, political, and social benefit. As the Black Panthers began providing free breakfasts to ghetto children, Cleaver started a lecture series on racism at the University of California at Berkeley. Cleaver also ran for president as the candidate of the Peace and Freedom Party.

In November 1968, an appeals court overturned the earlier judge's order to release Cleaver. Ordered to return to prison, Cleaver instead went underground and fled the country. After several months in Cuba, Cleaver lived for six years in exile in Algeria. Cleaver, who declared himself a born-again Christian, voluntarily returned to the United States in 1975. Cleaver remained free on bail while awaiting trial on charges of assault and attempted murder in the 1968 conflict with Oakland police. The state dropped the attempted murder charge when Cleaver pleaded guilty to assault in 1979. Cleaver was sentenced to five years of probation and community service.

Cleaver has continued to struggle with the law since his return to the United States. In 1988, he received probation for charges of burglary and cocaine possession. In 1992, he was again arrested for possession of cocaine after leaving a "crack house" in Oakland. Charges were later dropped when a judge ruled that the police had wrongly arrested him. *See* CHARMICHAEL, STOKELY; KING, MARTIN LUTHER, JR.; NEWTON, HUEY P.

Coffin, William Sloane, Jr.

(1924–   )

PRESBYTERIAN CLERGYMAN AND ACTIVIST AGAINST
WAR AND RACISM

> All of life is risk exercise. That's the only way to live more freely, and more interestingly.
>
> —Coffin (1977)

Social activist and risk-taker, William Sloane Coffin, Jr. has called himself a "Christian revolutionary." A member of the Presbyterian clergy, Coffin has spoken out against racism, the Vietnam War, and the nuclear arms race. In 1979, he became one of four clergy members chosen to celebrate Christmas with Americans taken hostage by revolutionary students in Iran.

William's uncle, the Reverend Henry Sloane Coffin, was for twenty years president of New York's Union Theological Seminary, a school that trains clergy members. His father, a vice president of the W. & J. Sloane furniture store, died when William was nine. The family moved from Manhattan to Carmel, California. As a teenager, William entertained hopes of becoming a concert pianist. He studied in Paris, France from 1938 to 1939, but returned to the United States when World War II erupted in Europe. After graduating from Phillips Academy, a private school in Andover, Massachusetts in 1942, Coffin spent a year studying music at Yale University.

Service in the U.S. Army during and after World War II transformed Coffin. His language skills led to an assignment as a liaison officer—in charge of communicating with allied armies to promote understanding and unity. Coffin worked first with the French army, then with the Soviet army. After the war ended, Coffin in 1946 was ordered to assist in a program called Operation Keelhaul. Run jointly by the English and American armies, the program aimed to return captured soldiers who opposed Soviet leader Josef Stalin to the Soviet Union. These soldiers, regarded as traitors by Stalin and his government, would then be put to death or sentenced to life in a brutal prison camp. When the day came to turn over the unsuspecting soldiers to the Soviet authorities, Coffin saw three commit suicide rather than return to their native country. In his memoirs, Coffin wrote that his participation in this operation left him with a lifelong "burden of guilt."

After his discharge from the army in 1947, Coffin returned to Yale, where he studied government. Before receiving his undergraduate degree in 1949, Coffin had already accepted a job with the Central Intelligence Agency (CIA). Before starting with the CIA, however, he attended a conference on the ministry in New York. The conference convinced Coffin that the church could take a prominent role in social reform. He postponed his commitment to the CIA for a year to study at the Union Theological Seminary, where his uncle had once served as president. From 1950 to 1953, Coffin worked in Germany for the CIA. When he returned to the U.S., he completed his studies for the ministry, receiving a bachelor of divinity degree from Yale in 1956.

Coffin served as chaplain at Phillips Andover Academy and then at Williams College. From 1958 to 1976, he was chaplain of Yale University. Coffin led a group of students to Guinea (Africa) in 1960. There, they helped build a community center in Mamou. In 1961, Coffin was appointed an adviser to the newly formed Peace Corps. This government agency was designed to do on a large scale what Coffin had done on a small scale the year before: working with the people of poorer nations to improve their living conditions. Coffin directed a training center in Puerto Rico for Peace Corps field workers.

Coffin also became involved in the **civil rights movement** in 1961. He was arrested for his participation in the "Freedom Rides": groups of African Americans and whites riding the buses together through the South to protest against **segregation** (separation of the races) in bus terminals. Coffin was arrested twice more—in 1963 and 1964—for his part in protests against segregation. He saw this activism as part of his duty as a clergy member. He believed that the clergy must disturb the peace in order to challenge and change the existing order of society.

Coffin became a prominent anti-war activist during the 1960s. He co-founded Clergy and Laity Concerned about Vietnam, which brought Jews and Christians together to promote the cause of peace. In 1967, he began providing **sanctuary** (protection from the law) in the Yale Chapel to those who refused to serve in the military. That year, Coffin and Dr. Benjamin Spock collected nearly one thousand draft cards turned in at a Boston antiwar rally. Coffin then delivered the cards to the U.S. Justice Department. Coffin and Spock wanted to show their support for the rights of those whose conscience would not allow them to fight in a war they saw as unjust. The following year, Coffin, Spock and three others were convicted of conspiring to aid and abet resistance to the draft. The convictions were overturned by an appeals court in 1970.

After leaving Yale in 1976, Coffin worked for a year combatting world hunger. He also completed *Once to Every Man*, a memoir published in 1977. That year, he was appointed senior minister at New York's Riverside Church. The church had built a reputation for social concern and activism in local, national, and global issues. Coffin carried on this tradition, advocating arms control with Clergy and Laity Concerned, the group he had helped found during the Vietnam War. Coffin also led Riverside Church—already known for its tolerance of differences in creed, race, and ethnic background—in welcoming the participation of homosexuals in the church.

In November, 1979, Iranian students stormed the U.S. embassy in Teheran, Iran and took the diplomatic staff hostage. Iran's government, the Revolutionary Council, supported the students in their action and their demand for the return and trial of their former dictator, the Shah Mohammad Reza Pahlavi. The Iranian government invited Coffin and three others to lead the hostages in Christmas services. Both before and after his trip, Coffin urged the U.S. to adopt a new stance toward Iran. He called for the U.S. to admit its past wrongs (including its support of the Shah) against the people of Iran. In this, as in so many of his stands, he did not fear to voice a view simply because it was unpopular. *See* SPOCK, BENJAMIN

Commoner, Barry

(1917–   )

ENVIRONMENTAL ACTIVIST

Barry Commoner's interest in biology began as a teenager, when he collected nature specimens in Brooklyn parks and studied them under a microscope. In 1937, he earned an undergraduate degree in zoology from Columbia University. He followed this in 1941 with a doctoral from Harvard University in cellular **physiology**: the study of the functions and processes of cells. After military service and a brief stint as associate editor of *Science Illustrated*, Commoner became an associate professor of plant physiology at Washington University in St. Louis in 1947. A respected lecturer and researcher, Commoner studied the effect of viruses on the process of cell reproduction in plants. This and his later work with laboratory rats contributed to the development of techniques used for the early detection of cancer in humans.

Commoner's environmental activism began in the early 1950s. Commoner was alarmed by the dangers of nuclear-bomb tests and the government's indifference to the effects of radioactive fallout on the atmosphere. He helped found the St. Louis Committee for Nuclear Information, which later broadened its scope and changed its name to the Committee for Environmental Information. As vice president of the committee from 1958 to 1965 and president from 1965 to 1966, Commoner built support for the international Nuclear Test Ban Treaty signed by more than one-hundred nations in 1963.

Commoner served as an informed spokesperson for the growing **environmental movement**, warning the public that unless changes were made, the world would soon be unsuitable for human life. From 1960 to 1966 he acted as chair of a committee formed by the American Association for the Advancement of Science to study how science could help promote human welfare. In 1966, his book *Science and Survival* explored human problems in a society ruled by its technology. In 1966, Commoner was named director of Washington University's newly formed Center for the Biology of Natural Systems, which conducts research on the relationship between humans and their natural environment. In 1969, he urged the government to test the impact on the environment of any new chemical prior to allowing its use. In 1970, he warned that at its present rate of growth, the world's population would outstrip its food supply by the year 2000. During the 1980s and 1990s, Commoner criticized the administrations of Ronald Reagan and George Bush for regulating pollution instead of preventing it. His 1990 book, *Making Peace with the Planet,* calls for an end to the war against the earth and its environment.

Converse, Harriet M.

(1836–1903)

ACTIVIST FOR NATIVE AMERICAN RIGHTS AND CULTURE

Harriet Arnot Maxwell Converse, whose grandfather traded with Native Americans and whose father was adopted by the Seneca's Wolf Clan, committed herself to the cause of preserving Native American culture and defending Native American rights. Thomas Maxwell, Harriet's father, had grown up among the Seneca tribe and later maintained his concern for the welfare of Native Americans as a member of the House of Representatives.

Harriet Maxwell Converse did not take up the cause of defending Native American rights and culture until she was forty-five years old. In 1881, she became friends with General Ely S. Parker, sachem (Native American chief) of the Six Nations of the Iroquois Confederacy. Parker introduced her to Iroquois culture and took her on frequent visits to reservations in New York and Canada. Fascinated with their folklore, Converse became determined to preserve the Iroquois people and their culture. Converse had already established her reputation as a poet with a highly praised collection, *Sheaves*, published in 1882. Two years later, she wrote an ode, "The Ho-de-no-sau-nee: the Confederacy of the Iroquois." In 1891, Converse helped defeat a state bill to end tribal ownership of New York's Native American reservations and parcel the land out to individual tribe members. Adopted by the council of the Seneca Nation as a member, Converse in 1892 became the first white woman named honorary chief of the Six Nations.

To help preserve Native American culture, Converse used grants from the New York State Museum and her own money to establish collections of Native American artifacts. In addition to donating her father's collection of relics to the museum, she acquired pieces from private collectors and individual tribespeople. Converse also built collections for the American Museum of Natural History, New York's Museum of the American Indian, and Harvard's Peabody Museum. Her folklore collection, *Myths and Legends of the New York State Iroquois*, was published in 1908, five years after her death.

Davis, Angela

(1944–   )

ACTIVIST FOR BLACK LIBERATION

Angela Yvonne Davis, the daughter of teachers and later a teacher herself, became an international symbol of the black-liberation movement while on trial for conspiracy and murder charges in the early 1970s. Growing up in a **segregated** middle-class neighborhood in Birmingham, Alabama, Davis joined her mother in civil rights demonstrations as a young girl. While attending a private school in New York in 1959, she lived with the family of Reverend William Howard Melish. Melish, a prominent civil rights activist, served as chair of the American-Soviet Friendship Council, which promoted peace and improved relations between the United States and the Soviet Union.

As a student at Brandeis University, she spent her junior year (1963–64) at the University of Paris. There, she formed friendships with Algerian students who described their revolution against the French—who had established colonies in their country—and complained of their second-class treatment in France. Davis's radical leanings increased when she returned to Brandeis. There, she studied with renowned political philosopher Herbert Marcuse. Marcuse promoted the ideas of Karl Marx, who had advocated the revolution of workers against their capitalist oppressors. Marcuse saw modern industrial society as repressive and advanced the notion of challenging the system through individual acts of resistance and rebellion. Earning her undergraduate degree in French literature in 1965, Davis continued her studies under Marcuse, who had moved to the University of California at San Diego (UCSD), where she obtained a graduate degree in 1968.

Her career as a political activist began in 1967, when she helped found a Black Students Council at UCSD. She became active in two civil rights organizations: the Student Nonviolent Coordinating Committee (SNCC) and the more militant Black Panthers. In 1968, she left these organizations to join the Communist Party, which called for radical change in every aspect of society. Davis was hired to teach four philosophy courses at the University of California at Los Angeles (UCLA) in 1969. But when Governor Ronald Reagan learned of her membership in the Communist Party, he pressured his fellow members on UCLA's Board of Regents to fire her before she had taught a single class. A court order reversed the firing, but Davis was allowed to teach just one semester at UCLA. Despite excellent evaluations and the objections of faculty and students, the board fired Davis again in 1970.

Davis was fired, in part, due to speeches outside the classroom in support of the "Soledad Brothers": three African-American convicts charged with the murder of a guard at

Soledad Prison in California. Davis set up Soledad House, where she raised funds and organized protests to prevent what she called a "legal lynching." The target of repeated death threats, Davis legally bought three guns for her protection. On 7 August 1970, Jonathan Jackson, the teenage brother of one of the Soledad Brothers, went to the Marin County Courthouse and used Davis's guns to take hostages, which he hoped to trade for the release of the Soledad Brothers. Jackson, a judge, and two others were killed in a shootout.

Though Davis had not been present at the shootout, her ownership of the guns led to charges that she had planned the kidnapping. When Davis went **underground**, the Federal Bureau of Investigation put her on its list of ten-most-wanted criminals. Her capture, after two months in hiding, sparked "Free Angela" movements around the world. After sixteen months in jail, Davis was released on bail as her trial approached in 1972. Charged with kidnapping, murder, and conspiracy, Davis was found not guilty of all charges by the jury.

After her release, Davis called for the release of all political prisoners in the United States. She also continued to work for social and economic change. After running in 1980 as the Communist Party candidate for vice president, Davis left the party. As a teacher at the University of California at Santa Cruz, she has urged African Americans to defy racism on campus. In 1991, she took part in protests against the Persian Gulf War. As a member of the National Black Women's Health Project, Davis has focused her current efforts on the issue of the well-being of African-American women.

Day, Dorothy

(1897–1980)

SOCIAL REFORMER AND PACIFIST

> The ugliness of life in a world which professed itself to be Christian appalled me. . . . I felt my faith had nothing in common with that of Christians around me. . . . that I must turn from it as from a drug. . . . So I hardened my heart.
>
> —From Day's *The Long Loneliness* (1952)

In her autobiography, *The Long Loneliness*, Dorothy Day described why she turned away from the Christian church. Yet Day would return to the church, becoming a Roman Catholic a dozen years later. A crusader for social justice, Day founded and guided the Catholic Worker movement. In reaching out to the poor and promoting peace, she served as a model for social activists within the Roman Catholic church.

Day was born in Brooklyn, but grew up in California, Chicago, and New York. Her family was **agnostic**, meaning they doubted the existence of God but admitted that God might exist. Dorothy, however, became a believer in God. She had found a Bible in the attic of the house in Berkeley, California, where they lived. During her teens, she was baptized and joined the Episcopal church. Completing high school at age sixteen, Day attended the University of Illinois on a small scholarship from 1914 to 1916. While in school, she supported herself by writing for the local newspaper, babysitting, and housecleaning. Her lifelong commitment to social justice grew out of the heartrending sight of Chicago's poor. It was at this time that Day left the church, which seemed to her blind or insensitive to social injustice and human misery. Believing that **socialism** could do more than the church to achieve justice and relieve poverty, she joined the Socialist Party.

In 1916, Day quit school and moved to New York with her family. She began writing for *The Call*, a daily socialist newspaper. Day left home shortly after joining *The Call* because her father, a sportswriter and editor himself, objected to women newspaper reporters. For a short time, she wrote for *The Masses*, but the government stopped publication of the radical magazine when it opposed U.S. entry into World War I. Day then took a job with *The Liberator*, edited by Crystal Eastman. Day, who opposed the military draft, joined sixty other women in a White House protest against U.S. involvement in World War I. Arrested and jailed, the women were released only after a hunger strike in which they refused to eat for ten days.

During the 1920s, Day wrote a novel, feature articles for *The New Orleans Item*, and screenplays before settling in Staten Island, New York with her **common-law** husband. In 1927, the couple had a child. Concern for her daughter's upbringing led Day to baptize her as a Catholic. Later that year, Day herself entered the church. Over the next five years, Day found few Catholics who shared her commitment to radical social reform. She did manage to find work at *Commonweal*, a liberal Catholic journal. She wrote articles on the labor movement, life in Mexico, and the hunger of unemployed workers during the Depression. In 1932, the managing editor of *Commonweal* introduced her to Peter Maurin, a soap-box socialist. Maurin would stand on soap boxes in city parks calling for the creation of a new Christian social and economic order.

With Maurin, Day published the first issue of *The Catholic Worker* in 1933. The monthly journal promoted Maurin's call for a "green revolution." Day and Maurin wanted to bring workers and scholars together in "houses of hospitality" that served the city's poor and homeless people and in nonprofit communes devoted to farming and crafts. *The Catholic Worker* also called for the creation of discussion groups to help "the workers to become scholars and the scholars to become workers." To put this program into action, Day founded St. Joseph's House of Hospitality in New York's Bowery district. St. Joseph's, a **settlement house**, directly served those in the community who needed help: unemployed workers, poor families, and alcoholics.

The Catholic Worker movement attracted hundreds of volunteers and quickly spread throughout the country. The movement hoped to achieve social justice by directly attacking the economic problems of the Depression. As she herself had done, Day urged her followers to adopt voluntary poverty in serving the poor community. By the end of the decade, the nation had over thirty houses of hospitality and several farming communes. The *Catholic Worker* grew rapidly too, reaching one-hundred-thousand readers in 1934 and peaking at 150,000 readers two years later. The organization supported the creation of labor unions during the depressed economy of the 1930s. Day joined picket lines and operated soup kitchens to feed workers on strike. Day described the first years of the movement in *House of Hospitality*, published in 1939.

During World War II (1941–45), most Americans, including Catholics, favored U.S. involvement in the war. Day, however, refused to abandon her commitment to **pacifism**: the opposition to war and violence. As she had in World War I, Day supported resistance to the draft. During the war, the government's fear of spying led to the **internment** of Japanese Americans, who were confined in special camps for the duration of the war. Day and *The Catholic Worker* harshly condemned this action. Day's support for unpopular causes helped drop the readership of *The Catholic Worker* to forty-thousand.

Although Day supported striking Catholic cemetery workers in a labor struggle with the New York Archdiocese in 1949, she seldom directly opposed the Roman Catholic church. The publication of her autobiography, *The Long Loneliness*, in 1952, helped increase the demand for Day as a public speaker. Her annual speaking tours continued into the 1970s.

From 1955, Day annually protested against government attempts to prepare people for a nuclear war. A New York law required everyone to take shelter once a year for a nuclear-attack drill. Day refused to comply, leading other protesters into City Hall Park. For challenging this law, Day spent short terms in jail every year for six years. Day wrote a history of the Catholic Worker movement, *Loaves and Fishes*, in 1963. Her activism would continue into her seventies. In 1973, Day was arrested with Cesar Chavez in a demonstration on behalf of striking farm workers. She died in Mary House, a hospice for women established by *The Catholic Worker. See* CHAVEZ, CESAR; EASTMAN, CRYSTAL

Decter, Midge

(1927–   )

CONSERVATIVE ACTIVIST

Midge Rosenthal Decter has consistently challenged the liberal ideas of modern times. Although she never graduated from college, Decter studied for a year at the University of Minnesota and three more years at the Jewish Theological Seminary of America in New York. Decter's first job was as secretary to the managing editor of *Commentary*, an intellectual journal published by the American Jewish Committee. There, she would meet and later marry her second husband, editor Norman Podhoretz. For twenty years, Decter rose through the publishing ranks, serving in various editorial positions at *Midstream*, *Commentary*, and CBS Legacy Books before becoming executive editor of *Harper's Magazine* from 1969 to 1971.

During these years, Decter also wrote dozens of articles that demonstrated her gradual shift from **liberal** ideas to **conservative** ones. Her first book, *The Liberated Woman and Other Americans*, published in 1970, questioned the assumptions of the women's liberation movement. Decter argued that the movement had itself put down women by considering childrearing and housework as inferior tasks. In her 1972 book, *The New Chastity and Other Arguments Against Women's Liberation*, Decter again took aim at women's liberation and the new sexual freedom it had helped win. In 1975, her *Liberal Parents, Radical Children* argued that overly lenient parents had paved the way for their children's rebellion against society in the 1960s. She criticized this **countercultural movement** for producing a generation of dropouts, drug addicts, and sexual revolutionaries. Decter also continued to write articles targeting liberal causes. Because she believes they lead to a loss of self-respect among women and minorities, she opposes **affirmative action**: job, housing, and education programs that offer favorable treatment to past victims of racism or sexism. She also opposes the movement to secure equal rights for homosexuals.

Around 1980, Dexter founded and became executive director of the Committee for the Free World. Decter's organization opposed to both Communism and the rise of terrorism throughout the world. Decter saw the former Soviet Union—and the agents of terrorism she believed they sponsored—as a threat to peace, freedom, and private rights. Throughout the 1980s, the Committee for the Free World actively supported the rigidly anticommunist positions of President Ronald Reagan.

Dellinger, David

(1915–)

ANTIWAR AND CIVIL RIGHTS ACTIVIST

Peace activist and author David Dellinger began working for the cause of peace as a ministry student at the Union Theological Seminary in New York in 1940. For refusing to register for the military draft, Dellinger was sentenced to a year and a day in the Lewisburg, Pennsylvania Federal Penitentiary. While in prison, Dellinger went on a two-month hunger strike to protest against **segregation**: the separation of prisoners by race. In the 1940s and 1950s, Dellinger actively supported such causes as the destruction of all nuclear weapons, the growing **civil rights movement**, and preserving fundamental freedoms of speech, press, and assembly. In 1956, Dellinger helped found *Liberation*, a magazine which aimed to inspire readers to act for peace and against injustice.

Dellinger gained his greatest fame protesting against the Vietnam War throughout the 1960s. When Dellinger traveled to Hanoi and met with the North Vietnamese leader Ho Chi Minh, the United States temporarily revoked his passport. As chair of a number of committees opposing the Vietnam War, Dellinger organized major demonstrations in New York (1965), Washington (1967, 1969, and 1971), and at Chicago's Democratic National Convention (1968).

The Chicago protest led to a violent confrontation between city police and demonstrators. Dellinger, Tom Hayden, Abbie Hoffman, and four others were charged with conspiring to commit violence and crossing state lines to incite a riot. In 1970 five of the seven defendants, the Chicago Seven, were found guilty of inciting a riot. Dellinger and three others were also found guilty of contempt of court for swearing and mockery in the courtroom. Dellinger received a five-year sentence and a $5,000 fine, but an appeals court overturned the riot convictions in 1972. Although the appeals court upheld the contempt charge, no sentence was ever imposed.

Dellinger, editor of *Seven Days Magazine* since 1975, has written extensively in support of nonviolent but radical change. His books include *Revolutionary Nonviolence* (1966), *More Power Than We Know: The People's Movement Toward Democracy* (1975), and *Vietnam Revisited: From Covert Action to Invasion to Reconstruction* (1986). *See* HAYDEN, TOM; HOFFMAN, ABBIE

Dix, Dorothea Lynde

(1802–1877)

MENTAL-HEALTH CRUSADER

Dorothea Lynde Dix worked to improve the care and treatment of the mentally ill throughout the nation. The daughter of a traveling Methodist minister who preached among the people of the Maine frontier, Dix devoted her early activism to the cause of education. Dorothea spent her early teen years living with a great-aunt in Worcester, Massachusetts. There, at age fourteen, she opened her own school for small children in 1816. In Boston from 1819 to 1821, Dix educated herself through public lectures, visits to museums, and long days in the city's libraries. While teaching at a private school, she opened her own school for young girls in 1821. Dix published an elementary natural-science text, *Conversations on Common*

Things, in 1824. A year later, she published *Hymns for Children*, a collection of uplifting poetry, and *Evening Hours*, a collection of meditations. In 1827, however, Dix had to give up her teaching due to the onset of **tuberculosis**.

After several summers as the caretaker and tutor for a Unitarian pastor, Dix regained her health. She opened a school in Boston in 1831, then a Sunday school for poor children in 1832. The Sunday school had grown to more than seven-hundred students by 1836, when Dix's health again broke down.

In 1841, Dix began teaching a Sunday School class for women in an East Cambridge prison. The discovery that insane women were living in unheated, dirty rooms among alcoholics, prostitutes, thieves, beggars, and other inmates horrified Dix. She brought the inmates food, blankets, and warm clothing, and obtained a court order forcing the prison to install heating stoves and renovate the women's quarters. For the next eighteen months, Dix visited every jail and workhouse in Massachusetts, investigating their treatment of the mentally ill. Although she observed humane care and therapy at a few costly private hospitals, Dix saw only abuse and neglect at most of the state's mental institutions.

Presenting her findings to the state legislature in 1843, Dix convinced the state to provide funds needed to enlarge the Worcester State Lunatic Hospital. Over the next two years, Dix conducted similar surveys in Rhode Island and New York. Again her efforts led to increased funding for the improvement of conditions in mental institutions. In 1845, she oversaw the creation of a model mental-health facility in Trenton, New Jersey—the state's first mental hospital. That same year, Dix wrote *Prisons and Prison Discipline in the United States*, which called for widespread reform in the nation's prisons.

From 1845 to 1848, Dix continued her investigative work in the Midwest and the South, reporting to state legislatures on the poor conditions in their mental-health facilities and urging them to take action. For the next six years, Dix worked to rally support for the creation of a federal land trust that would provide funds for the care of the insane. Approved by Congress in 1854, the land trust was vetoed by President Franklin Pierce, who believed that the states, rather than the federal government, should care for the mentally ill. Dix next took her crusade to Europe. Between 1854 and 1856, her reports on European prisons and mental hospitals prompted action by both Queen Victoria of England and Pope Pius IX in Italy.

In 1861, when war broke out between the northern and southern states, Dix organized the Women's Volunteer Nursing Corps. When the war ended in 1865, Dix returned to her mental-health work. Her unceasing efforts led to the founding of new mental-health institutions in thirty-two states, Canada, and Europe.

Douglass, Frederick

(1817–1895)

ANTI-SLAVERY LEADER

> Why am I a slave? Why are some people slaves and others masters? These were perplexing questions and very troublesome to my childhood.
>
> —Douglass,
> in *Life and Times of Frederick Douglass*

Frederick Douglass was an eloquent and dedicated opponent of slavery. His book *Life and Times of Frederick Douglass* is a candid account of his early life in which he precisely described his childhood in bondage.

When he was born in 1817, Frederick Douglass was named Frederick Bailey by his mother, a slave who lived on a plantation on the eastern shore of Maryland. His father was a white man whom he never knew. As a slave, young Frederick's life was not easy, filled with hunger, regular beatings and hard work. When he was eight years old, his mother died and he was sent to live with his master's relatives in Baltimore. There he became the special property of a boy his own age, Thomas Auld. His new master's mother, Mrs. Auld, began to teach him to read. At the time, it was against the law to teach a slave to read. When Mr. Auld discovered the reading lessons, he stopped them at once. But Frederick had learned enough to continue studying on his own.

When he was seventeen, he was sent to live with another member of the Auld family. On this plantation, there was a small Sunday school for slaves and Frederick was asked to teach in it. But when his new masters found out that he was teaching the other slaves to read, the classes were suspended and Frederick was beaten again. Frederick was sent to live with a farmer named Edward Covey who had a reputation for subduing defiant slaves. Covey beat him regularly with a whip until one day, Frederick fought back. After that, Covey never beat Frederick again.

Still, he longed to be free and made plans to escape. One attempt was thwarted by a slave who betrayed him. But finally he succeeded and made his way to New York. There, he turned to other free blacks for help and support. While there, he fell in love with a free black woman named Anne Murray, and they married. Together, they set off for New Bedford, Massachusetts. It was around this time that he changed his name, because as an escaped slave, he could be captured and sent back to his slave master. He chose the name Frederick Douglass, which he used for the rest of his life.

In New Bedford, Douglass had to work hard, taking any job he could find. He got work handling and loading cargo in a shipyard. His wife did laundry. But when he joined the Abolitionist Society (a group which believed that slavery was wrong and wanted to **abolish** or do away with it) he found a new direction for his life. In 1841, at the age of 24, he made his first anti-slavery speech in Nantucket. Soon, he was making speeches on a regular basis and gaining quite a large following.

In 1845, he published *Narrative Life of Frederick Douglass*, which described life as a slave. The publication of this book was a daring act, for it let people know where he was and how to find him; since he was still technically a slave, he could have been sent back to his master. So he left the United States and spent the next two years in England. Before returning home, he bought his freedom from his old master for the sum of $710.96. While some antislavery supporters felt this was wrong because it meant he was going along with rules established by slave owners, Douglass took a more practical approach: he had important work to do and couldn't afford to spend time worrying about being sent back into slavery.

Back in America, Douglass bought a home in Rochester, New York. He continued speaking out against slavery, and became involved in the **Underground Railroad**, a secret organization that helped bring slaves from the South to the liberty of the North. This was a dangerous thing to do because under the Fugitive Slave Act, anyone caught helping runaway slaves would be severely punished. Douglass also launched a newspaper called the *North Star*.

When the Civil War broke out in 1861, Douglass had to rethink his position against violence. He finally agreed to support the war and urged black men to join the Union army. The first answer to his plea were his own two sons, Charles and Lewis. During the war, he was dismayed to learn that black soldiers received half the pay of whites; moreover they were not promoted as quickly and as prisoners, they were often tortured or killed by Southerners angry that they dared fight against their old masters. Douglass arranged to meet with President Abraham Lincoln in the White House. Lincoln was responsive to the points Douglass raised. He promised to increase the salaries of the soldiers and warned Southern leaders that he would execute one rebel or Southern prisoner for each black who was killed in a southern prison. Douglass and Lincoln liked each other and met two additional times during the war. After President Lincoln was assassinated, his widow sent his favorite walking stick to Frederick Douglass.

When the Civil War was over, Douglass continued to work for the rights of black Americans. He worked with congressmen to secure voting rights and education for blacks. He spoke against **segregation**—the separating of blacks and whites in public places. Nor did he neglect the civil rights of others: he was one of the few male supporters of women's suffrage (the right to vote). He was also active in politics.

With the money he earned from his lectures, Douglass bought a house in the capital of Washington D.C. It was here that he spent his last years, never ceasing to work to secure freedom and opportunity for his fellow black Americans.

Dumont, Gabriel

(1838–1906)

ACTIVIST FOR METIS RIGHTS

Gabriel Dumont became a leader in the fight for the rights of the Metis—people of mixed French-Canadian and Native-American ancestry—in Canada. Dumont was born along the Red River in what was then known as Rupert's Land: the vast territory from Hudson Bay to the Saskatchewan River Valley. The son of a Metis hunter, Gabriel became a skilled buffalo hunter and wilderness guide. Though he never learned to read or write, Dumont could speak and understand six languages. At that time, the peoples of the western Canadian prairie had no government to protect them. At age thirteen, he helped defend a Metis camp against Sioux attackers in 1851. Dumont and his father later established a treaty between the Metis and the Sioux in 1862 that helped insure peaceful settlement of the Canadian prairie. The following year, Dumont was elected to lead Metis hunters along the Saskatchewan River. He led the hunt until 1881, when the buffalo were nearly extinct.

In 1873, Dumont was elected president of the first local government between Manitoba and the Rockies. Dumont realized that the buffalo hunt would soon end and that the Metis would need to depend on farming in order to live on the prairie. He therefore tried to set up a system to establish ownership of the land. The North West Mounted Police (NWMP) took control of the land for Canada and ended Dumont's government in 1875. Land speculators and government surveyors from Canada poured into the region. For the next ten years, Dumont led the Metis in their struggle to win Canadian recognition of their rights, especially to own land. Canada, however, repeatedly delayed awarding the people land grants. In 1884, Dumont traveled to Montana as a representative of the settlers, the Metis, and people of mixed Native American and English ancestry. He sought the help of Louis Riel, who had secured the rights of Metis in Manitoba fourteen years earlier, to present their grievances to the Canadian government.

When Riel declared his own government of the Saskatchewan River region in 1885, Dumont was placed in charge of the military. He led the small Metis army—three hundred poorly trained, poorly armed men—in the North West Rebellion. The rebels, Metis and Cree tribemembers, fought for the independence of Sasketchewan from Canada. Although Dumont won victories in battles with the NWMP at Duck Lake and Fish Creek, the rebel headquarters at Batoche fell within two months. After defending Batoche to the end, Dumont fled to Montana, joining Buffalo Bill's traveling Wild West show. After Canada pardoned all rebels not already under sentence, Dumont returned to the Saskatchewan district in 1888. There, he hunted, traded, and narrated his account of the rebellion. *See* RIEL, LOUIS

Eastman, Crystal

(1881–1928)

SOCIAL REFORMER AND WOMEN'S RIGHTS ACTIVIST

The daughter of two ordained Congregational ministers, Crystal Eastman inherited a commitment to women's rights and social reform from her mother. After earning a law degree from New York University in 1907, Eastman took part in a landmark study of industrial accidents in Pittsburgh, Pennsylvania. Eastman's *Work Accidents and the Law*, published in 1910, helped fuel the movement for laws that would establish benefits programs for workers, compensate injured workers, and improve job safety. The only female member of the New York State Commission on Employers' Liability from 1909 to 1911, Eastman helped draft the state's Workers' Compensation Law. At this time, she also began calling for a **socialist** revolution against a society that repressed its workers.

In addition to her work for labor reform, Eastman also took up the cause of equal rights for women. After managing the Political Equality League's campaign to win the vote for women in Wisconsin in 1912, Eastman helped found the Congressional Union for Woman Suffrage in 1913. As war broke out in Europe in 1914, Eastman campaigned for peace. She organized and headed the New York branch of the Women's Peace Party and directed the American Union Against Militarism (AUAM). Eastman gave speeches and wrote articles opposing the buildup of U.S. military industries prior to the nation's entry into World War I. In 1917, she helped organize AUAM's Civil Liberties Bureau. This bureau (renamed the American Civil Liberties Union when AUAM disbanded after the war) pledged to defend basic freedoms of speech, press, assembly, and conscience. Also in 1917, Eastman became managing editor of *Liberator*, a radical journal she had founded with her brother Max.

When the war ended, Eastman returned to the cause of women's rights. Eastman, who had refused to accept financial support from her ex-husband when they divorced in 1916, called for the abolition of laws favoring women as well as those favoring men. In 1919, she helped organize the first U.S. Feminist Congress in New York, where she demanded the vote, equal opportunities for jobs, and birth control. From 1921 to 1925, Eastman lived in England, where she helped found a London branch of the National Woman's Party.

Evans, Elizabeth Glendower

(1856–1937)

SOCIAL REFORMER

For nearly thirty years, Elizabeth Gardiner Glendower Evans served on the board of trustees of the Massachusetts reformatory system. Under her progressive leadership from 1886 to 1914, the reformatory system changed its goals. No longer content merely to lock away and punish young criminals, reform schools and prisons began attempting to rehabilitate them. Evans introduced training programs into the reform system and advocated the "casework" approach to offenders. This approach treats each person as an individual rather than just as an offender—a thief or a murderer.

Beginning in 1908, Evans also devoted her energies to labor reform. A four-month study of trade unionism in England converted Evans to **socialism**. In 1909, she joined the National American Woman Suffrage Association because she believed that giving women the vote would help advance the socialist movement. Evans also joined the Women's Trade Union League, initiating a long career as a labor reformer. Evans demonstrated with women weavers on strike in Roxbury in 1910. For the next two years, she led the Massachusetts drive to enact the nation's first minimum-wage law. In 1919, Evans was arrested for picketing with textile workers in Lawrence.

From 1913 to 1935, Evans provided financial support and acted as contributing editor of the progressive *La Follete's Magazine* and its successor, *The Progressive*. She also joined the peace movement, going to the Netherlands in 1915 to attend the International Congress of Women, which condemned war as a means of settling disputes among nations.

In the 1920s, Evans became the national director of the American Civil Liberties Union (ACLU), a group dedicated to preserving basic freedoms. Under Evans, the ACLU defended the freedom of speech and other rights of immigrants. This cause led her to provide financial aid and public support for

Nicola Sacco and Bartolomeo Vanzetti. In one of the most notorious trials of the decade, Italian immigrants Sacco and Vanzetti were convicted of murdering two men and stealing a payroll. Evans and the ACLU appealed the verdict, arguing that the men were denied a fair trial. They contended that the jury convicted Sacco and Vanzetti not for the crime itself, but for their **anarchist** beliefs: the opposition to all forms of government. Despite Evans' efforts on their behalf, Sacco and Vanzetti were executed in 1927. In the final decade of her life, Evans took up the cause of striking coal miners in Harlan County, Kentucky. She also joined in protests against medical experimentation on live animals, a practice she saw as inhumane.

Fauntroy, Walter E.

(1933–)

CIVIL RIGHTS ACTIVIST

Having grown up in a Washington, D.C. ghetto, Baptist Reverend Walter Edward Fauntroy returned to renew and reform his old neighborhood after earning his divinity degree from Yale University Divinity School in 1958. Fauntroy turned down an offer to stay at Yale as the dean of its divinity school and instead became pastor of the New Bethel Baptist Church in his hometown. In 1960, Fauntroy was named director of the D.C. bureau of the Southern Christian Leadership Conference (SCLC), the largest and most powerful group in the **civil rights movement**. In 1961, Fauntroy helped organize the "Freedom

Rides," which protested against **segregation** in interstate bus terminals. He also helped organize protest marches, including the massive March on Washington by 250,000 demonstrators in 1963. As the SCLC's chief spokesperson in Washington, Fauntroy urged members of Congress to pass the Civil Rights Act of 1964 and Voting Rights Act of 1965. He would later advise President Lyndon Johnson on how best to implement these civil rights acts.

In 1965, Fauntroy turned his attention to urban renewal: the improvement of inner city neighborhoods. He co-founded the Coalition of Conscience, which called for additional welfare assistance for people who were forced out of their homes by urban-renewal programs. From 1966 to 1971, Fauntroy volunteered as executive director of Model Inner City Community Organization (MICCO). MICCO allows the residents of ghettos to participate directly in the planning and rebuilding of neighborhoods, and then puts unemployed members of the community to work in the rebuilding efforts. In 1969, Fauntroy and MICCO helped direct the nation's first urban-renewal project entirely planned and run by community residents.

In 1971, Fauntroy was elected to a newly created nonvoting seat in the House of Representatives. As the city's representative, Fauntroy pushed for the self-government of Washington, a district ruled by the federal government. He won a limited victory in 1973, when Congress granted city residents the right to elect directly their own mayor and council members. Yet Congress retained control of city spending and voted itself veto power over all council legislation. His efforts led to a second victory in 1977, when Congress granted statehood status to Washington in congressional and presidential elections. In 1982, Fauntroy was elected to serve in Congress as the representative from the District of Columbia. Fauntroy was still calling for full statehood in 1990, when he ran unsuccessfully for mayor of Washington.

Fletcher, Alice Cunningham

(1838–1923)

ANTHROPOLOGIST, ACTIVIST FOR NATIVE AMERICAN
RIGHTS AND CULTURE

One of the first female anthropologists in the United States, Alice Cunningham Fletcher helped preserve Native American culture and worked for the reform of the government's policy toward Native Americans. Fletcher's activism began in the early 1870s, when she joined Sorosis, a pioneering New York women's club. As the club's secretary in 1873, she helped found the Association for the Advancement of Women and organized the association's annual Woman's Congress. She also worked actively for the **temperance** and antitobacco movements as a speaker, organizer, and fund raiser.

Her interest in the new science of **anthropology** began when Fletcher started a career as a public lecturer on American history. Researching new topics, she visited Harvard University's Peabody Museum of American Archaeology and Ethnology in 1878. Examining Native American artifacts for the museum, Fletcher became fascinated. In 1879, she joined the Archeological Institute of America.

That same year, Fletcher met Susette La Flesche Tibbles, who was leading a group of Omahas on a nationwide tour, speaking out against the forced removal of Native Americans from their lands. With Tibbles's help, Fletcher arrived on the Omaha reservation in Nebraska in 1881.

Living among the Omahas, she lived in teepees and ate Native American food. Her experience led Fletcher to begin working to save Native American lands. Fletcher believed that the reservation system stifled Native American development by encouraging dependence on government support, made poor use of the land, and exposed Native Americans to the corruption and inefficiency of the Bureau of Indian Affairs agents. So she petitioned Congress to break up the Omaha reservation—lands owned collectively by the tribe—and instead give land titles to individual tribe members. When Congress passed the bill Fletcher had helped draft, she was hired to oversee the distribution of land to tribe members from 1883 to 1884. Believing that Native Americans would have to adopt white ways in order to survive, Fletcher also helped arrange for Native Americans to go to far-away "Indian schools," and helped secure loans to build frame houses on Native American lands.

After studying the educational needs of natives of Alaska and the Aleutian Islands in 1886, Fletcher wrote *Indian Education and Civilization*, which assessed the needs and progress of the Native American population. Her continuing efforts to break up the reservation system helped secure Congressional passage of the Dawes General Allotment Act in 1887. This law was designed to move Native Americans toward citizenship by parceling out reservation land and allowing Native Americans to support themselves as farmers and small tradespeople. Although well-intentioned, this act ended up encouraging swindles and abuse. The majority of land covered by the act soon fell into non-Indian hands. From 1887 to 1893, Fletcher acted as a special agent of the Interior Department, implementing the Dawes Act first among the Winnebago tribe in Nebraska, then among the Nez Perces in Idaho.

Fletcher next turned her attention to Native American music. With the help of Susette Tibbles's brother, Francis La Flesche, she began transcribing—and thus preserving—hundreds of Native American songs. In 1900, Fletcher wrote *Indian Story and Song from North America* and in 1904, *The Hako: A Pawnee Ceremony*, the sole complete record of a ceremony from a Plains tribe. In 1911, she examined an entire tribal culture in *The Omaha Tribe*, written with La Flesche. With these books, Fletcher attempted to increase white understanding of Native American cultures—in the belief that greater knowledge would lead to better treatment. *See* TIBBLES, SUSELTE LA FLESCHE

Fox, Robert

(1930–1984)

SOCIAL REFORMER

A Roman Catholic priest and social worker, Robert John Fox dedicated his life to improving the quality of life in New York's Spanish Harlem. Ordained as a Catholic priest in 1955, Fox received a graduate degree in social work from Catholic University of America in 1958. After several months at the University of Ponce, Puerto Rico, where he learned the Spanish language, Fox returned to New York, where he worked for Catholic Charities until 1961. From 1963 to 1969, Fox served as coordinator of Spanish Community Action, a program of the Roman Catholic Archdiocese of New York.

Fox reached out to the city's 1,500,000 Spanish-speaking Catholics, many of them poor. Fox focused his efforts to improve the community's religious, economic, and social welfare at a neighborhood level. His "Summer in the City" programs in 1964 and 1965 brought the residents of Spanish Harlem together for such activities as street dances, mural painting, bingo, and discussion groups. In 1967, when rioting broke out in Spanish Harlem, Fox quickly organized a peace march of 1,300 residents who carried candles, sang hymns, and gave flowers to onlookers. The rioting stopped overnight.

In 1968, Fox organized a program he called "The Thing in the Spring." The program united suburbanites and city residents who worked together to clean up forty-three blocks in Manhattan and the Bronx. Participants swept, scrubbed, painted, did carpentry and plumbing, then came together for an outdoor feast. The success of the program led to the creation of Full Circle Associates, a nonreligious group devoted to renovating the inner city. As director of Full Circle Associates, Fox oversaw the construction of new playgrounds in vacant lots, coordinated street performances and festivals, and helped open recreational, educational, and artistic centers in Spanish Harlem and other poor New York communities. Some participants turned abandoned buildings into cooperative apartments and stores. Fox regarded as his most important contribution the human relationships and sense of their own power that this cooperation helped build.

Friedan, Betty

(1921–   )

FEMINIST, WRITER, COFOUNDER OF NOW

First, she must unequivocally say 'no' to the housewife image. This does not mean, of course, that she must divorce her husband, abandon her children, give up her home. She does not have to choose between marriage and career; that was the mistaken choice of the feminine mystique.

—From Friedan's The Feminine Mystique (1963)

Writer Betty Friedan helped launch the women's movement with her 1963 book, *The Feminine Mystique.* She exploded the myth that all women could find fulfillment solely through their husbands and children. Yet while expanding the opportunities available to women, she warned her readers not to reject the family. Though not the sole source of fulfillment for women, the family could and should remain one source, she insisted.

Betty Naomi Goldstein Friedan was born in Peoria, Illinois. Her father, an immigrant Jew, began his life in the United States by selling buttons on street corners, but through hard work became owner of a jewelry store. Her mother edited the women's page of a Peoria newspaper, but was forced to quit her job when she married. Her discontent with life solely as a housewife and mother made a lasting impression on Betty. Peoria's treatment of Jews also raised her awareness of injustice. Regardless of their wealth, Jews could not join the local country club or high-school sororities.

Betty Goldstein began writing in high school, where she started a literary magazine. After graduating in 1938, she edited the college newspaper at Smith College in Northampton, Massachusetts. She received an undergraduate degree in psychology in 1942, then worked for a year as a researcher in psychology at the University of California at Berkeley.

She moved to New York in 1943, taking a job with a news service. When men returning from World War II re-entered the economy in 1945, Goldstein was forced to leave her job. Except when on maternity leave in 1949, Betty Friedan, who got married in 1947, worked as a reporter from 1945 to 1954. When she requested a second maternity leave in 1954, Friedan was fired and her job was given to a man. The injustice of both firings fueled Friedan's dawning **feminism**. Yet from 1954 to 1957, Friedan unwittingly supported the myth that women were happy confining themselves to domestic affairs through the articles she contributed to women's magazines.

Frustrated by this work, she began a survey of her Smith classmates in 1957. She set out to prove that education did not destroy a woman's femininity or create conflict and frustration in their lives. As she wrote in *The Feminine Mystique*, "I discovered that the critics were half-right; education *was* dangerous and frustrating, but only when women did not use it." Friedan published her findings in *The Feminine Mystique* in 1963. The book attacked the myth, which she called "the feminine mystique," that women should define themselves solely as wives, mothers, and consumers. This myth, Friedan argued, made women feel guilty and inhibited their growth, preventing them from forming their own identities, fully using their talents, and realizing their goals. The bestseller helped spark the nationwide women's movement. Friedan became a prominent spokesperson, appearing in television interviews and going on national speaking tours.

While teaching courses on non-fiction writing at New York University and the New School for Social Research from 1965 to 1970, Friedan increased her political activism. She determined that social changes would not come without political action. So in 1966, she co-founded the National Organization of Women (NOW) and served as its first president. Under Friedan, NOW called for greater enforcement of existing laws—especially a section of the Civil Rights Act of 1964 that outlawed **discrimination** (unequal treatment) in hiring and promotions based on sex. NOW also urged the passage of new laws to protect the rights of women. It supported the proposed Equal Rights Amendment to the Constitution as well as the legalization of abortion. To help achieve this latter goal, Friedan co-founded the National Conference for Repeal of Abortion Laws in 1968. The group later changed its name to the National Abortion Rights Action League after the 1973 Supreme Court decision in the case of *Roe v. Wade* established a woman's right to a safe, legal abortion. Rejected by younger, more radical feminists, Friedan declined to seek reelection to the NOW presidency in 1970. That same year, however, she called for a one-day national women's strike for equality to mark the fiftieth anniversary of women gaining the vote. The event became the largest U.S. demonstration for women's rights in fifty years.

After Congress passed the Equal Rights Amendment in 1972, Friedan spent the next ten years campaigning for state approval of the amendment. Despite the efforts of Friedan and other feminists, the amendment fell three votes short of approval. In 1973, she helped found the First Women's Bank and Trust Company in New York. Three years later, she published *It Changed My Life*, an account of her campaigns for women's rights since the publication of *The Feminine Mystique*.

In the struggle for women's equality, Friedan had always insisted that men should be regarded as allies. Although she believed women should not have to limit their interests to family and home life, she also recognized their importance to most women. Her 1981 book, *The Second Stage*, reflected this emphasis on the family. In outlining an agenda of issues for feminists, Friedan focused on the family and home life. Feminists in the 1980s and 1990s, she suggested, should attempt to win changes in job policies and home life. To allow men and women to share household and family duties, she advocated more flexible work schedules and allowing either parent to take a leave of absence from work for pregnancy and childbirth. She also called for improvements in child care. Friedan's emphasis on home and family drew a heated response. Many feminists accused her of turning her back on the movement she had helped initiate. Others criticized her for ignoring issues of rape and violence against women. Friedan insisted that she was merely dealing with the reality of changing family life. The family, she contended, was too important an issue to leave to conservative activists like Phyllis Schlafly.

The differences between Friedan and many other feminists became clear in 1986. A California bank had challenged a law guaranteeing women that they would not lose their jobs during maternity leaves. In the interests of equality, NOW wanted the law extended to men who took "paternity leaves," too. Friedan—and in 1987, the Supreme Court—disagreed. Friedan favored equal treatment of men and women. But she also believed that because women carry and deliver babies, they needed the added protection of the law. This, she insisted, would insure that equal rights would not be held hostage to biology.

In 1988, Friedan began teaching such courses as "Women, Men and the Media" at the University of Southern California. She has continued to write articles and to promote issues of concern to women and families. These include affordable day care for all women, a law requiring employers to allow all employees—women and men—time off from work following the birth of a child, and the protection of women's choices regarding abortion. In 1989, Friedan turned her attention to what she calls the "age mystique": the myths Americans have about aging. Friedan objects to American culture's tendency to portray the natural process of aging solely in negative terms, using such words as "decay" and "decline". To counter this, Friedan has begun offering her view of aging as a source of freedom and as an opportunity for older Americans to discover hidden strengths. *See* SCHLAFLY, PHYLLIS

Glasser, Ira

(1938–   )

CIVIL RIGHTS ACTIVIST

Ira Glasser became a leading voice in the struggle to defend basic rights as head of the American Civil Liberties Union (ACLU). At age sixteen, Ira spent the first of nine summers working at a holiday camp for adults who were blind, deaf, or mute. By 1963, he had become the executive assistant to the camp director. While working as a math instructor at Sarah Lawrence College in 1962, Glasser served as associate editor and then editor of *Current*, a liberal magazine concerned with public affairs. Glasser left *Current* in 1967 to become associate director of the New York Civil Liberties Union (NYCLU). Glasser's work with the NYCLU focused on attempts to fight **segregation** (the separation of races) in schools and to defend student rights. In 1968, Glasser delivered a paper to a conference of the national organization, the ACLU. The paper sparked an ACLU campaign to force the military to treat its personnel according to the Bill of Rights: the Constitutional amendments that guarantee freedom of speech, press, religion, and assembly.

From 1970 to 1977, as executive director of the NYCLU, Glasser headed efforts to defend the rights of African Americans, homosexuals, prisoners, patients in mental hospitals, foster children, and the poor. He also spoke out against the death penalty and President Richard Nixon's orders to bomb Cambodia from 1970 to 1973.

In 1978, Glasser was elected executive director of the ACLU, whose membership had dropped from 275,000 in 1974 to 185,000 in 1978. Glasser set about to restore the organization's financial health, win back old members, and recruit new members. He pledged to continue the ACLU's efforts to guarantee that the Bill of Rights benefits everyone, regardless of sex, race, religion, color, or politics. Under Glasser's leadership, the ACLU has embraced the cause of women's rights—

especially a woman's right to privacy in her choice of whether or not to have an abortion. Glasser, a former teacher, has spoken out against the censorship of school textbooks. He opposes state laws that, under pressure from religious groups, forbid the teaching that the human race evolved from apes. He has also continued to campaign against the death penalty. As the Supreme Court grew increasingly conservative in the 1980s, Glasser steered the ACLU's efforts in new directions. The ACLU now challenges laws that erode the Bill of Rights in state courts, state legislatures, and Congress. By 1985, Glasser's efforts had rebuilt ACLU membership to 250,000.

Goldman, Emma

(1869–1940)

SOCIAL ACTIVIST AND REFORMER, ANARCHIST

The right to vote, or equal civil rights, may be good demands, but true emancipation [freedom] begins neither at the polls nor in the courts. It begins in woman's soul.

—Goldman "Women Suffrage", *Anarchism and Other Essays* (1911)

Rebel, writer, lecturer, and organizer Emma Goldman opposed anything that hindered the freedom of the soul: government, church, private property. A driving force in many reforms, she rallied support for the labor movement, the birth-control movement, and, during World War I, the antiwar movement. Her activism and speeches made her the nation's foremost **anarchist**: a person opposed to all forms of government or authority. Throughout her life, she worked to make others aware of injustice and to take direct action to correct it.

Born in Kaunas, Lithuania (then ruled by the Russian Empire), Goldman had an unhappy childhood. Her Orthodox Jewish parents ran an inn while her father also managed the stage coach in Popelan (also called Papile), Lithuania. She felt unloved by her mother and rejected by her father due to her sex. As a young girl, she regularly witnessed the brutality of Russian officers. She saw Lithuanian peasants beaten and young boys forced into the army. Jews were targeted for especially brutal abuse at the hands of Russian military police. These injustices helped fuel her lifelong hatred of the military and authority. She became convinced that all government was corrupt and unjust.

From 1877 to 1882, the Goldmans lived in Konigsberg, the capital of Prussia, where Emma received most of her formal schooling. The family then moved to St. Petersburg, the capital of Russia. After a few months of school, the family's poverty forced young Emma to leave school and work in a cousin's glove factory. In 1885, she and her half-sister emigrated to Rochester, New York. At age sixteen, she took a low-paying job in a clothing factory. After a brief marriage and divorce, Goldman moved to New York City in 1889. By this time, she had already begun to embrace the cause of anarchy. While working as a garment worker, she began to promote anarchy in speeches before unions and workers and to organize anarchist meetings and protests. Goldman called for the creation of a society of equals, ruled by no authority, where people would be united solely by a concern for equal justice.

Unlike many anarchists, Goldman did not see violence as the only route to anarchist goals. However, she did not condemn anarchist acts of violence. In 1892 in Homestead, Pennsylvania, striking steelworkers battled armed guards hired by Henry Clay Frick, head of Carnegie Steel. With Goldman's assistance, her partner, anarchist Alexander Berkman, went to Homestead in an attempt to murder Frick and kill himself. Although he shot and stabbed Frick, Berkman failed to kill either Frick or himself. Berkman was sentenced to twenty-two years in a Pennsylvania prison. Goldman's health suffered, and she was soon diagnosed as having tuberculosis, a lung disease.

After regaining her health, Goldman herself was arrested the following year. In a time of high unemployment, Goldman urged a crowd of unemployed workers to "take bread" to keep themselves from starving. Convicted of inciting the crowd to riot, Goldman served one year in prison. Goldman, who worked as a practical nurse in the prison hospital, studied midwifery (assisting in births) and nursing in Vienna, Austria from 1895 to 1896. Returning to New York, she began to serve poor immigrant women as a midwife and nurse.

Goldman's prison term had brought her fame, however, and in 1897, she began a twenty-year career of lecture tours throughout the United States. In her lectures, Goldman called for a revolt against the government, the church, private property, and conventional morality—all of which she saw as hampering human growth. In addition to promoting anarchism, however, she also encouraged the forming of trade unions. She stressed the importance of education as a means of raising the awareness of social injustice. Goldman called for the liberation of women from conventional sexual morality, marriage, and forced pregnancies. She saw a strong link between anarchism and **feminism** (women's rights). The capitalist economy, she insisted, burdened women and children most heavily. She urged women to join unions, championed sexual freedom, and advocated increased access to birth control.

Through her lecture tours, Goldman became an ardent advocate of freedom of speech. When police or angry mobs attempted to silence her, freedom of speech would become the issue of the day. By pointing out the threat to free speech posed by such bullying tactics, Goldman won the support and defense of many liberals and radicals.

When an anarchist killed President William McKinley in Buffalo, New York in 1901, Goldman was arrested in Chicago. After two weeks in jail, she was released. No evidence ever linked her to the assassination. In response to the killing, Congress passed a law in 1903 to prevent foreign anarchists from entering the country and to deport alien anarchists already in the U.S. When Berkman was released from prison in 1906, Goldman began publishing a monthly anarchist magazine, *Mother Earth*. While continuing her lecture tours, she also wrote several books, beginning with *Anarchism and Other Essays*, published in 1911. The following year, she helped Berkman write *Prison Memoirs of an Anarchist*. She also wrote

The Social Significance of Modern Drama, published in 1914. This book brought together her lectures on the social protest dramatized in the plays of such European playwrights as Henrik Ibsen, George Bernard Shaw, Anton Chekhov, and August Strindberg.

With **Margaret Sanger**, Goldman in 1915 broke the law that prohibited the distribution of information on birth control. The protest led to fifteen days in jail the following year. In 1917, the government stopped publication of Goldman's newspaper for printing its opposition to World War I. Goldman and Berkman soon organized a league to help draft resisters. For these actions, both were sentenced to two years imprisonment for interfering with the military draft process. Upon their release in 1919, Goldman, Berkman, and hundreds of other anarchist immigrants were deported to the Soviet Union.

Goldman spent the rest of her life as an American exile in the Soviet Union, Sweden, Germany, France, England, Canada, and Spain. In Germany in 1923, she wrote *My Disillusionment with Russia*, in which she criticized the Bolsheviks (Soviet revolutionaries) for crushing freedom of speech and thought. *Living My Life*, her autobiography, was published in 1931. Three years later, she conducted a three-month lecture tour throughout the United States. Denied permission to remain, she returned to her life in exile. *See* SANGER, MARGARET

Greeley, Horace

(1811–1872)

SOCIAL REFORMER, ABOLITIONIST,
AND PIONEERING JOURNALIST

> The . . . all-embracing reform
> of our age is the Social Re-
> form—that which seeks to lift
> the Laboring Class, as such—
> not out of labor, . . . but out of
> ignorance, inefficiency, depen-
> dence and want.

—Greeley *Recollections of a Busy Life* (1868)

Idealistic editor and crusader Horace Greeley used the power
of the press to advance American social reform. Considered
the most accomplished newspaper editor of his time, Greeley
waged his fiercest fight against slavery in the 1850s.

Greeley was born in Amherst, New Hampshire. His father,
a poor farmer, soon took his family to Vermont to stay out of
debtor's prison. Horace's mother urged her son to begin reading at an early age. By age five, Horace had dutifully read the
entire Bible. At age fourteen, Horace moved to East Poultney,
Vermont, where he served as an **apprentice** printer under the
editor of *The Northern Spectator*. When the *Spectator* closed
down in 1830, he moved to Erie, Pennsylvania to rejoin his
parents. A year later, he moved to New York, where he became
a printer and typesetter with *The New York Evening Post*. In
1833, Greeley—just twenty-one years old—established *The
New York Morning Post*. The paper sold for two cents a copy,
becoming the first newspaper sold for cash instead of by yearly
subscription. The newspaper folded, however, after only three
weeks. After contributing articles to New York newspapers for
a year, Greeley founded and edited *The New Yorker* in 1834.
This weekly news and literary journal established Greeley's
reputation—and survived for considerably longer than the

Morning Post. In 1838 and 1840, Greeley edited two weekly newspapers that campaigned for the Whig Party. The two papers helped rally support that contributed to the election of New York Governor William Seward in 1838 and President William Harrison in 1840.

Competing with fourteen other daily newspapers in New York, Greeley began publishing *The New York Tribune* in 1841. In its first issue, Greeley pledged "to promote . . . moral social, and political well-being." Greeley edited the newspaper and contributed articles and editorials until his death. The paper quickly became a success, reaching eleven-thousand readers after just two months. Later that year, he published the first issue of *The Weekly Tribune*, which absorbed his other weeklies (*The New Yorker* and his Whig campaign paper).

The Tribune became the first nationally significant newspaper in the country. During the paper's first decade, Greeley proclaimed his support for state laws prohibiting liquor. He also called for an end to the use of tobacco, gambling, and prostitution. He opposed the death penalty for criminals. Greeley supported the creation of labor unions and the passage of laws limiting the number of hours in a workday. He also urged reforms in education, including making education free and available to all children.

Greeley strongly encouraged the westward expansion of the United States. However, he opposed the expansion of slavery into these new territories. For this reason, he opposed the Mexican War (1846–48), which he saw as an attempt to gain a foothold for slavery in the West. In 1848, Greeley reported on the first women's rights convention in Seneca Falls, New York, organized by Elizabeth Cady Stanton, Lucretia Coffin Mott, and Martha Coffin Wright. Although Greeley did not support giving women the vote, he came out in favor of most of the other goals of the women's rights movement.

While serving briefly in Congress from 1848 to 1849, Greeley introduced the first Homestead Bill to foster westward expansion. Under the bill, the U.S. offered cheap government land in the west to settlers. To discourage land grabs by railroad companies and land speculators, Greeley proposed that any land not sold to individual settlers be sold at four times the price offered to homesteaders.

Greeley showed his support for organized labor by becoming the first president of the New York Printers' Union in 1850. That same year, he published *Hints Toward Reform*, a collection of his lectures on **temperance** (giving up liquor), **abolition** (ending slavery), vegetarianism, and other suggested reforms. During the 1850s, Greeley developed the concept of an editorial page: a presentation of his views on social, political, and economic issues. Greeley's published opinions exercised a powerful influence on thought throughout the United States.

Greeley's attack on slavery became heated in the mid-1850s. He strongly opposed the Kansas-Nebraska Act in 1854. The law allowed the population of these territories to determine whether they would allow slavery when they became states. The law helped initiate "Bleeding Kansas," a virtual civil war between proslavery and abolitionist settlers from 1854 to 1859. In the struggle, Greeley supported those fighting to keep slavery out of Kansas with both words and arms supplies. In 1856, Greeley helped organize the new Republican Party, which opposed the westward expansion of slavery. In the years leading up to the Civil War (1861–65), Greeley also called for the use of force to resist bounty hunters in search of fugitive slaves.

During this time, Greeley also introduced a number of innovations into American newspapers. In 1856, he created a book review department, the first of its kind in a U.S. newspaper. Three years later, he invented the technique of using direct quotes obtained through interviews to tell a newspaper story. His innovations and continuing high standards helped *The Weekly Tribune* reach two-hundred-thousand readers in 1860.

Although Greeley supported Abraham Lincoln in the 1860 presidential election, he soon grew impatient with the new president's slowness to free the slaves. In 1862, he urged Lincoln to free all slaves who managed to escape to the North. When Lincoln's Emancipation Proclamation declared all slaves freed in 1863, Greeley celebrated the announcement in *The Tribune*. After the war ended, Greeley urged that freed slaves be granted full equality under the law. He also supported offering a general pardon to all soldiers who fought for the

South. He hoped this measure would heal the wounds of the Civil War. To promote this ideal, Greeley in 1867 signed a bail bond to obtain the release of Jefferson Davis, the former president of the southern Confederacy. The unpopular stand caused *The Weekly Tribune* to lose half its subscribers. Greeley, who published his autobiography, *Recollections of a Busy Life*, in 1868, ran for president in 1872. He lost the election to Ulysses S. Grant in a landslide, and died less than four weeks after the election.

Green, Mark

(1945–   )

CONSUMER ACTIVIST

Mark Joseph Green, consumer activist, public interest lawyer, and author, graduated from Cornell University in 1967. While earning a law degree at Harvard, Green acted as editor-in-chief of the liberal *Harvard Civil Rights–Civil Liberties Law Review.*

After graduating in 1970, Green joined consumer advocate Ralph Nader in Washington, D.C., and was a leading member of "Nader's Raiders" for the next ten years. His work with Nader began as legal consultant to the Center for the Study of Responsive Law, which examined ways in which the law could better serve public interest. From 1971 to 1976, Green directed the Corporate Accountability Research Group, another Nader organization designed to hold big business responsible for its abuses of consumers. In 1972, Green coauthored *The Closed Enterprise System*, which exposed price and product fixing in American business and criticized government officials and members of Congress who ignored these practices. In the same year, he also coauthored *Who Runs Congress?*, which criticized the power of political action committees. These "PAC's"—established by special-interest groups, such as gun owners, oil drillers, labor unions, religious groups, and the medical establishment—use political contributions to influence members of Congress to vote for laws that favor their special interests, regardless of the overall public interest.

From 1977 to 1980, Green served as director of Public Citizen's Congress Watch, the largest consumer-rights lobbying group in the United States. Green rallied support for 1980s "superfund" law, which provided money for cleaning up toxic waste sites. He also worked to strengthen the Occupational Safety and Health Administration, which monitors working conditions in the United States. In 1980, Green left Nader's organization to run unsuccessfully for a New York seat in Congress. After the election, Green founded the Democracy Project, a group of academics and thinkers devoted to generating new ideas to advance liberal causes. Green ran for a New York seat in the Senate in 1986, and declared that he would refuse all money from political action committees, which he criticized as enemies of free speech and democratic rule. Green lost the election to his Republican opponent, Alfonse D'Amato, who spent nine times as much money as Green did on the campaign.
See NADER, RALPH

Hale, Clara

(1905–1992)

SOCIAL REFORMER

> I love children. I think all children are born with something special. And you can bring it out and make them good people. But they need love. We give out love and they give love in return.
>
> —Hale, interview with Tom Seligson, "How Mother Hale Saves Young Lives," in *Parade*, November 18, (1984)

Social activist Clara McBride Hale offered love and care to babies that others ignored. For more than twenty years, "Mother Hale" rocked, nurtured, and nursed back to health babies born to drug-addicted mothers. Since pregnant addicts pass on their addictions to their babies through the bloodstream they share, the babies Hale tended were born addicted, too. Hale offered comfort and love to hundreds of babies while helping them through the pain of **withdrawal** (getting the drugs out of their system).

Clara McBride was born and reared in Philadelphia, Pennsylvania. Her father died during her infancy. Clara's mother supported the family by cooking and renting out rooms in their home. Clara later credited her mother with teaching her to take pride in herself and to love others. After graduating from high school, she married and moved to Harlem in New York. Clara Hale worked nights for several years, cleaning theaters to add to the income from her husband's floor waxing business. When Thomas Hale died in 1932, Clara Hale was left a widow with three children. While continuing to clean theaters at night, Hale cleaned homes during the day. In order to stay home with her children, Hale started a day-care center in her home. She also began taking foster children into her home. The city paid Hale $2 a week to take care of each child. In addition to those receiving day care, Hale usually housed seven or eight foster children. Over twenty-seven years, she cared for forty foster children.

In 1968, Hale decided to retire. After just one year, however, she began caring for drug-addicted children. Hale's new career began in 1969, when her daughter, who holds a doctoral degree in child development, noticed a young heroin addict falling asleep one day in a Harlem park. A two-month-old baby was falling out of the young woman's arms. Lorraine Hale talked to the addict, gave her her mother's address, and told her she could get help there. The next day, the addict agreed to turn the baby over to Clara Hale while she underwent drug treatment. Word of Hale's action spread quickly, and two months later, Mother Hale had crammed cribs in every room of her apartment to care for twenty-two addicted babies.

For eighteen months, Hale's work was financed solely by her three children, who worked overtime to raise the money needed to care for the babies. In the early 1970s, the New York City Department of Social Services for Children began to provide funding. With money provided by the federal government, the Hales renovated a five-story home in Harlem. In 1975, Hale House—the only institution in the country that treated victims of their mothers' drug abuse—officially opened in its new location. Hale House could care for as many as fifteen children, ranging in age from ten days to four years, at a time. Hale began to hire and train child-care workers and sleep-in aides to help her care for the addicted babies. In time, Hale House also employed a social worker, a teacher, and a part-time staff of doctors and nurses.

Hale House usually began its program of care within ten days of a baby's birth. The babies would receive comfort in Hale's room until the withdrawal symptoms ended weeks or even months after their arrival. The addicted babies would often suffer from diarrhea and vomiting; they would scratch themselves until they bled and cry endlessly until withdrawal was completed. She would walk with the babies, talk to them, sing to them, or rock them—whatever worked to stop their crying. After withdrawal had ended and the babies slept through the night, they would be moved to the nursery where the child-care staff would take care of them.

Mother Hale always stressed that Hale House was not an orphanage. Her goal was to reunite healthy parents and children. Ninety-seven percent of the babies were returned to their mothers after completed drug treatment. An average of less than one child a year was ultimately put up for adoption.

In 1985, President Ronald Reagan saluted Mother Hale as "a true American hero" in his State of the Union address before Congress. The recognition brought national attention to Hale House. Although the government cut funding to Hale House in 1989, private donations increased rapidly following Reagan's address. Hale House expanded its program in the 1990s to offer housing and education to mothers who have completed their drug-treatment programs. Hale also opened a home for infants and mothers with the deadly disease AIDS (Acquired Immune Deficiency Syndrome). Although Clara Hale died in 1992, Hale House, today run by Lorraine Hale, has continued to provide love and care to the babies of addicts and of mothers with AIDS.

Harrington, Michael

(1928–1989)

SOCIAL REFORMER AND CIVIL RIGHTS ACTIVIST

Michael Harrington, who would later become cochair of the Democratic Socialists of America (DSA), was first exposed to social activism in 1951, when he joined the Catholic Worker, a radical Catholic organization led by **Dorothy Day**. For two years, Harrington lived at the St. Joseph's House of Hospitality in New York, where the Catholic Worker housed and fed the poor. He wrote for the *Catholic Worker*, which promoted the ideas of aid to the poor and **pacifism**: the opposition to war and violence. Pacifism was not new to Harrington, who had refused to carry a gun for the U.S. Army Medical Reserves that year. In 1953, Harrington left the Catholic Church and the Catholic Worker. He joined the Workers Defense League, which defended the civil liberties of trade union members. The following year, Harrington joined the Young Socialist League, an anti-communist group committed to defending civil liberties. He also investigated **blacklisting** (the refusal to hire suspected communists) in the entertainment industry.

Harrington took part in most of the social protests of the next decade. He joined the **civil rights movement**, organizing demonstrations against racism and marches in support of equal rights. He helped organize trade unions. He served on the national executive board of the Socialist Party from 1960 to 1968. He spoke out against the involvement of the U.S. military in Vietnam. Harrington, who would go on to write fourteen other books on poverty, radicalism, and socialism, published *The Other America: Poverty in the United States* in 1962. The widely praised book exposed an underclass of people trapped in poverty, unable to help themselves. The book sparked the "War on Poverty" programs initiated by Presidents John Kennedy and Lyndon Johnson.

In 1972, Harrington, a professor of political science at Queens College in New York, resigned from the Socialist Party.

The next year, he founded the Democratic Socialist Organizing Committee (DSOC), a less radical alternative to the Socialist Party. Growing from two-hundred members in 1973 to four-thousand by 1980, the DSOC brought together peace activists, trade unionists, **environmentalists**, **feminists**, and minorities. In 1981, the DSOC merged with the New American Movement to form the Democratic Socialists of America, the largest socialist group in the country. As cochair, Harrington urged the DSA to work with the Democratic Party to win liberal reforms of the tax and welfare systems. He hoped to move the nation gradually toward socialist goals of full employment, the abolition of poverty, and a national health-care program. In 1988, a year before his death, Harrington founded the Next America Foundation, which funds research on poverty. *See* DAY, DOROTHY

Hayden, Tom

(1940–   )

ANTIWAR AND CIVIL RIGHTS
ACTIVIST

Thomas Emmett Hayden became a student activist as the editor of the *Michigan Daily*, the campus newspaper of the University of Michigan, in 1960. Hayden wrote editorials supporting the **civil rights movement** and other social reforms. After graduating in 1961, Hayden helped register African-American voters in Georgia and Mississippi as a member of the Student Nonviolent Coordinating Committee, a leading civil rights organization. Later that year, Hayden co-founded the Students for a Democratic Society (SDS), a national organization formed to coordinate student political movements throughout the nation. Hayden wrote the "Port Huron Statement," outlining the goals of the SDS, in 1962. The "Port Huron Statement" attacked racism in hiring and housing, the nuclear arms race, and the government's failure to address poverty and the living conditions of the poor. To deal with these issues, Hayden called for the creation of a participatory democracy in which everyone has a share in decision making.

The first president of the SDS, Hayden in 1964 helped create its Economic Research and Action Project (ERAP). Hayden went to Newark, New Jersey as an ERAP organizer, helping poor residents set up community groups. Hayden helped organize rent strikes and welfare demonstrations, and put pressure on the city government to build new playgrounds. Hayden's ghetto experience contributed to his *Rebellion in Newark* (1967), which explored the frustration with racism that helped lead to the Newark riots of 1967.

In 1965, Hayden traveled to North Vietnam to help build a link between the North Vietnamese and the American peace movement. Two years later, he cowrote *The Other Side*, which offers a North Vietnamese perspective of U.S. military involvement. His contacts and later meetings with North Vietnamese leaders helped bring about the release of three American prisoners of war, whom Hayden escorted home in 1967. At the Democratic National Convention in Chicago in 1968, Hayden organized demonstrations by the National Mobilization Committee to End the War in Vietnam. When violence erupted between police and demonstrators, Hayden and seven others—including David Dellinger and Abbie Hoffman—were arrested for inciting a riot. In 1970, five of the so-called Chicago Seven defendants, were sentenced to five years in prison for inciting riot and contempt of court. Two years later, however, a court of appeals overturned the riot convictions due to the presiding judge's improper rulings and conduct. Freed of legal worries, Hayden returned to the antiwar movement, writing articles and speaking at antiwar rallies. When direct U.S.

military involvement ended in 1973, Hayden called on the government to end covert (secret) actions in Southeast Asia and cut off aid to the South Vietnamese government.

In the mid-1970s, Hayden entered mainstream politics, attempting to introduce reforms from inside the system. Calling himself a "grass-roots Democrat," Hayden in 1976 unsuccessfully sought the Democratic nomination for Senator from California. From 1983 to 1993, he served in the California state assembly, where he focused especially on environmental issues and encouraged people to build a sense of connectedness with the planet. In 1990, Hayden introduced the nation's most wide-reaching environmental bill in California. The bill would have ended the use of cancer-causing chemicals to kill insects on fruits and vegetables, banned oil development in state waters, an imposed strict limits on car pollution, industrial pollution, and the number of trees that the lumber industry could cut down each year. The state's voters, fearing the loss of jobs and the high cost of the bill, defeated it in a statewide vote that fall. Hayden, however, elected to the California state senate in 1992, continues to promote the protection of the planet. *See* DELLINGER, DAVID; HOFFMAN, ABBIE

Hayes, Robert

(1952–   )

ACTIVIST FOR CIVIL RIGHTS AND SOCIAL REFORM

Lawyer Robert Michael Hayes led the fight for the rights of homeless people in the 1980s. An investigative reporter for the *Long Island Catholic Newspaper* from 1973 to 1975, Hayes wrote exposés on mental health and social service issues, nearly getting fired for a sympathetic article he wrote on the gay rights movement. While attending the New York University School of Law from 1975 to 1977, Hayes volunteered as a legal aide, handling welfare and housing complaints for poor residents of the city's slums. Accepting a position with a Wall

Street law firm, Hayes could not ignore the homeless people he passed every day on his way to work. In talking to them, Hayes learned that most preferred living on the streets to sleeping in city shelters. Visits to shelters angered and horrified Hayes, since he saw as many as 250 people, some mentally ill or criminal, sleeping in a single room.

In 1979, Hayes sued the Governor of New York and the Mayor of New York City on behalf of the city's homeless people. He charged them with not providing the aid, care, and support of the needy guaranteed by the state's constitution. The landmark case, which Hayes won in 1980, established the right to shelter for all who needed it. Hayes filed further suits forcing the city and state to provide adequate food and health care to the homeless as well.

In 1980, Hayes founded the nonprofit National Coalition for the Homeless and named himself the coalition's counsel (lawyer). Hayes raised funds for the coalition by appealing to corporations that his law firm handled. In 1982, he left the law firm to work full time with the coalition. Throughout the decade, Hayes won a series of lawsuits on behalf of the homeless. Hayes' victories established the right of homeless women and children to shelter and the right of the homeless to vote. He forced local governments to provide counseling and day-care services for homeless families. He won appropriate housing and medical care for homeless patients suffering from Acquired Immune Deficiency Syndrome (AIDS). Hayes also established the New York Coalition for the Homeless, which operates soup kitchens, lunch programs, and a summer camp for homeless children.

In addition to his legal victories, Hayes lobbied members of Congress on behalf of the nation's three-to-four-million homeless people. His efforts led to the Homeless Assistance Act of 1987, which provided nearly $1 billion to fund improved housing and services for the homeless. Hayes stressed that the only permanent solution to the homeless problem lies in the construction of affordable housing. After a long string of successes, Hayes resigned from the Coalition for the Homeless in 1989 to join a private law firm.

Hill, Joe

(1879–1915)

ACTIVIST FOR LABOR MOVEMENT AND COMPOSER
OF LABOR SONGS

> Goodbye Bill. I die like a true rebel. Don't waste time in
> mourning. Organize.
>
> —Hill

On the night before his execution in 1915, Joe Hill, also
known as Joseph Hillstrom, sent this telegram to labor leader
Bill Haywood. Hill, a labor organizer and writer of labor songs,
was convicted of murder despite a weak case brought by prosecutors. The labor movement in the United States immediately
hailed him as a folk hero and a **martyr**: someone who dies for
a noble cause.

Joe Hill was named Joel Emmanuel Hagglund at his birth in
Gavle, Sweden. His parents, both amateur musicians, encouraged Joel's love of singing and musical instruments. During his
childhood and early adulthood, Joel learned to play the piano,
guitar, organ, violin, and accordion. In 1902, he emigrated to
the United States. For the next twelve years, Hill drifted from
town to town and job to job.

While working in San Pedro, California in 1910, he joined
the local of the Industrial Workers of the World (IWW). The
IWW, also known as the Wobblies, was a radical labor group
that called for workers' control over industries. It supported
the creation of industrial unions and sought shorter hours,
higher pay, and a better life for workers. To achieve these ends,
it often advocated strikes, **boycotts**, and acts of sabotage. Hill
began contributing letters, articles, and songs to the IWW paper, *Industrial Worker*. He soon became the most popular of
the IWW songwriters and was appointed secretary of his local.

In writing his labor songs, Hill would set them to familiar
melodies. This allowed workers to join in singing them on
picket lines and in union halls. His songs, almost always hu-

morous, told of the lives of immigrant workers in sweatshop factories, railway workers, and those who sought work wherever they could find it. His most famous song, printed in the IWW's *Little Red Song Book* in 1911, was called "The Preacher and the Slave." The song poked fun at preachers who failed to serve the needs of the poor and hungry on earth:

> You will eat, bye and bye,
> In that glorious land above the sky;
> Work and pray, live on hay,
> You'll get pie in the sky when you die.

With the song, he invented the now-familiar phrase, "pie in the sky," which means a far-off promise.

While working in Salt Lake City, Utah, Hill was arrested for the robbery and murder of a grocer and the grocer's son in 1914. On the night of the murder, Hill had been treated for a bullet wound in the chest. But he insisted that he had gotten the wound in a fight over a woman. He refused to cooperate with his lawyers by naming the woman, however, and ultimately fired them. Hill's membership in the hated IWW created automatic suspicion. The police ignored leads that might have pointed to other suspects. And after a ten-day trial, the jury found him guilty despite the fact that prosecutors had presented no hard evidence of his involvement in the crime. Hill was sentenced to execution by firing squad.

Hill spent more than a year in prison during attempted appeals of the verdict. Thousands of people—including President Woodrow Wilson and Helen Keller—urged the governor of Utah to stay the execution. The appeals went unheeded. Hill was shot by a firing squad on 19 November 1915.

Funeral services were held in both Salt Lake City and in Chicago, where the IWW had its headquarters. The Chicago funeral attracted five-thousand mourners. Proclaimed a martyr for the cause of labor, Hill's body was cremated. The IWW sent envelopes containing the ashes of Hill's body to locals in every state but Utah, as well as to locals on every other continent but Antarctica. The Hill legend continued to grow with poet Alfred Hayes' 1925 song, "I Dreamed I Saw Joe Hill Last Night." The song, later recorded by such popular folk singers as Pete Seeger and Joan Baez, proclaimed that Joe Hill would never die. *See* KELLER, HELEN; SEEGER, PETE

Hoffman, Abbie

(1936–1989)

SOCIAL REFORMER AND ANTIWAR ACTIVIST

> Kids today live with awful nightmares: AIDS will wipe us out; the polar ice cap will melt; the nuclear bomb will go off at any minute; even the best tend to believe we are hopeless to affect matters. . . . Young people are detached from history, the planet and, most important, the future.

—Hoffman, Speech to jury during trial on trespassing charges, April 15, (1987)

Writer and prankster Abbott Hoffman, who saw himself as a revolutionary, tried to inspire young people to join in protest movements. His politically inspired pranks and outlandish behavior in the 1960s and early 1970s regularly placed him on the nation's evening news broadcasts. A best-selling author and celebrity, Hoffman also founded the Yippies (Youth International Party), a social protest group.

Born in Worcester, Massachusetts, Hoffman later admitted being a troublemaker throughout his childhood. Expelled from high school for fighting with an English teacher, Hoffman in 1955 graduated from a private school, Worcester Academy. After receiving an undergraduate degree from Brandeis University in 1959, he earned a graduate degree in psychology the following year from the University of California at Berkeley. Hoffman, the son of a pharmacist, then returned to Worcester, where he worked selling medicinal drugs from 1963 to 1966.

At this time, he began to work as a political organizer in the **civil rights movement**. In 1964, Hoffman was arrested for taking part in "Freedom Summer," a massive campaign to register African-American voters in the state of Mississippi. Despite the arrest, Hoffman returned to Mississippi and Georgia the following year to continue his organizing activities on behalf of African Americans. In 1966, Hoffman left Worcester for New York City. There, he opened Liberty House, a store that sold crafts made by poor people he had met in Mississippi.

As U.S. involvement in the Vietnam War deepened, Hoffman shifted the focus of his activism to the growing antiwar movement in 1967. He also staged the first of what he called "happenings": symbolic acts that sent a message of protest. To demonstrate how mindless greed drove the American economy, Hoffman led a group who showered hundreds of dollar bills on the floor of the New York Stock Exchange. Television news cameras captured the frenzy of stock traders scrambling for the bills. Later that year, Hoffman organized 1,200 people to encircle the Pentagon in a mock attempt to lift it by mental force. He claimed that this action would help drive the evil spirits out of the military. These and similar demonstrations and attacks on powerful targets showed a profound understanding of the new power of television and attempted to point out the pointlessness of some firmly held points of view.

Using the pen name "Free," Hoffman published *Revolution for the Hell of It* in 1968. The book aimed to stir revolutionary feelings in teenagers and young adults. That year, Hoffman and a group of friends decided to call themselves "Yippies." After coming up with the name, he founded the Youth International Party (YIP). Hoffman joked that the group had "no leaders, no members, and no organization." Led by Hoffman and his friend Jerry Rubin, the Yippies protested against the Vietnam War, the U.S. economy, and the existing political system. Hoffman led the Yippies in a protest against the war outside of Chicago's Democratic National Convention. During violent attacks between police and protesters, Hoffman was arrested for appearing in public with an obscenity written on his forehead.

In the wake of the convention violence, Hoffman and seven others—including Rubin, David Dellinger, and Tom Hayden—

were charged with conspiracy and crossing state lines to incite a riot. One of the eight, Black Panther leader Bobby Seale, was later tried separately, but the others were tried as a group. The trial of the "Chicago Seven" quickly turned into a farce. Hoffman and Rubin sometimes refused to stand when the judge entered the courtroom. They once wore judge's robes to mock the court. Hoffman even accused the judge, Julius J. Hoffman (no relation), of being his illegitimate father. The staged events put the justice system itself on trial. The infuriated judge over-reacted, abusing the defendents' rights. At one point, before Seale had been separated from the others, the judge ordered him bound, gagged, and removed from the courtroom. The jury found all of the defendents innocent of the conspiracy charges. Five, however, including Hoffman, were found guilty of inciting a riot. The judge charged the seven defendents with an additional 175 counts of contempt of court. Hoffman was sentenced to eight months in jail. But he regarded the trial as a triumph of political protest.

While appealing to higher courts to reverse the convictions, Hoffman rallied opposition to the war on a nationwide tour of college campuses and in countless television appearances. His celebrity made him a target of the FBI and local police, who broke his nose during a Washington, D.C. protest in 1971. Frustrated by the inability of the antiwar movement to end the Vietnam War, Hoffman began to withdraw from activism.

In 1971, he published *Steal This Book*. The book jokingly described how to shoplift, create false identification, make explosives, and rip off the telephone company and other large companies that provided goods and services. When more than thirty publishers rejected the book because it told how to commit illegal acts, Hoffman himself published the book, which sold 260,000 copies. Meanwhile, an appeals court overturned Hoffman's conviction in 1972. Nine months later, however, Hoffman was again arrested for taking part in a scheme to sell cocaine to undercover agents. Facing a life sentence if convicted, Hoffman vanished just before the trial was scheduled to begin in 1974.

For the next six years, Hoffman lived a secret, underground life. He changed his appearance through plastic surgery and used at least two dozen different names. Life on the run contributed to two nervous breakdowns, but Hoffman was never caught. Occasionally he surfaced for interviews and in 1976 published *To america with Love: Letters from the Underground*, a collection of letters to his son america. Around 1977, he settled in the upstate New York town of Fineview. Posing as freelance writer "Barry Freed," Hoffman laid low for a short time. When plans were announced to dredge the nearby St. Lawrence River, however, he organized the Save the River Committee. The group's success in stopping the project made him a local hero among **environmentalists**. As "Barry Freed," Hoffman gave interviews on both radio and television and in 1979, even testified before a Senate environmental panel.

In 1980, Hoffman surrendered to federal authorities. As he had done before, he used the publicity to promote himself and his new autobiography, *Soon to Be a Major Motion Picture*. Hoffman pleaded guilty to reduced charges in 1981 and received a three-year sentence for the drug offense and for jumping bail before trial. Paroled after a year in prison, Hoffman toured college campuses, lecturing on the environment and racism in South Africa during the 1980s. In 1989, he died, possibly as a result of suicide.

Howe, Julia Ward

(1819–1910)

ACTIVIST FOR WOMEN'S RIGHTS

> Of the diversity of human gifts we [women] had, no doubt, our full share. But the talents which we were not permitted to exercise were folded and laid away in a napkin, to moulder useless and unknown, even to ourselves.
>
> —Howe, "Speech on Equal Rights," *Julia Ward Howe and the Woman Suffrage Movement*, ed. Florence Howe Hall (1913).

Woman's club leader and activist for women's **suffrage** (the right to vote), Julia Ward Howe gained her greatest fame as author of "The Battle Hymn of the Republic." The song, which conveyed the grave emotional concerns of a nation at war, became popular in the North during the Civil War (1861–65). The modest fame allowed Howe to embark on nationwide lecture tours. Her speeches on **feminism** helped bring the "radical" issue of women's rights to a mainstream audience.

Julia Ward grew up in New York, where her father worked as a banker and her mother wrote poetry. When their mother died in 1824, the children were cared for by their mother's sister, also a poet. Their strict, Episcopalian father believed strongly in the virtue of discipline. He taught his children that worldly pleasures would lead them to the endless torments of hell after death. Julia was educated by governesses, private tutors, and in private girls' schools. She demonstrated an eagerness to learn, but was frustrated by the lack of formal schooling available to girls in her time.

After her father died in 1839, Julia Ward began writing and publishing critical essays on poets. In 1843, she married Samuel Gridley Howe, head of the Perkins Institution for the Blind in Boston. A year later, the couple settled in South Boston. In addition to working with the blind, Samuel Howe devoted his time to a variety of social causes. He actively supported the movement for public schools, programs for prison reform, and the campaign to end slavery. Although he also believed in the right of women to vote, he did not apply his liberal views on women's rights to his own home and family life. Samuel Howe felt that his wife should devote her life to serving his needs and desires. Although Julia Howe wanted to join in her husband's reform and charity work, he believed that married women did not belong in public life. Julia Howe felt isolated and unhappy confining her interests to housework and parenting. To keep her mind active, she began to study languages, religion, and philosophy. Following the example of her mother and her aunt, Howe also began to write poetry.

In 1853, her husband briefly allowed Howe to assist him in editing *Commonwealth*, the journal of the Free Soil Party, which opposed the westward expansion of slavery. The following year, Howe published her first collection of poetry, *Passion-flowers*. A second collection, *Words for the Hour*, followed in

1857. Howe's first play, *Leonora, or the World's Own*, was produced in the same year. Attacked as immoral and indecent, the play closed within a week. Howe's husband disapproved of both her plays and her poetry, which focused on themes of passionate love, betrayal, and suicide. Although both poetry collections had been published without her name, he was especially furious that Julia Howe had explored their marriage in print. Twice he asked for a divorce, but Howe refused his demand to give up two of their five surviving children.

Howe continued to write, publishing accounts of her travels in popular magazines and as books. She did some volunteer work promoting health and hygiene during the Civil War. In 1861, she wrote "The Battle Hymn of the Republic." The poem, published the following year, was set to the music of another song ("John Brown's Body") and popularized throughout the North during the Civil War. Howe used her new fame to launch a brief series of lectures on religion and philosophy. While continuing to write poetry, she founded *Northern Lights*, a short-lived literary magazine in 1867.

In 1868, Howe finally found the means of fulfilling her ambition for a public career. With Lucy Stone, she co-founded the New England Woman Suffrage Association. She served as the association's president from 1868 to 1877 and again from 1893 to 1910. In the same year, she helped found the New England Women's Club. She headed the women's club from 1871 until her death in 1910. Howe saw both the suffrage movement and women's clubs as a way of bringing women together in order to improve society. She became one of the leaders of the American Woman Suffrage Association (AWSA), which Stone headed. Throughout the 1870s, Howe became increasingly devoted to the cause of feminism. She served as president of the Massachusetts Woman Suffrage Association from 1870 to 1878, and later from 1891 to 1893. In 1870, she founded *Woman's Journal*. Howe edited and contributed articles to the weekly magazine for the next two decades. Her "Appeal to Womanhood Throughout the World," written in the same year, called on women to initiate a worldwide peace movement. Howe herself attempted to organize an international peace conference of women in 1872.

In 1873, she co-founded the Association for the Advancement of Women and served as its president for many years. The association sponsored conferences of women educators, ministers, lawyers, scientists, and reformers to discuss the means for achieving equality for women. This involvement led her to edit *Sex and Education*, which urged the education of both sexes together. After her husband died in 1876, Howe embarked on a lecture tour, and published a collection of her lectures as *Modern Society* in 1880. On an 1888 lecture tour along the Pacific Coast, she founded the Century Club of San Francisco, a women's group. The following year, she helped negotiate the merger of the American Woman Suffrage Association with its rival the National Woman Suffrage Association. In 1890, she helped found the General Federation of Women's Clubs, which she directed from 1893 to 1898. A second collection of lectures, *Is Polite Society Polite?*, appeared in 1895. In her eighties, Howe lectured less frequently, but in 1900, published an autobiography called *Reminiscences*. *See* STONE, LUCY

Jackson, Jesse

(1941–   )

PREACHER, CIVIL RIGHTS AND POLITICAL ACTIVIST

> Leadership has a harder job to do than just choose sides. It must bring sides together.
> —Jackson, on *Face the Nation*, April 9, (1988).

Civil rights leader, preacher, and political activist Jesse Louis Jackson has attempted to bring people together to forge a more just world. Although he claims to be just a "country preacher," Jackson is an inspired and inspiring public speaker. Through his words, he has encouraged the poor, the forgotten, and the oppressed to take pride in themselves. A friend and follower of Martin Luther King Jr., Jackson became the first African American to mount a serious campaign for the presidency of the United States.

Jackson was born in Greenville, South Carolina, the son of an unmarried domestic worker, Helen Burns. His adoptive father, Charles Henry Jackson, a postal employee and janitor, married his mother when Jackson was two. An excellent student and athlete, Jesse also began to show a talent for leadership. He attended local Sunday school conventions on behalf of his Baptist church. And he led the offense as quarterback of his football team, which won a state championship. He graduated from an all-black high school in 1959.

Jackson attended the University of Illinois on an athletic scholarship for a year. The football team, however, refused to allow Jackson to compete for the quarterback slot. Jackson transferred to an all-black college, North Carolina Agricultural and Technical State College in Greensboro. There, he starred as quarterback, was elected student body president, and excelled in sociology and economics. While at Greensboro, he joined the campus **civil rights movement**, working toward equal rights for African Americans. Jackson staged demonstrations and **sit-ins** at restaurants, hotels, and theaters to protest against **segregation**, the separate and unequal treatment of different races of people. After earning his undergraduate degree in 1964, Jackson won a scholarship to study for the ministry. After two years at the Chicago Theological Seminary, Jackson left school to work for the Southern Christian Leadership Conference (SCLC), a leading civil rights group. Martin Luther King, Jr., head of the SCLC, asked Jackson to run "Operation Breadbasket" in Chicago. Operation Breadbasket aimed to increase the number of jobs and improve services for the African-American community. Jackson's biggest victory in Chicago involved the large A&P chain of supermarkets. The company agreed to hire 268 more African Americans, some as store managers, and to sell twenty-five brands of goods manufactured by African Americans. In recognition of his success, Jackson was appointed national director of Operation Breadbasket in 1967. The following year, Jackson was with King in Memphis when an assassin killed the civil rights leader. Although some suggested that Jackson should follow King as leader of the SCLC, the job went to Ralph Abernathy.

Perhaps unhappy with Abernathy's leadership, Jackson left the SCLC in 1971. He founded and served as president of Operation PUSH (People United to Save Humanity). Like Operation Breadbasket, PUSH used boycotts and pickets to achieve its goals: a bigger share of economic and political power for African Americans, other non-whites, and the poor. PUSH also aimed to promote a revival of racial pride among African Americans. In 1976, Jackson initiated a new program called PUSH–Excel (PUSH for Excellence). Jackson felt that without improved education, African Americans would never progress toward economic, social, and political equality. So PUSH–Excel launched a crusade against the forces that interfered with the education of African Americans, especially those in city slums. PUSH–Excel campaigned against drug abuse, teenage pregnancy, vandalism, truancy, and high dropout rates. Jackson himself carried this message to many inner-city schools. He told students that by working hard, they could achieve their highest aims. PUSH–Excel made no attempt to recommend a particular course of studies. His primary aim was to motivate students to stay in school—and to excel.

Jackson also worked to achieve greater social justice in other nations. On a 1979 trip to South Africa, Jackson urged blacks to maintain their pride in the face of racism. He encouraged blacks to refuse peacefully to comply with the nation's **apartheid** laws: laws which unfairly withhold equal rights from non-whites in South Africa. Jackson also pursued a peaceful, just solution to tensions in the Middle East. He urged Israelis and Palestinians, longtime enemies, to recognize each other's right to exist. Extremists on both sides criticized Jackson for his visit that year.

In 1983, Jackson took a leave of absence from PUSH. He organized a massive drive to register new voters, especially among African Americans and other non-white ethnic groups. With this act, Jackson launched his campaign for the 1984 Democratic Presidential nomination. No one, he insisted, could better represent the interests of ethnic minorities and the poor. He promised to pull together those neglected by President Ronald Reagan into a "rainbow coalition." Jackson campaigned in person and through interviews with reporters from magazines, newspapers, and television news bureaus. His campaign got a boost when he personally obtained the release of a U.S. Navy pilot who had been shot down over Lebanon. He went to Cuba, where he won the release of twenty-two imprisoned Americans as well as twenty-six Cubans jailed for opposing the government.

Although Jackson had hoped to include Jews in his "rainbow coalition," he had problems winning the Jewish vote. In an off-handed remark, he referred to Jews using an ethnic slur. His closeness to Louis Farrakhan, head of the Nation of Islam, also hurt Jackson in the Jewish community. Farrakhan had reportedly once called Judaism a "gutter religion." Winning 21 percent of the popular vote in the primaries, Jackson finished a distant but respectable third. Jackson considered the race a victory, however, because he had inspired millions to register to vote and take part in the election.

After the election, Jackson returned to PUSH. However, he continued to work to expand voter registration among poor people and non-whites after the election. In 1985, Jackson was arrested in front of the South African embassy in Washington for protesting against that nation's apartheid laws. The following year, he resigned as director of PUSH. He later announced the formation of the National Rainbow Coalition. This group aimed to bring together African Americans and other non-whites, members of labor unions, farmers, **environmentalists**, peace activists, and women to work for progressive reforms within the Democratic Party. Backed by the Rainbow Coalition, Jackson again ran for the Democratic presidential nomination in 1988. Receiving much more support, he finished second to Michael Dukakis. Jackson then unsuccessfully sought the vice presidential nomination. He did, however, win the Democratic Party's official support for some of his reform policies. More recently, Jackson has served as the non-voting representative to the Senate from Washington, D.C. He has been active in the attempt to win statehood for the nation's capital. *See* ABERNATHY, RALPH; KING, MARIN LUTHER, JR.

Jacob, John

(1934–   )

SOCIAL REFORMER AND CIVIL RIGHTS ACTIVIST

Raised in poverty in Houston, Texas, John Edward Jacob would become head of the National Urban League, an interracial community service organization that attempts to improve the social and economic standing of African Americans and other minorities. From 1960 to 1965, Jacob worked for the Baltimore Department of Public Welfare, providing poor families with social services and signing them up for welfare programs. Jacob earned a graduate degree in social work from Howard University in 1963. Two years later, he became director of Education and Youth Incentives for the Washington Urban League, a local branch of the National Urban League. By 1968, he had risen to acting executive director of the Washington Urban League. Jacob oversaw projects for ghetto teenagers, fought for fair housing programs, and trained ghetto residents to work with community social workers. After directing the San Diego Urban League from 1970 to 1975, Jacob returned to serve as president of the Washington Urban League. Named executive vice president of the National Urban League in 1979, he was elected president in 1982.

Jacob took over the league at a difficult time. The Reagan Administration had sharply cut back on social programs and job training, putting a strain on poor city residents. Jacob criticized President Reagan and the conservatives he had appointed to the Civil Rights Commission for opposing **affirma-**

tive action. He accused the president of abandoning the government's commitment to protect **civil rights.**

Jacob identified five major economic and social problems in African-American urban communities: the increase in pregnancies among unwed teenagers; the large number of households headed by single women; the high rate of crime; the low percentage of voters; and the quality of education. Taken together, Jacob concluded, these problems trap many African Americans in a never-ending cycle of poverty. Under Jacob, the National Urban League has begun to develop self-help solutions to these problems. In 1983, local branches began introducing programs on birth control designed to educate urban teenagers and prevent teen pregnancies.

But Jacob also led the National Urban League to shift its focus to the problems of the poor, rather than just the problems of African Americans. The need for jobs, housing, education, and welfare is shared by all poor people, regardless of race. Jacob therefore called for increased job-training programs and government-sponsored construction projects—two steps that would move the nation closer to full employment.

Johnson, Sonia

(1 9 3 6 –   )

ACTIVIST FOR WOMEN'S RIGHTS

In 1979, Sonia Harris Johnson, whose family had been members of the Mormon church for five generations, was **excommunicated** (stripped of church membership) for her support of women's rights. Johnson, who taught Mormon missionaries in Samoa from 1960 to 1961, received a doctoral degree in education from Rutgers University in 1965. For the next ten years, she continued her missionary work and teaching in California, Korea, Malawi, Malaysia, and Virginia. In 1977, she became a **feminist**, supporting women's rights and the proposed Equal Rights Amendment (ERA) to the United States Constitution.

The amendment called for equal treatment of men and women under the law. The Mormon church (also called the Church of Jesus Christ of Latter-Day Saints) opposed the amendment. Johnson, who founded Mormons for ERA, began to recognize sexism in church teachings that called on women to serve men. In 1978, Johnson's testimony before a Senate Subcommittee on Constitutional Rights helped win an extension of the period in which states were allowed to approve the amendment. A year later, the Mormon church excommunicated her for opposing church programs, undercutting support for church leaders, and spreading false doctrine.

The publicity of her church trial only increased the demand for Johnson as a lecturer. Her speeches called on women to transform society through nonviolence and cooperation. In 1981, a year after addressing the Democratic National Convention, Johnson published her autobiography, *From Housewife to Heretic*. In 1982, she took part in the "Women's Fast for Justice," a demonstration intended to win support for the ERA in Illinois. For thirty-seven days, Johnson and seven other women ate nothing and drank only water. Johnson was hospitalized three times during the fast.

In 1984, Johnson was chosen by the Citizens Party to run for president of the United States. Johnson called for social justice, laws guaranteeing equal pay for equal work, homosexual rights, an end to nuclear power, and protection of the environment. In foreign affairs, Johnson was a **pacifist**. She supported cutting the military budget in half, an end to nuclear arms, and basing all foreign-policy decisions on issues of human rights. To protest military spending, Johnson announced that she would refuse to pay income taxes. That same year, Johnson founded the Women's International Disarmament Alliance, an organization that coordinates women's peace movements throughout the world. Johnson has continued to write, lecture, and conduct workshops to promote feminism. Her work has focused on her own life as a way of highlighting women's struggle to free themselves from a culture and society created and dominated by men. In 1989, Johnson founded Wildfire Books in order to publish her own work free of the influence of male-dominated publishing houses. Wildfire's first publication, *Wildfire: Igniting the She/Volution*, collected Johnson's essays on feminist activism. *The Ship That Sailed into the Living Room*, published in 1991, explores Johnson's attempt to create and sustain a lesbian relationship with her lover that avoids the power struggles that she sees as typical of male-female relationships in western society.

Jones, Mary Harris

(1830–1930)

LABOR ACTIVIST

Not even my incarceration in a damp underground dungeon will make me give up the fight in which I am engaged for liberty and for the rights of the working people. To be shut from the sunlight is not pleasant but . . . I shall stand firm. to be in prison is no disgrace.

—Jones, letter from the cellar of the Walsenberg, Colorado courthouse, (1914)

Mary Harris Jones, better known as Mother Jones, stirred up laborers for over half a century. An uncompromising crusader, Jones fought for the rights of miners, mill workers, railroad workers, working children, and other workers.

Mary Harris was born to poor Irish peasants outside Cork, Ireland. Because her parents ardently opposed British rule in Ireland, Mary was instilled with a spirit of revolt. When Mary was five, her father left Ireland to escape British authorities. Three years later, his wife and children joined him in Toronto, Canada. Mary attended public schools in Toronto, where her father helped build the railway. Mary Harris graduated from a Toronto normal school, where she was trained as an elementary school teacher, in 1847. After teaching in schools in Canada and the United States for several years, she became a dressmaker in Chicago. Returning to teaching, she moved to Memphis, Tennessee. Her marriage to George Jones, a fervent member of the local Iron Molders' Union, first exposed her to the trade union movement.

Two tragedies helped propel Mary Jones into the labor movement. In 1867, a yellow fever epidemic raged through the Irish-American community in Memphis. Mary's husband and all four of her children died in less than a week. Jones served as a volunteer nurse until the epidemic died down, then returned, alone, to dressmaking in Chicago. Four years later, the Chicago fire of 1871 destroyed everything she owned. Seeking shelter in a church basement with hundreds of others, Jones happened upon a meeting of the Knights of Labor. An industrial union, the Knights called for improved working and living conditions for American laborers. Stripped of her family, her home, and her possessions, Jones embraced the cause of labor with a religious zeal. At age forty-one, she decided to devote her life to seeking economic and social justice.

For the next fifty years, "Mother Jones" joined in the struggle for higher wages, shorter hours, and better working conditions. Jones traveled from one industrial area to the next, where she secretly investigated working conditions, organized and educated workers, and called for strikes or assisted striking workers. Her first major effort came during a national railroad strike in 1877. Jones traveled to Pittsburgh to provide assistance to striking workers and to protest against the use of federal troops to subdue the strikers. When the Knights of Labor began to decline in the late 1880s, Jones shifted the focus of her organizing efforts to the textile industry in the South. She took a job in an Alabama cotton mill in order to get a firsthand look at child-labor conditions. At that time, nearly one-third of all mill workers in the South were less than sixteen years old. Jones was appalled at the unhealthy conditions and ten- to twelve-hour workdays. The experience strengthened her commitment to work toward outlawing child labor.

In the 1890s, Jones began her most significant work as a

union organizer for the newly formed United Mine Workers of America (UMWA). Her work with coal miners would continue for the next twenty-five years. She took part in her first coal strike in Norton, Virginia in 1891. As an outside labor organizer—an **agitator**—Jones was arrested and forbidden from using town meeting halls to promote unionization. Undaunted, Jones gathered crowds of miners around her in the streets. During a 1900 coal strike, Jones organized a women's brigade among miners' wives in eastern Pennsylvania. The women marched to the mines pounding on pots and pans. They swung mops and brooms at strikebreakers and at the mules that pulled the coal cars. Drawing women into the struggle allowed Mother Jones to turn her opponents' sexism against them. She herself often took advantage of this tactic, defying strikebreakers and security guards to attack a woman.

During the first fifteen years of the twentieth century, Mother Jones focused her organizing efforts on coal miners in West Virginia and Colorado. Jones took part in five major strikes in West Virginia. The isolation of mining towns and the complete dependence of workers on the mining companies made it difficult to organize unions. During a statewide walkout of sixteen-thousand miners in 1902, Jones headed organizing efforts in the north of the state. Disguised as a peddler, she went to Colorado in 1903 to gather information on local mining conditions. After completing her investigation, Jones called for a strike. Authorities in Colorado attempted to mute her influence by personally taking her out of the state several times. Her efforts in Colorado failed, however, in part because UMWA leader John Mitchell refused to acknowledge or support the strike. The dispute prompted Jones to leave UMWA near the end of the year.

In 1903, she led a "Children's Crusade." Children on strike against textile mills in Kensington, Pennsylvania marched to Oyster Bay, New York, where President Theodore Roosevelt lived. There, Jones urged passage of a federal child-labor law. From 1903 to 1911, Jones organized unions for anyone who needed her. She supported strikes by railway workers and copper miners. She helped the Socialist Party organize workers for seven years, although she herself never joined the party.

She helped found the radical Industrial Workers of the World (Wobblies), but then rejected the association as too radical.

In 1911, she returned to organizing local unions for miners in West Virginia. During the mine wars of the next two years, she urged miners to protect themselves from violence by using violence themselves. Fifty people died in the fourteen-month battle. Jones was arrested, tried before a military court, and found guilty of conspiring to murder the state's governor. Although she insisted she had only wanted to meet with him, Jones was sentenced to twenty years in prison. The decision was soon set aside, however, and Jones returned to activism.

She helped organize workers during the Colorado mine wars from 1913 to 1915. Again escorted out of the state, Jones returned to lead a march of two-thousand labor officials to the state capital in Denver. There, she protested the use of troops to quell the dispute. Jones was arrested and held in a charity hospital for nine weeks. Typically, after her release, she immediately set out to return to the strike area. Authorities then locked her in the cellar of the Walsenberg, Colorado courthouse for a month, where Mother Jones defended herself against rats by throwing old beer bottles at them. Her testimony in 1914 before a House of Representatives committee on mining helped lead to the settling of the strike by federal government mediators. The following year, she met with John D. Rockefeller, Jr., whose family owned many mines in Colorado. After their meeting, Rockefeller dropped charges against some miners and later supported the creation of a company union.

Mother Jones actively supported streetcar and garment workers' strikes in New York City in 1915 and 1916. In 1919, her participation in a major steel strike led to her last jailing at the age of 89. Except for several public speeches on behalf of unions, Jones curtailed her organizing activities during the 1920s. Her life story, *Autobiography of Mother Jones*, was published in 1925.

Keller, Helen

(1880–1968)

SOCIAL REFORMER, FEMINIST,
PACIFIST, AND ADVOCATE FOR
THE BLIND AND DEAF

> I look upon the world as my fa-
> therland, and every war has to
> me a horror of a family feud. I
> look upon true patriotism as
> the brotherhood of man and the
> service of all to all.
>
> —Keller, "Menace of the Militarist Program",
> *New York Call*, Dec. 20, (1915)

Helen Keller overcame deafness, muteness, and blindness to achieve her ideal of serving others. Having overcome so much herself, she took on a mission to help the disadvantaged—especially as an advocate for the blind and deaf—through lectures, fund-raising and personal appeals to lawmakers. Although she became a symbol of the triumph of courage, will, and intelligence over adversity, Keller was a writer and educator, a social reformer, and a **feminist**.

Helen Keller was born in Tuscumbia, Alabama. She could see, hear, and by the time she was one, speak. In 1882, Helen suffered from a severe illness that left her deaf, blind, and mute at nineteen months. A wild, willful child, Keller invented sixty signs on her own as a way of making her desires known. In 1886, Keller's mother sought help from the Perkins Institution for the Blind in Boston. The institution recommended Anne Sullivan, a recent Perkins graduate, as Keller's teacher and governess. Sullivan, partially cured of her own blindness, would exercise the greatest influence on Keller as a child—and throughout her life.

Using a combination of love and discipline, Sullivan in 1887 tamed Helen's wildness within two weeks. Sullivan taught Helen the "manual alphabet": an alphabet for the deaf that uses the positioning of fingers to form letters. Within a month,

Helen realized that everything had a name, and that the manual alphabet was her path to knowledge. This moment of realization was later portrayed in the famous water-pump scene in William Gibson's play and movie, *The Miracle Worker*. By spelling out the names of objects in Helen's hand, Sullivan taught her more than three-hundred words in a few months. After four months of teaching, Helen wrote her first letter—to her mother.

In 1888, Sullivan brought Helen to Boston to live at the Perkins Institution. By this time, the press had already begun to praise Helen's accomplishments. While at Perkins from 1888 to 1894, Helen learned to read and write in **Braille**: an alphabet for the blind formed by raised dots on paper. Helen begged Sullivan to teach her how to speak, eventually convincing her teacher to cooperate. Helen learned to speak by placing her fingers on Sullivan's throat to "hear" (through her fingers) the vibrations when she spoke. From 1890 to 1894, she took speech classes at the Horace Mann School for the Deaf in Boston. During this period, she demonstrated her first charitable impulses. She helped raise money for a deaf, blind, and mute boy to receive schooling at Perkins. In 1894, Sullivan brought Helen to New York to attend the Wright-Humason School, which taught deaf children how to speak.

After Helen's father died in 1896, Sullivan raised funds to allow her student to enroll in the Cambridge School for Young Ladies. Through this school, and two years of work with a private tutor, Helen Keller gained admission to Radcliffe College—with advanced credit in Latin—in 1900. Keller took on a full course load at Radcliffe. Sullivan attended all classes with her, spelling lectures into Keller's hands. With the help of Sullivan and Harvard University literature instructor John Macy, Keller wrote an autobiography, *The Story of My Life*, published in 1902. Keller used the money earned from the book to buy a farm in Wrentham, Massachusetts. The following year, she published a second book, *Optimism*, an essay that conveys her faith in life's essential goodness. In 1904, she received honors and applause upon her graduation from Radcliffe.

In 1905, Sullivan married Macy, who joined her in working with Keller. The following year, the governor of Massachusetts appointed Keller to the nation's first State Commission for the Blind. Keller soon raised eyebrows by campaigning against sexually transmitted disease, a previously unmentionable subject. Keller, however, insisted on addressing it, because it caused blindness in newborn infants. *The World I Live In*, a collection of essays about the way Keller perceived the world was published in 1908.

At this time, Keller became active in other social reforms as well. She joined the Socialist Party in 1909 and was also committed to the cause of women's **suffrage**: the right to vote. She supported striking textile workers in Lawrence, Massachusetts in 1912. The following year, Keller published a collection of socialist essays, *Out of the Dark*.

Anne and John Macy separated in 1913, though they never divorced. That year, Keller and Anne Sullivan Macy began a series of cross-country lecture tours. They were joined by Polly Thomson, a young woman who served as Keller's secretary, housekeeper, and hairdresser. Thomson would remained with Keller for almost fifty years.

Keller continued to work toward social reforms. In 1915, she called for a general strike against war when the U.S. began to abandon its neutrality in World War I. Keller joined Industrial Workers of the World, and she appealed to the governor of Utah to spare the life of IWW organizer and songwriter Joe Hill. As a feminist, she endorsed the birth-control movement promoted by Margaret Sanger. She also supported the National Association for the Advancement of Colored People, founded in 1909 to work toward the goal of equal rights for African Americans. She also urged the passage of laws that would prohibit child labor and outlaw the death penalty.

In 1924, Keller began serving as a spokesperson for the American Foundation for the Blind (AFB). In addition to helping the foundation raise funds, Keller in the 1930s sought out lawmakers to win new laws to benefit the blind. Her lobbying helped secure federal money to fund reading services for the blind, as well as other laws benefiting the blind. Keller helped insure the inclusion of a section of the Social Security Act of 1935 that allows the blind to receive federal grant money.

When Anne Macy died in 1936, Keller and Thomson went

abroad. She lectured throughout Japan, the first of a series of international tours. *Helen Keller's Journal*, published in 1938, expressed her feelings since Macy's death and explored who she was without Macy. During World War II (1941–45), Keller toured military hospitals to build morale. After the war ended, Keller spent ten years lecturing on blindness throughout the world: in Europe, Australia, New Zealand, South Africa, the Middle East, Latin America, and India. In 1961, the year after Thomson died, Keller suffered the first of a series of small strokes. Three years later, President Lyndon Johnson awarded her the Medal of Freedom. *See* HILL, JOE; SANGER, MARGARET

Kenyon, Dorothy

(1888–1972)

SOCIAL REFORMER AND WOMEN'S RIGHTS ACTIVIST

Lawyer Dorothy Kenyon devoted over forty years to the American Civil Liberties Union (ACLU), where she championed the cause of women's rights. After earning a law degree at New York University in 1917, Kenyon worked for the government for a year, researching wartime labor. In private practice, Kenyon's commitment to social justice led to appointments on government commissions on minimum-wage laws, welfare, and public housing. A leading voice in the women's rights movement in the 1920s and 1930s, Kenyon called for increased educational and economic opportunities, the right of women to serve on juries, equality in marriage, and access to birth control.

In 1930, Kenyon began serving on the board of directors of the ACLU, a position she held until her death in 1972. The ACLU is dedicated to protecting the basic freedoms spelled out in the U.S. Constitution's Bill of Rights: freedom of speech, and freedom of press, freedom of assembly, and freedom of religion. Kenyon served briefly as a New York municipal court judge from 1939 to 1940. From 1938 to 1943, she also served on a League of Nations committee established to study the legal status of women in different nations of the world. She continued this work as the U.S. delegate to the United Nations Commission on the Status of Women from 1946 to 1950.

In 1950, Kenyon defended herself against charges of membership in Communist organizations before a Senate Foreign Relations Subcommittee. Kenyon asserted that although she had liberal views and opposed dictatorship, she was neither a Communist nor disloyal to the United States. In the 1950s, Kenyon became one of the first voices to protest against laws that restricted a woman's right to choose to have an abortion. Kenyon also helped advance the **civil rights movement**, joining protest marches and preparing legal opinions for lawsuits filed by the ACLU and the National Association for the Advancement of Colored People, and demonstrated against U.S. military involvement in Vietnam. Kenyon was also an active social reformer on the local level. In 1968, she helped found the first agency in her New York neighborhood that offered legal services to the poor.

King, Martin Luther, Jr.

(1929–1968)

CIVIL RIGHTS ACTIVIST

> I have a dream that one day this nation will rise up and live out the true meaning of . . . 'all men are created equal.'
>
> —King, in a speech August 28, (1963)

Martin Luther King, Jr., spoke these words looking out at the more than 250,000 people who gathered in front of the Lincoln Memorial in Washington D.C. on August 28, 1963. As the leader of the non-violent wing of the American **civil rights movement** and youngest recipient of the Nobel Peace Prize, King had begun the historic speech that would live in the hearts and minds of Americans for generations to come.

Martin Luther King, Jr., was born in Atlanta, Georgia on January 15, 1929. His father, Martin Luther King, Sr., was a minister of the Ebenezer Baptist Church. His mother, Alberta King, had been a teacher before her children—Christine, Martin Luther, Jr., and Alfred Daniel—were born.

The church was a very important part of Martin's early life. With his father's guidance, he studied the Bible. He spent time in church listening to his father preach. Martin enjoyed reading and was an excellent student. He skipped two grades in school and at the age of fifteen was accepted by Morehouse College in Atlanta, where his father and grandfather had both gone. At first, he planned to become a doctor. But at Morehouse, he decided to become a minister, like his father. At seventeen, he gave his first sermon, in his father's church.

After college, King went to Crozer Theological Seminary, where he studied to become a minister. Once again, he was a brilliant student and was given a scholarship to attend Boston University in Massachusetts. In Boston, he met a young woman named Coretta Scott and they were married. By this time, several churches in Boston were familiar with King's powerful, charismatic preaching and asked him to be a minister there. But he turned them down and instead returned to the south.

He and Coretta chose to live in Montgomery, Alabama, where he preached at the church on Sundays. Soon King became an important community leader. He talked with other leaders about the problems of segregation.

On December 1, 1955, a black woman named Rosa Parks refused to give up her seat on the bus to a white person in defiance of the current law. The driver called a police officer, took her to the police station where she was arrested. Soon, black people all over town were talking about it. They were very angry and wanted to **boycott** the bus company to protest the unfair law.

When Martin Luther King heard about Mrs. Parks, he immediately began working to spread the word about the boycott. He wrote a letter which was distributed in every part of the city where blacks lived. A newspaper heard about the boycott too, and even though the publishers printed a story condemning it, they still brought attention to what King was planning.

The people who planned the boycott formed a group called the Montgomery Improvement Association. Martin Luther King was elected president. Instead of riding the bus, the people walked, rode on mules or in wagons or on bicycles. Everyone agreed the boycott should continue.

As the boycott stretched on, many whites grew angry. King was arrested several times. One night, a bomb was thrown into his house. News travelled fast, and soon an angry crowd of blacks had gathered out front, ready to hurt or even kill those who had thrown the bomb. But King stood on the ruined porch, preaching that their struggle must continue without violence. Someone had tried to kill him, and yet King had spoken of love. In amazement they went home quietly.

The boycott continued for several more months. King was jailed over and over. But finally, in November of 1956, the United States Supreme Court ruled that segregation in city buses was illegal. The blacks had won their struggle.

King was inspired to try similar methods in other segregated cities. Along with other black ministers, he formed the Southern Christian Leadership Conference (SCLC) and began lecturing all over the country, telling blacks how to resist segregation laws in peaceful yet effective ways. He taught them to stage **sit-ins** by going into restaurants where blacks were not served and simply sitting at the counter until they were given something to eat. Since many Southern blacks were prevented from voting, he organized registration drives so that they could vote for candidates who would support their fight for equality.

In April of 1963, he led a group of 40 blacks to city hall in Birmingham, Alabama, and demanded to talk to white leaders. He was thrown in jail, but soon released. The marches continued, though police were brutal, using clubs, police dogs and the powerful streams from fire hoses to subdue the blacks. But they kept on marching, in Birmingham, and all over the country.

King gained respect and recognition for his work, although many still hated him and what he represented. In August of 1963, he led a march on Washington D.C. to ask Congress to pass the civil rights bill, which would guarantee blacks the same freedoms as whites. In 1964, at the age of 35, he was awarded the Nobel Peace Prize, an international award given to those who make outstanding contributions towards the cause of peace. On April 4, 1968, King's work was abruptly stopped when he was shot and killed by a white man outside his motel room in Memphis, Tennessee. *See* PARKS, ROSA

Kovic, Ron

(1946–   )

VIETNAM VETERAN AND PACIFIST

Born on the Fourth of July, 1946, Vietnam veteran Ron Kovic became a leading voice in the peace movement of the 1960s and 1970s. Hoping to become a hero, Kovic joined the U.S. Marine Corps in 1964, when the United States expanded its military involvement in Vietnam. In Vietnam, Kovic experienced the horrors of war. During a confusing retreat, he accidentally shot and killed one of his own men. On another occasion, his company shot up a hut in which they thought they saw rifles. Assigned to count the bodies of the dead, Kovic entered the hut to find only an old man and several children, dead or dying. No rifles were found.

In 1968, Kovic became a statistic: one of the 305,000 Americans wounded in Vietnam. (Another 47,000 Americans died in the conflict.) A shot shattered Kovic's spinal cord, leaving him

paralyzed below the chest. Kovic was sent home to recuperate in a dirty, rat-infested Veterans Administration hospital in the Bronx, New York. Awarded the Purple Heart and the Bronze Star, Kovic began wondering what purpose he had served in losing the use of his legs.

In 1970, Kovic attended a rally in Washington, D.C. to protest the United States invasion of Cambodia. The demonstrators also mourned the deaths of four students who had been shot and killed by the National Guard during an antiwar protest at Kent State University a week earlier. The rally inspired Kovic to begin speaking out himself. Kovic voiced his anger at the public and the government, which did not seem to care about wounded veterans. He opposed U.S. military intervention into the affairs of other nations. In 1971, Kovic joined the Vietnam Veterans Against the War. The next year, Kovic and two other veterans disrupted President Richard Nixon's speech at the Republican National Convention by chanting, "Stop the bombing! Stop the war!" Kovic's protests against the actions of the government and the military continued throughout the 1970s. He called for better medical care for veterans. Kovic also spoke out against the nuclear arms race, the involvement of the United States in the affairs of Central American countries, and the law requiring all eighteen-year-old boys to register for the **draft**. His 1976 autobiography, *Born on the Fourth of July*—and the 1989 movie based on the book—made Kovic's story familiar to millions.

Kozol, Jonathan

(1936–   )

SOCIAL AND EDUCATIONAL REFORMER

Teacher Jonathan Kozol published his first book, a novel called *The Fume of Poppies*, in 1958, the same year he graduated from Harvard University. Kozol spent most of the next five years in Paris, where he tried to write a second novel.

After returning to Boston, Kozol became a substitute teacher. For most of the 1964–65 school year, Kozol taught fourth-graders in Roxbury, an African-American ghetto in Boston. Kozol saw the poor children at the school as victims of neglect, abuse, and injustice. He objected to teachers that did not seem to care about their poor students nor to be bothered by text-books and teaching materials that supported racist ideas. Near the end of the year, Kozol was fired for teaching his students about African-American poet Langston Hughes.

A year later, Kozol started tutoring poor children at a Roxbury church. His program soon became the New School for Children, a creative alternative school run by the community. Kozol's *Death at an Early Age: The Destruction of the Hearts and Minds of Negro Children in the Boston Public Schools* was published in 1967. When the account of his experience as a substitute teacher won a National Book Award, Kozol donated the $1,000 prize to community leaders in Roxbury. From 1968 to 1971, Kozol served as educational director of the Storefront Learning Center, another alternative school in Boston. In 1972, his *Free Schools* outlined how parents and teachers could create their own alternative-education programs.

In 1978, Kozol published *Children of the Revolution: A Yankee Teacher in the Cuban Schools*. The book detailed his research on the success of a project to teach all adults in Cuba how to read and write. As Kozol learned more about the Cuban program, he became determined to combat **illiteracy** (the inability to read and write) among adults in the United States. *Prisoners of Silence: Breaking the Bonds of Adult Illiteracy in the United States* was published in 1980. Five years later, Kozol's *Illiterate America* detailed how illiteracy traps adults in poverty and humiliation. Illiterate adults find themselves unable to do even the most ordinary day-to-day tasks. They cannot read poison warnings on household products or instructions on prescription drugs. They cannot fill out application forms for jobs. In shedding light on the everyday problems of illiterate adults, Kozol urged the federal government to finance a massive literacy program. While continuing to teach, Kozol visited both rich and poor schools to study teaching conditions. In 1991, he published his findings in *Savage*

Inequalities: Children in America's Schools. Kozol contended that in the twenty-four years since *Death at an Early Age*, the gap between rich and poor had grown even wider. He urged reform in the way the nation funds public schools. By using taxes on property as the main source of educational funds, Kozol insists, rich communities build excellent schools while poor communities struggle just to keep their schools open. Kozol advocates the funding of public schools primarily through the state and federal governments, which would provide the same amount of money for every pupil in the state. Only through equal funding, Kozol contends, will the nation be able to create true equality in education and the schools.

Kuhn, Maggie

(1905–   )

ACTIVIST FOR THE RIGHTS OF THE ELDERLY

> Old people constitute America's largest untapped and undervalued human energy source. Yet I have observed only token effort to give us a chance to be self-determining and . . . involved in planning and developing the programs that are designed to help us.
>
> —Kuhn in testimony before the House of Representatives (1977).

Older people, so often ignored, neglected, and forgotten in American society, found an advocate and spokesperson in Margaret E. Kuhn. The founder of the Gray Panthers, Kuhn launched an attack against **agism**: prejudice and unequal treatment based on a person's age.

Kuhn was born in Buffalo, New York. Her mother moved the family from Memphis, Tennessee to Buffalo just before her daughter's birth. She did not want Maggie to grow up in the South, because she hated the region's **segregation**: separation and unequal treatment of people due to their race. Her father, a credit manager, however, was soon transferred back to Memphis. Maggie grew up in Memphis and Cleveland, Ohio, where she graduated from high school in 1922. Kuhn then attended the Flora Stone Mather College of Case-Western Reserve University in Cleveland. Women had just won the right to vote in 1920, and Kuhn helped organize a campus chapter of the League of Women Voters. She trained as a teacher—one of the few professions open to women in the 1920s—in a Cleveland junior high school. In 1926, she earned an undergraduate degree in English and sociology.

After leaving school, she worked as a volunteer for the Cleveland Young Women's Christian Association (YWCA) for a year. In 1927, she was hired as a YWCA staff member. Her work with young employed women at the YWCA helped turn Kuhn into a **feminist**: an advocate of women's rights. "So many of our members at the YWCA in Cleveland were women working for rotten-paying clerical or commercial jobs," she later explained. "They were working six days a week for ten dollars. . . . My work with these women as they started to organize and unionize cemented my radicalism." After doing similar work in Philadelphia, Kuhn became an editor for the national YWCA in New York.

In the late 1930s, Kuhn resigned from the YWCA to work with the General Alliance of Unitarian Women in Boston. She returned to New York in the mid–1940s to take a job with the United Presbyterian Church. As associate secretary in the office of church and society, she helped manage church social programs. She also helped develop the church's policy on race relations. As an editor and writer for the church magazine, *Social Progress* (later called *The Journal of Church and Society*), Kuhn helped build support within the church for women's rights and for liberal stands on housing, medical care, and the problems of older Americans.

This last issue took on a particular importance to Kuhn in 1970, when the church forced her to retire at age 65. That year Kuhn had lunch with five friends, all of whom were being forced into retirement. They felt it was unjust for them to have to abandon their work for the social causes to which they had dedicated their lives. The group recognized that because older people no longer need to worry about losing their jobs or ruining their careers, they have much more freedom to become activists than younger people do. Resolving to act on their beliefs, Kuhn and her friends founded an organization dedicated to action for social change. Within a year, the group, which would later become known as the Gray Panthers, had grown to include one hundred retired men and women.

The first issue that united the group was opposition to continuing U.S. involvement in the Vietnam War. They supported young people who protested against the war and the military draft. This stand helped bring young volunteers into the organization, which was originally called the Consultation of Older and Younger Adults for Social Change. Kuhn brought the two age groups together because she felt that both younger adults and older Americans were ignored by decision makers in both government and business.

At the White House Conference on Aging in 1971, Kuhn led a group of older adults who called for redirecting money from fighting the Vietnam War to providing social services. With the help of college students, Kuhn established the first headquarters of the Gray Panthers in a Philadelphia church basement. The group had been given the name Gray Panthers by a TV news reporter who compared their radical activism to that of the Black Panthers.

From the beginning, the Gray Panthers has fought against agism. Kuhn has compared agism to sexism and racism in its destructive and demeaning impact. In 1971, the Gray Panthers began working with the Retired Professional Action Group, a public citizen lobbying group founded by Ralph Nader. The two groups, which merged in 1973, promoted laws regulating such businesses as the hearing-aid industry and the nursing-home industry. From 1973 to 1976, the Gray Panthers conducted a study of nursing homes. Kuhn recognized the importance of health-care issues to older Americans. At meetings of the American Medical Association, the Gray Panthers have protested against doctors who get rich treating the medical complaints of older people. Since 1972, Kuhn has called for the creation of a national health-care system that eliminates doctors' profit motive. She has also testified on health-care issues before a Senate committee on aging.

One of the biggest challenges facing the Gray Panthers was prejudice against older Americans. To combat this problem, the Panthers founded Media Watch. This group has monitored the image of older people presented on radio and television and in advertising. When they saw older people portrayed as useless, helpless, or senile, the Gray Panthers' Media Watch complained directly to broadcasting executives.

The Gray Panthers have insisted that the talents and resources of older Americans be put to good use. Kuhn has advocated retraining older people to use their skills to promote public interests. She has suggested "recycling" older Americans to serve as public-interest watchdogs. In this role, they could monitor the performance of courts, banks and insurance companies, and local government agencies.

At the group's second convention in 1977, the Gray Panthers once again supported the creation of a national health-care system that would provide medical services to everyone without charge or bias. They affirmed the rights of older Americans to express their sexuality and they opposed all mandatory retirement policies based on age. *See* NADER, RALPH

Lathrop, Julia

(1858–1932)

SOCIAL REFORMER AND CREATOR
OF OCCUPATIONAL THERAPY

Julia Clifford Lathrop learned activism from her parents. Julia's father, an **abolitionist**, had helped organize the Republican

Party in Illinois and later served as a member of Congress. Her mother had long been an advocate of women's **suffrage**. After graduating from Vassar College in 1880, Lathrop worked in her father's law office for a decade. In 1890, she joined Hull House, the new **settlement house** in Chicago founded by **Jane Addams**. In 1893, Lathrop became the first woman appointed to the Illinois State Board of Charities. Her efforts on the board led to the removal of mentally ill persons from state poorhouses. She also prompted state hospitals to begin hiring female doctors and nurses. In 1899, the efforts of Lathrop, Addams, and others led to the creation of the first juvenile court in the nation. In 1901, to protest the poor training of staff members at state institutions and the routine awarding of staff jobs as political favors, Lathrop resigned from the Board of Charities. In an address to the National Conference of Charities and Correction the following year, she called for the creation of new state institutions for delinquent children and for the mentally ill.

In 1903 and 1904, Lathrop helped found the Chicago School of Civics and Philanthropy, which trained social workers. At this school, Lathrop introduced a pioneering program of **occupational therapy** (physical and mental activities designed to speed recovery) for mental patients. Reappointed to the Board of Charities in 1905, Lathrop continued to urge reforms in the process of hiring workers at state institutions. A founder of the Illinois Immigrants' Protective League in 1908, Lathrop would remain a league trustee until her death in 1932.

In 1912, President William Taft appointed Lathrop as the director of the newly created Children's Bureau. Lathrop directed studies on the death rates of infants and mothers, juvenile delinquency and the juvenile courts, mentally retarded children, the rights of illegitimate children, and child-labor laws. From 1918 to 1919, Lathrop also served as president of the National Conference of Social Work. In 1921, she helped gain passage of a law that provided federal funds for state-run health-care programs for infants and mothers. That same year, she resigned from the Children's Bureau due to illness. She remained active, however, serving as president of the Illinois League of Women Voters from 1922 to 1924 and as a member of the Child Welfare Committee of the League of Nations from 1925 to 1931. *See* ADDAMS, JANE

Lewis, John

(1940–   )

CIVIL RIGHTS ACTIVIST

John Robert Lewis embraced nonviolence as a way of life. Reared in Alabama, he experienced the destructive impact of **segregation**: the separation of the races. African Americans attended poor schools and were prohibited from borrowing books from the public library. As a teenager, Lewis began preaching in local Baptist churches. While attending Fisk University in 1959, he attended workshops on nonviolence sponsored by the Nashville (Kentucky) Christian Leadership Conference. Like most others in the **civil rights movement**, Lewis adopted nonviolent protest as a tactic to win social change.

In 1960, Lewis was arrested six times for organizing **sit-ins** at all-white diners and lunch counters in Nashville to protest segregation. Later that year, he helped found the Student Nonviolent Coordinating Committee (SNCC), a national network established to coordinate local efforts to end segregation. In 1961, Lewis joined in the first of the "Freedom Rides," which protested segregation in interstate bus terminals. The Freedom Riders suffered from repeated attacks on their bus ride from Washington, D.C. to New Orleans. In Montgomery, Alabama, one racist clubbed Lewis until he lost consciousness. Yet the protest led to a 1961 ban on racial segregation in bus terminals.

Lewis dropped out of college in 1963 to become chairperson of SNCC. The next year, he organized the "Mississippi Freedom Summer," a massive drive to register African-American voters in the state. In 1965, Lewis helped Dr. Martin Luther King, Jr., organize a march from Montgomery to Selma, Alabama. The demonstrators demanded the right to vote for African Americans in the state. Although the clubbing of Lewis and others by state troopers halted the demonstration, the march resumed two weeks later. The marchers were escorted by federal troops and joined by hundreds of white Americans who had been outraged at the violence of the Alabama police. Lewis criticized the military draft, which forced young men who were denied freedom at home to fight for freedom in a foreign country. In 1966, he co-founded the Southern Coordinating Committee to End the War in Vietnam.

Lewis was defeated in his bid for a fourth term as SNCC chair by the more militant Stokely Carmichael in 1966. Lewis resigned from SNCC later that year to protest its rejection of nonviolence. In 1967, he directed community organization programs for the Southern Regional Council (SRC), an agency that served poor, rural communities. As executive director of the SRC's Voter Education project from 1970 to 1977, Lewis helped more than 2,500,000 African Americans register in the South. From 1977 to 1980, Lewis directed domestic operations for ACTION, the agency that oversaw federal antipoverty programs, including Volunteers in Service to America (VISTA) and the Peace Corps. After leaving the federal government upon election of President Ronald Reagan in 1980, Lewis turned to local politics. From 1982 to 1986 he served on the city council of Atlanta, Georgia. His attempt to meet the needs of the city's poor and elderly helped win him election to the House of Representatives in 1986. In Congress, Lewis has continued to advance the struggle for African-American civil rights. Although some African-Americans criticized the 1991 civil-rights bill for failing to meet the group's economic needs, Lewis supported the measure. *See* CARMICHAEL, STOKELY; KING, MARTIN LUTHER, JR.

Lovejoy, Elijah

(1802–1837)

ABOLITIONIST

In life, Elijah Parish Lovejoy defended the rights of all people to be free. In fact, he died trying to defend the freedom of the press to print antislavery articles. After studying at the Princeton Theological Seminary, Lovejoy became a Presbyterian preacher in St. Louis, Missouri in 1833. As editor of *The St. Louis Observer*, a Presbyterian weekly journal, Lovejoy regularly condemned habitual drinking and Roman Catholicism. Although he opposed slavery, Lovejoy also criticized **abolitionists**, whom he regarded as extremists. Lovejoy instead advocated a more gradual approach to freeing the slaves. Yet he also condemned the church for failing to take a stand against slavery. A local lynching (mob killing) in 1835 strengthened his opposition to slavery. That same year, responding to a letter urging him to tone down his editorials against slavery, Lovejoy wrote an editorial asserting his right to publish his views and repeating his opposition to slavery.

In 1836, hoping to avoid mob violence, Lovejoy moved his newspaper from the slave state of Missouri to Alton, Illinois. Lovejoy's press was immediately dumped into the Mississippi River, but community members—many of whom shared his support for gradually freeing the slaves—raised money for a new press. In what was now called *The Alton Observer*, Livejoy called for the establishment of an Illinois branch of the American Anti-Slavery Society. Angry proslavery mobs tossed Lovejoy's presses in the river two more times in 1837. Although many abolitionists opposed even the defensive use of force, repeated attacks on his home had convinced Lovejoy of his right to defend himself against the violence of proslavery mobs. When his fourth press, provided by the Ohio Anti-Slavery Society, arrived in Alton, Lovejoy and other abolitionists armed themselves to guard it. In front of a riverfront warehouse where the press was stored, an exchange of gunfire killed a person in the proslavery mob. In the violence that followed, Lovejoy too was shot and killed. The death of Lovejoy, who became known as the "martyr abolitionist," helped rouse and strengthen antislavery feelings in northern states.

Lowery, Joseph

(1925–   )

CIVIL RIGHTS ACTIVIST

Joseph E. Lowery, ordained as pastor of a United Methodist church in Birmingham, Alabama in 1952, joined a group of African-American preachers to found the Southern Christian Leadership Conference (SCLC) in 1957. Led by co-founders Dr. Martin Luther King, Jr., and Ralph Abernathy, the SCLC developed a nonviolent strategy to advance the **civil rights movement**. The SCLC employed the tactic of **civil disobedience**: peacefully refusing to comply with unjust laws as a way of drawing attention to injustice. Lowery served as vice president of the SCLC from its founding until 1967. While serving as administrative assistant to the United Methodist bishop in Nashville, Tennessee from 1961 to 1964, Lowery directed protests against **segregation** (the separation of people based on race) in the city's restaurants and hotels. In Minneapolis, Minnesota, from 1964 to 1968, Lowery campaigned against police brutality and called for the hiring of African Americans as police officers.

In 1967, Lowery was elected chair of the SCLC board of directors. On a community level, Lowery's United Methodist Church in Atlanta, Georgia, sponsored a housing development for poor and middle-income families. In 1977, Lowery was elected president of the SCLC, rejecting the calls of the conference's more militant members and winning the votes of its moderate members. Lowery steered the SCLC away from its previous focus on winning basic rights for African Americans. Lowery instead sought access to the social, economic, and political mainstream. In 1979, he led a protest march in Decatur, Alabama on behalf of a mentally retarded African American convicted of raping a white woman. Shots fired on the crowd by members of the Ku Klux Klan, a white racist group, injured four demonstrators.

Under Lowery's direction, the SCLC expanded its scope to include international affairs. In the 1970s and 1980s, Lowery sharply criticized American businesses that continued to deal with South Africa, a nation governed by racist laws. In 1979, he attempted to mediate between Palestinians and Israelis in order to bring peace to the Middle East. Lowery announced his support of the Palestinian right to a homeland, but urged Palestinians to recognize the right of Israel to exist. He believed that African Americans have a significant interest in global peace, and reasoned that a war would cause the deaths of a higher proportion of African Americans than white Americans. Furthering the cause of peace, Lowery hoped, would also free up money from the U.S. military budget that could be redirected to housing and unemployment programs that would benefit African Americans and other poor people.

In the 1980s, Lowery was highly critical of the cutbacks in social programs by the administration of President Ronald Reagan. He regularly accused the president of being out of touch with the reality of the African-American experience. After serving for sixteen years, Lowery resigned from the presidency of SCLC in 1993.

Mackenzie, William Lyon

(1795–1861)

ACTIVIST FOR LABOR MOVEMENT AND SOCIAL
REFORM IN CANADA

The leader of the unsuccessful Rebellion of 1837, William Lyon Mackenzie was born in Dundee, Scotland. After educating himself, he arrived a poor immigrant in English-speaking

Upper Canada (now Ontario) in 1820. For several years, he supported himself as a clerk, a druggist, a bookseller, and a shopkeeper. In 1824, he founded *The Colonial Advocate*, a weekly newspaper advocating reform, to promote the cause of laborers and farmers ignored by the Canadian government. He repeatedly criticized the greed and self-interest of the Family Compact: the group of wealthy, pro-British families that ruled Upper Canada. He called for the building of long-promised roads, bridges, and schools to benefit settlers. He also opposed laws favoring the Church of England, especially the setting aside of huge land reserves for the church. Supporters of the Family Compact raided the newspaper offices in York (now Toronto) in 1825. They destroyed the press and threw the type into Toronto Bay. After collecting over $2,000 in damages, Mackenzie resumed printing. The incident had made him a hero and radical leader of ordinary settlers.

By exposing the government's wasteful spending and neglect of settler's rights, Mackenzie and other Reformers were elected to the Assembly of Upper Canada in 1828. Although they controlled the Assembly, the Reformers found they had little real power. The Executive Council of Upper Canada, appointed by the British colonial governor, controlled all spending. When the Executive Council repeatedly ignored the Reformers' demands, Mackenzie went to England to present a list of complaints to the British government. The Reformers sought the creation of a "responsible government," one that represented the interests of the people. They demanded the right to elect—and recall—all office-holders. Most importantly, they wanted the Executive Council to answer to the elected Assembly or be removed from office. Due to his opposition to the government, Mackenzie was expelled from the Assembly six times between 1832 and 1836. Each time, the people of York returned him to office. In 1834, the new City Council of Toronto named Mackenzie the city's first mayor. He also continued to serve in the House of Commons, writing a five-hundred-page list of grievances that exposed the neglect and abuses of colonial government. Shortly after publishing a letter from British radical Joseph Hume that seemed to call for Canadian independence, he sold *The Colonial Advocate*.

After losing his seat in the Assembly in 1836, Mackenzie founded and edited a second radical newspaper, *The Constitution*. An economic depression the following year ruined many businesses and farms and increased popular support for Mackenzie's radical ideas. He met with followers to develop a proposed constitution for a new nation. Mackenzie wanted the new state to outlaw powerful corporations and create a public school system. Late in 1837, most Canadian forces were sent to Lower Canada (Quebec) to suppress a rebellion prompted by **Louis-Joseph Papineau**. Mackenzie saw the opportunity to strike: to take arms to create a new, responsible, democratic government. He led eight-hundred rural supporters toward Toronto, planning to seize the governor and establish a new government. The rebels, however, did little more than damage the property of those who supported British rule. The rebel forces scattered after guards fired several shots. The next day, the rebel force was crushed at their headquarters in Montgomery's Tavern.

Mackenzie fled to the United States, where supporters of his democratic revolution promised him money, arms, and volunteers to carry on his campaign. On Navy Island in the Niagara River, he planned further rebellions. But when the Canadian militia fired on the island, captured and burned a rebel supply ship, and killed an American, the rebellion was over. The U.S. government charged Mackenzie with violating neutrality laws with Canada. Found guilty in 1839, he spent eleven months in prison. Mackenzie remained in the U.S., writing several books and reporting for *The New York Daily Tribune* until 1849. After the government pardoned all rebels, he returned to Canada. He served in the Canadian Parliament from 1851 to 1858, but never again exercised the influence he had before the rebellion. *See* PAPINEAU, LOUIS-JOSEPH

Malcolm X (Malcolm Little)

(1925–1965)

CIVIL RIGHTS ACTIVIST

> Power in defense of freedom is greater than power in behalf of tyranny and oppression.
>
> —Malcom X, in a speech in New York City, (1965)

The black Muslim leader Malcolm X was a powerful leader in the civil rights movement. He searched for ways to end racial oppression, and for ways to foster black identity and pride.

He was born Malcolm Little in Omaha, Nebraska on May 19, 1925. His father was a minister who preached about black pride, and encouraged blacks to remain separate from whites. The Ku Klux Klan, a secret society of whites who hated blacks, were angered by his preaching and the Little family was forced to move several times to escape their repeated threats of violence. When Malcolm was six years old and living with his family in Lansing, Michigan, his father was killed; Malcolm always believed that he had been murdered by members of the Ku Klux Klan.

With her husband gone, Malcolm's mother now had to fend for herself and seven children. The family was very poor and often did not have enough to eat. They were forced to go on welfare, which meant that government gave them money to live on and sent social workers to their house. When they saw that Mrs. Little was less and less able to cope with caring for her family, and learned that Malcolm had been caught stealing food, they decided he should be sent to live with another family.

But without parents to watch out for him, he soon got into

trouble and was expelled from school. He was sent to a detention home, where boys in trouble were sent to get special help and guidance. The couple who ran the home liked Malcolm, and sent him to the public junior high school in Mason, Michigan; he was the first boy from the detention home to attend school and one of the very first blacks to attend that school.

At first, he liked it and did well in his classes. A summer trip to Boston to stay with his half-sister Ella introduced him to the ways of a larger city. Boston was a whole new world to him; there were entire African-American neighborhoods, something he hadn't seen before. When he returned to school that fall, he was dissatisfied. Malcolm began to notice that people assumed blacks were inferior to whites. He began to withdraw from his classmates, and at the end of school year, when he was released from the detention home, he boarded a Greyhound bus for Boston to live with Ella.

Malcolm lived in Boston for a time, selling sandwiches on the New York to Boston railroad. This allowed him to go to Harlem, a New York neighborhood populated by African Americans. Malcolm felt immediately at home in Harlem. When he was fired from the railway company, he moved there.

In Harlem, he began committing crimes: selling drugs and stealing. When he knew the police were looking for him, as they often were, he went back to Boston. Eventually he was caught and convicted for burglary; and in 1946, when Malcolm was twenty years old, he was sent to the Charlestown State Prison in Massuchusetts.

Prison life was brutal; Malcolm Little's cell was tiny and dingy. There was no running water and the toilet was a covered pail in the corner. After three years, he was transferred to Norfolk Prison Colony, a newer and better-run prison that had an excellent library. He began taking books out of the library. He read for as long as fifteen hours a day—so much that he strained his eyes, and had to start wearing the glasses that later became his trademark.

During this time, he received a visit from his brother Reginald, who lived in Detroit. Reginald talked to him about a new religion he had joined called the Nation of Islam. Its followers were called "Black Muslims." They believed that blacks should be respected by whites, but live separately from them, with their own communities and businesses. Reginald also told him about the leader of the Black Muslims, the Honorable Elijah Muhammed. Muhammed called white people "devils" who had tried to enslave black people. Malcolm was stirred by these thoughts and began to correspond with Muhammed. He also became a convert to the Muslim religion, and changed his name to Malcolm X. Because black Americans didn't know the African name of their ancestors, the Muslims used the letter "X", which is used in mathematical equations to stand for an unknown number, to show that their true names could never be known.

Malcolm X was let out of jail in the summer of 1952. He went to Detroit to live with his brother Wilfred, who was also a Muslim. He held jobs in a furniture store and on the assembly line in a factory. He adopted the Muslim customs of wearing a neat dark suit, refusing liquor and pork, and attended a Muslim Temple. In September of that year, he went to the Nation of Islam's headquarters in Chicago. There he met Elijah Muhammed and was impressed by his powerful talk about the black man's situation in America. Now Malcolm X knew what he wanted to do with his life: he was going to work for the Nation of Islam.

By the summer of 1953, Malcolm X was the assistant minister in Detroit Temple Number One. He spent his time visiting black neighborhoods, talking and trying to convert them to the Muslim faith. For the next six years, he worked hard, establishing new temples in Philadelphia, New York and other cities. When Elijah Muhammad became ill, Malcolm X took over many of his responsibilities. It seemed that he might be the Nation of Islam's next leader, for he was known as their most important spokesperson. While many people felt Malcolm X hated whites, he tried to correct their thinking: he was angry with them because of the crimes against blacks that they had committed, not just because they were white.

During his travels, he met a woman named Betty X in a temple and fell in love with her. They were married in 1958, and went on to have four daughters. Malcolm X and his family moved to a house in Queens, New York.

In 1964, Malcolm X made two trips to Africa and the Middle East. First he made a pilgrimage, or holy trip to the holy city of Mecca in Saudi Arabia. Mecca was the birthplace of the prophet Muhammad, founder of the Muslim religion. In Mecca, he took the name El-Hajj Malik El-Shabazz, a title of honor given to Muslim who had made the trip to the holy city.

When he returned to America, he decided to leave the Nation of Islam. While in Mecca, he had noticed that blacks and whites were able to get along peacefully together, and he began rethinking some of his ideas about white people. He also saw how black Christians and Muslims worked together. Now he wanted to head such a movement in America, which he called the Organization of Afro-American Unity (OAAU).

But Malcolm X Shabazz had made enemies as well as friends: many Muslims were angry with him for leaving the Nation of Islam and many whites did not want him to lead a movement of blacks. He received threatening phone calls and one night, a firebomb was thrown through the window of his house. No one was hurt, but the house was badly damaged and many of his family's things were destroyed. A week later, on February 25, 1965, the OAAU held a meeting at the Audubon Ballroom in Harlem. Malcolm X was scheduled to speak. When he appeared on the stage, there was a burst of applause, followed by angry shouting. He tried to calm the angry voices, but suddenly, gunfire rang out. Malcolm X had been shot. He fell backward onto the floor and was dead at the age of thirty-nine.

Mankiller, Wilma

(1945 –   )

FEMINIST, ACTIVIST FOR NATIVE AMERICANS' RIGHTS,
AND CHIEF OF THE CHEROKEE NATION

> Early historians referred to our government as petticoat
> government because of the strong role of the women in the
> tribe. Then we adopted a lot of ugly things that were part
> of the non-Indian world and one of those things was sexism.
> This whole system of tribal government was designed by
> men. So in 1687 women enjoyed a prominent role, but in
> 1987 we found people questioning whether women should
> be in leadership positions anywhere in the tribe. So my elec-
> tion was a step forward and a step backward at the same
> time.
>
> —Mankiller, from a *Ms.* magazine
> interview (1988)

In 1985, Wilma P. Mankiller became the first woman in modern
history to serve as the chief of a major Native American tribe.
As principal chief of the Cherokee Nation, Mankiller has
served as a role model for both Native Americans and women.
She has used the celebrity of her historic status to bring new
attention to the painful history and modern challenges faced
by Native Americans.

Born to a white mother and a full-blooded Cherokee father
in Tahlequah, Oklahoma, Wilma Mankiller and her ten brothers
and sisters grew up in poverty. Charlie Mankiller, whose last
name indicates a high rank in the Cherokee military, had inherited 160 acres of land from his father. In 1838, thousands of
Native Americans had died on the "Trail of Tears": a forced
relocation of the Cherokee from their lands in the southeastern
United States to the new Indian Territory, which later became
the state of Oklahoma. The land owned by the Mankillers had
been part of a settlement package later provided to the Cherokee tribe by the U.S. government. Wilma spent the first twelve
years of her life on this land, known as Mankiller Flats. But
when the family farm failed due to a two-year drought, the
Mankillers were forced to move. The U.S. government's Bu-

reau of Indian Affairs (BIA) relocated the family to San Francisco, California. The Mankillers' move was part of a BIA program intended to bring rural Native Americans into the mainstream of American urban life. Wilma and her family found it difficult to adapt to life in the modern city. After finding work in a warehouse, Wilma's father became an activist union organizer in the city.

In the 1960s, Wilma Mankiller began to study **sociology** and took a job as a social worker. Not until 1969 did she become involved in the Native American rights movement. That year, Native American college students seized the property and building of a former prison on Alcatraz Island in San Francisco Bay, and used the action to call attention to nearly five centuries of inhuman treatment of Native Americans by white Americans. During the eighteen months that the protesters held the island, Wilma Mankiller helped raise funds to support them.

The event sparked Mankiller's activism on behalf of Native Americans. In the early 1970s, while attending college at night, she began overseeing Native American programs for the public school system in Oakland, California. In 1971, the government helped put the Cherokee Nation back together by legally designating seven-thousand square miles as tribal land. In 1907, this land had been parcelled out to individual tribe members. But the policy had been a disaster: Breaking up the commonly owned land destroyed the basis for tribal culture, and many Cherokees lost their land to banks and land grabbers. In the mid-1970s, Mankiller returned to Oklahoma to reclaim her share of her grandfather's land. She began working for the betterment of the 92,000 members of the Cherokee Nation, the second largest tribe in the U.S.

In 1977, she was hired to help stimulate the economy of the Cherokee Nation, most of whom lived on the edge of poverty. In this job, she began to urge Cherokees to rebuild their self-esteem by helping themselves. After earning an undergraduate degree in social science from Flaming Rainbow University in Stilwell, Oklahoma, Mankiller began developing economic programs for the Cherokee Nation in 1979. Two years later, she raised funds for the Community Development Department of the Cherokee Nation, which she founded and directed. Through this agency, Mankiller introduced a series of successful rural development projects. She oversaw the installation of rural water systems and the rebuilding of houses. These projects, based on the notion of a community helping itself to improve, received national attention and served as a model for other North American tribes. Mankiller also won several government grants to finance these community development projects and other social services.

In 1983, Cherokee Chief Ross O. Swimmer asked Mankiller to be his running mate in that year's election. Their victory made Mankiller the first woman to serve as deputy principal chief of the Cherokee tribe. She supported Swimmer's programs designed to decrease the dependency of the Cherokee Nation on federal assistance. During the next two years, the Cherokee Nation established a cattle and poultry ranch, founded an electronics company, and opened a motel and a restaurant. Swimmer and Mankiller also urged full-blooded and mixed-blooded members of the tribe to live together in peace.

In 1985, Swimmer left office to become the head of the federal BIA in Washington, D.C., Mankiller filled the vacancy as principal chief of the Cherokee Nation. As Swimmer had done, Mankiller emphasized the importance of self-reliance. To realize her goal of economic self-sufficiency for the Cherokee Nation, she realized that improved education and jobs had to receive the highest priority. Promising to continue her efforts to improve the Cherokee economy, Mankiller was elected to a full four-year term as principal chief in 1987. As chief, she founded the Cherokee Nation's Chamber of Commerce, a group dedicated to linking tribal business ventures to the larger economic development of northeastern Oklahoma. She also promoted the building of a hydroelectric power plant on Cherokee lands. Rebuilding pride in Cherokee culture was another important concern. Mankiller promoted the Institute for Cherokee Literacy to preserve tribal language and culture. The institute offers summer school courses in reading and writing in the Cherokee language. In turn, students who have completed the course teach their communities these same skills.

Mankiller, who was reelected as principal chief of the Cherokee Nation in 1991, has attempted to balance the past and
future in the Cherokee Nation's present. She has emphasized
preserving the tribal language and culture while modernizing
education and the economy. In doing so, as she has explained,
"We have kept the best of our old ways of life and incorporated
the sounder elements of today's non-Indian world."

Marshall, Thurgood

(1908–1993)

CIVIL RIGHTS ACTIVIST AND FIRST AFRICAN
AMERICAN TO SERVE ON THE SUPREME COURT

After winning dozens of court battles that extended fundamental rights and freedoms to African Americans, Thurgood
Marshall became the first African American to serve on the
United States Supreme Court. After graduating from the all-
black Lincoln University in Oxford, Pennsylvania, Marshall
graduated first in his class from Howard University Law
School in 1933. Marshall took a job as legal counsel for the
Baltimore chapter of the National Association for the Advancement of Colored People (NAACP). In 1935, Marshall
brought a lawsuit that forced the all-white University of Maryland Law School, which had rejected his own application six
years earlier, to admit its first African-American student. Marshall's successes in Baltimore led to his 1936 appointment as
assistant to the national counsel (lawyer) for the NAACP, and
later his promotion to national counsel.

In 1939, Marshall helped found the NAACP Legal Defense
and Educational Fund (LDF). The LDF brought the battle
against **segregation** into the nation's courtrooms. As chief
counsel of the LDF, Marshall was in charge of developing the
group's overall legal strategy. He also argued **civil rights** cases
that were brought before the United States Supreme Court.
Over the next twenty-two years, Marshall won an impressive

twenty-nine of the thirty-two cases he argued before the Supreme Court for the NAACP. His most notable victory came in 1954, in the case of *Brown v. Board of Education of Topeka.* Marshall argued against an 1896 Supreme Court ruling that allowed states to establish "separate but equal" schools for whites and African Americans. Contending that separation leads to inequality, Marshall insisted that segregated schools violated the Fourteenth Amendment to the U.S. Constitution. The Fourteenth Amendment, passed in 1868, guarantees equal protection of the law to all citizens. The court agreed with Marshall's arguments, ruling that segregation of schools was unconstitutional. Marshall's other court victories helped eliminate unequal treatment of the races in voting laws, housing, public facilities, and graduate and professional schools.

In 1961, President John Kennedy named Marshall a judge on the U.S. Court of Appeals. Despite a year of stalling by Senators who favored segregation, Marshall was confirmed by the Senate in 1962. As a judge, Marshall ruled that it was illegal to force teachers to take an oath proclaiming their loyalty to the government of the United States. He also protected the rights of immigrants by preventing immigration authorities from deporting them without legal cause. From 1965 to 1967, Marshall served as U.S. Solicitor General: the nation's chief prosecuting attorney and the third highest post in the Justice Department. Appearing again before the Supreme Court, Marshall defended the government's right to carry out the Voting Rights Act of 1965. The act banned tests of reading ability, poll taxes, and other restrictions used to prevent African Americans and the poor from voting. Marshall won that case, as well as thirteen of the other eighteen cases he argued before the Supreme Court for the Justice Department.

Appointed to the U.S. Supreme Court by President Lyndon Johnson in 1967, Marshall's rulings on the Court demonstrated his continued commitment to individual rights. He consistently upheld the concept of equal justice under the law and ruled against the government's attempts to chip away at fundamental freedoms. During his tenure on the Court, new justices appointed by Presidents Nixon, Ford, Reagan, and Bush made the court increasingly conservative. More and more often,

Marshall and Justice William Brennan wrote opinions that disagreed with the ruling of the majority. Marshall opposed the death penalty as a violation of the Constitution's prohibition of "cruel and unusual punishment." He argued that the death penalty fails to provide "equal protection of the laws," because African Americans receive death sentences more often than white criminals. Marshall affirmed the right of privacy that prohibits states from limiting a woman's right to a legal, safe, and affordable abortion. Marshall defended the constitutionality of **affirmative action**: job, education, and housing programs that attempt to correct the longstanding denial of equal economic opportunity for women, African Americans, and other minorities. In 1991, Marshall resigned from the Court.

McClung, Nellie

(1873–1951)

SOCIAL REFORMER AND WOMEN'S RIGHTS ACTIVIST

Author, lawmaker, and reformer Nellie Letitia Mooney McClung long supported the cause of women's rights, especially a woman's right to vote. Born in Chatsworth, Ontario, Nellie grew up on a homestead in Manitoba, where her family moved in 1880. With no school on the frontier, she did not begin her schooling until age ten. In 1890, she received a teaching certificate from the Winnipeg Normal School. Nellie Mooney taught for six years in rural Somerset, Manitoba.

At the urging of her mother-in-law, the head of the Manitoba branch of the Women's Christian Temperance Union, Nellie McClung in 1907 began lecturing for the cause of **temperance**: giving up liquor. The following year, her first novel, *Sowing Seeds in Danny*, the portrait of a western town, became a bestseller. Her new fame allowed McClung to become a prominent spokesperson for both temperance and women's rights. Her next novel, *The Second Chance*, published in 1910, portrayed an idealistic teacher and her campaign for women's rights.

After moving to Winnipeg in 1911, McClung began lecturing on behalf of legal and political equality for women. She helped lead the Political Equality League's campaign for women's **suffrage** in Manitoba in 1914. She organized and presided over a famous "Mock Parliament" meeting in Winnipeg. The meeting mocked the opposition to women's suffrage in Manitoba. As "premier" of a parliament of women, McClung pretended to receive a delegation of men (actually women playing male roles) seeking the vote. She turned the men away, joking that the vote would distract them from their higher duty to support the family, break up homes, and wreck innocent lives. Women won the right to vote in Manitoba two years later.

After moving to Edmonton, Alberta, McClung joined Emily Murphy in the fight for women's suffrage in that province. She also promoted **prohibition** (a ban on the sale of alcohol), which all of the provinces but Quebec had enacted by 1916. After women won the right to vote in Alberta in 1916, McClung broadened the scope of her **feminism**. She called for the property rights of married women, laws to make factories safer for workers of both sexes, and other reforms to aid women and children. Her 1917 book, *Next of Kin*, offered a collection of sketches that portrayed the tragedy and waste of war.

From 1921 to 1926, McClung served in the Alberta legislature, continuing to promote liberal reforms. *Painted Fires*, published in 1925, depicts the cruelty of Canadian society toward poor immigrants. With Murphy and three other women, McClung petitioned the Supreme Court to rule on whether women were considered "persons" under the law. (As persons, women would be eligible for appointment to the Senate.) Although the Canadian Supreme Court ruled in 1928 that women were not persons, the five women appealed the ruling to Great Britain. The following year, the government recognized women as persons, leading to the first appointment of a woman to Canada's Senate in 1930.

In 1933, McClung moved to Vancouver Island, where she wrote books, short stories, and a newspaper column. The first volume of her autobiography, *Clearing in the West: My Own Story*, was published in 1935. McClung served as a delegate to the League of Nations in 1938. McClung, who wrote sixteen books in all, published the second volume of her autobiography, *The Stream Runs Fast*, in 1945. *See* MURPHY, EMILY

Means, Russell

(1939–   )

NATIVE AMERICAN CIVIL RIGHTS ACTIVIST

Russell Charles Means, born on the Pine Ridge Reservation in South Dakota, first encountered racism while attending high school in San Leandro, California. The target of racial insults, Means, a Sioux, turned to drugs and alcohol as an escape. By the late 1960s, Means had joined the American Indian Movement (AIM), a militant Native American **civil rights** group founded in 1967. Means founded the second AIM chapter in Cleveland. On Thanksgiving Day in 1970, Means led a group of Native Americans in seizing control of the *Mayflower II* in Plymouth, Massachusetts. The action, which ended peacefully, gave AIM its first national exposure. Means and AIM wanted to bring the plight of Native Americans to the attention of the American public. During the next two years, Means led an unsuccessful attempt to occupy the central information office of the government's Bureau of Indian Affairs and sued the Cleveland Indians baseball club for degrading Native Americans with its team logo, "Chief Wahoo."

In 1972, Means led a cross-country demonstration called the Trail of Broken Treaties to protest against a century of broken promises of land and social services for Native Americans. The Trail ended in Washington, D.C., where the protestors took over the Bureau of Indian Affairs building. They renamed the building the Native American Embassy to symbolize their demands for the rights of an independent nation rather than for civil rights within the existing white society. Five days later, when the White House promised to investigate the quality of federal programs for Native Americans and to consider allowing Native Americans to govern themselves, the protestors left the building.

Returning to the reservation, Means and other AIM members found themselves barred from attending public meetings of the Oglala Sioux tribal council. Means was arrested twice for challenging the court order obtained by the tribal president Dick Wilson. In 1973, Means sought to impeach Wilson for corruption and misuse of tribal funds. Means met briefly with Wilson, then suffered a beating at the hands of Wilson's "goons" (Guardians of the Oglala Nation). The next day, Means led two-hundred AIM members in seizing the village of Wounded Knee, South Dakota. Means announced that he had freed the village from a government that had violated 371 treaties with Native Americans. Declaring that AIM would establish a traditional tribal government, he demanded self-rule for Native Americans. After thirty-eight days, Means left Wounded Knee to negotiate a peaceful settlement with the White House.

Arriving in Washington, he found the White House unwilling to talk until AIM first surrendered the village. Means was arrested for announcing his intention to defy a court order and rejoin the protestors. After seventy-one days, the seige of Wounded Knee ended, when the government agreed to investigate broken treaties and the abuses of Wilson's tribal council. Means was charged with ten felonies for his part in the occupation of Wounded Knee. After a seven-month trial, in which lawyers for the defense showed that the government had conducted illegal wiretaps and lied in their testimony, the judge dismissed all charges against Means.

After Wounded Knee, Means continued to lead protests designed to raise awareness of injustices suffered by Native Americans. Several times, he was sentenced to prison for taking part in riots that erupted at protest sites. In 1985, he supported the struggle of Miskito Indians against the government of Nicaragua. Means appeared in the 1992 film *Last of the Mohicans*, which he hailed for its full, rounded depictions of Native American characters. That October, in Denver, Colorado, he organized and led a Native American protest of celebrations honoring the 500th anniversary of Christopher Columbus arrival in America. Means condemned Columbus for initiating five centuries of murdering and relocating Native Americans.

Millett, Kate

(1934–   )

FEMINIST

> I hope I pointed out to men how truly inhuman it is for them to think of women the way they do, to treat them that way, to act that way toward them. All I was trying to say was, look, brother, I'm human.
>
> —Millett, from a *Life* magazine interview (1970)

In *Sexual Politics*, teacher and sculptor Katherine (Kate) Murray Millett examined how men have controlled women throughout history. She argued that all dealings between men and women involve a struggle for power—a struggle she defines as "political." The best-selling book helped Millett become a leader among **feminists**: women's rights activists.

Born an Irish Catholic in St. Paul, Minnesota, Kate Millett attended Catholic schools as a girl. As a teenager, however, Kate lost faith in Catholicism and rebelled against the church and its teachings. When Kate was fourteen, her father abandoned the family. Left without support, her mother, a college graduate, tried to find work. Despite her education, her mother had difficulty finding a job, finally landing an offer to demonstrate potato peelers. Her mother ultimately got a job selling insurance, but earned only $600 in her first year. Kate was outraged at the sexual **discrimination** (unequal treatment based on sex) in her mother's new business. Men selling insurance earned a salary until they had won enough customers to support themselves through **commissions** (a percentage of each sale). Women like her mother, however, were given no salary and had to support themselves solely through commissions from the very beginning. Women were forced to prove their worth, while men were welcomed as valued employees.

Millett earned an undergraduate degree in English from the University of Minnesota in 1956. Hoping to curb Millett's rebellious nature, an aunt offered to pay for her graduate studies at England's Oxford University. Kate accepted the offer, studying English literature at Oxford's St. Hilda's College for two years. Returning to the United States in 1958, Millett accepted a job teaching English at the University of North Carolina. But she quit teaching after half a semester to move to New York. There, while working as a kindergarten teacher in Harlem, she began painting and sculpting. She held her first one-woman sculpture show in Tokyo, Japan, where she taught English at Waseda University from 1961 to 1963. When she returned to New York, she began creating whimsical sculpted furniture: beds with what looked like human feet, sofas with "human" legs.

During this time, Millett also became increasingly involved in social reform movements. She worked for the peace movement, protesting against U.S. involvement in the Vietnam War. She joined the Congress of Racial Equality, a group advancing the **civil rights movement** for African Americans and other ethnic minorities. But her greatest commitment was to the dawning women's movement. In 1966, she was appointed chair of the education committee of the National Organization of Women (NOW), founded that year by Betty Friedan. After investigating the education offered by women's colleges, Millett wrote a study called "Token Learning." As its title suggests, the work sharply criticized the quality of education then provided to college women.

In 1968, she began working toward a doctoral degree in English at Columbia University. She also taught English at the university's school for women, Barnard College. At Columbia, she organized campus demonstrations in support of women's rights, the reform of abortion laws, and students' rights. That fall, in a short speech before a feminist group at Cornell University in Ithaca, New York, Millett urged women to take action to free themselves from the control of men. The following month, apparently in response to her campus activism, Barnard fired her from her teaching position.

In 1969, Millett began expanding her Cornell speech into

a doctoral thesis. Barnard rehired her that fall to join in an experimental, communal teaching program. Living off campus with students and other faculty members, Millett taught philosophy for one semester. The following spring, she earned her doctorate from Columbia. Her thesis was published later that year as *Sexual Politics: A Surprising Examination of Society's Most Arbitrary Folly*. Millett outlined her view that all relations between men and women are political. The book began by exploring the history of male domination and control over women. The "political" institution of marriage and the family, Millett contended, regarded women as nothing more than property owned by men. She also showed how the male power structure exercised control over women in the economy as well. Millett aimed criticism not only at men, but at women as well. She accused women of accepting and even devoting themselves to the masters and institutions that enslave them.

Millett did admit the existence of differences between the male and female sexes. However, she contended that **gender** differences—contrasts between feminine and masculine attitudes and behavior—are not necessarily present at birth. The society's culture teaches men to think and behave aggressively and forcefully and to aim their lives toward specific goals and achievements. By contrast, women in this culture learn to behave passively, to submit to men, and to depend upon men for their survival. Millett admitted that some differences in attitudes, thinking, and personality might exist at birth. She insisted, however, that no one would ever know this with certainty until society began to treat men and women alike.

Millett's views were quickly embraced by the feminist movement. Women activists began to see their efforts as part of a larger political struggle for power and control over their own destiny. In 1971, Millett began teaching a course on women's roles and behavior in society at Bryn Mawr College. Since then, she has written several other books on women and society, which include the autobiographical *Flying* (1974) and *The Loony-Bin Trap* (1990). She continues to take an active part in NOW and many other women's liberation groups. *See* FRIEDAN, BETTY

Mott, Lucretia Coffin

(1793–1880)

ABOLITIONIST, ACTIVIST FOR WOMEN'S RIGHTS, AND
QUAKER MINISTER

After devoting half of her adult life to the struggle to outlaw slavery, Lucretia Coffin Mott spent the rest of her life as a pioneer in the women's rights movement. In 1808, Lucretia Coffin was given a job as assistant teacher at Nine Partners, a Quaker boarding school near Poughkeepsie, New York. Only fifteen years old, Coffin worked for no pay. Although she liked the male teacher at the school, James Mott, it seemed unjust to her that he earned more than twice what the female teacher was paid. In 1811, Coffin married James Mott, and they shared a mutual commitment to reform throughout their lives.

Lucretia Mott, who had begun speaking at Quaker meetings shortly after the death of her son in 1817, was recognized as an official Quaker minister in 1821. Around 1825, Mott began to protest against slavery by **boycotting** (refusing to buy) cotton cloth, cane sugar, and other products of slave labor. In her sermons, she urged her fellow Quakers to join her in buying only crops produced by free laborers. In 1833, the Motts attended an **abolitionist** convention in Philadelphia to organize the American Anti-Slavery Society. Since the society did not admit women members, Lucretia Mott helped organize the Philadelphia Female Anti-Slavery Society that year. The society wrote letters to Congress urging immediate freedom for all slaves, raised money to aid poor African Americans, and opened a school for African-American children. In 1837, Mott helped organize the Anti-Slavery Convention of American Women. She also helped maintain calm when a proslavery mob disrupted the Philadelphia convention and burned Pennsylvania Hall to the ground. Both Lucretia and James Mott went to London in 1840 as Philadelphia delegates to the World Anti-Slavery Convention. Along with all other female delegates, however, Lucretia Mott was refused recognition at the convention. Sitting in the rear of the convention hall, Mott met Elizabeth Cady Stanton, another woman excluded from the convention. This meeting would lead to the beginning of the women's rights movement.

Eight years later, Mott, Stanton, and Martha Coffin Wright (Mott's sister) organized the first Women's Rights Convention in Seneca Falls, New York. Mott, who delivered the opening and closing speeches, also helped write the convention's Declaration of Sentiments. The Declaration, which stated that "all men and women are created equal," urged women to organize and demand their rights. The convention passed twelve resolutions asserting the rights of women. Mott introduced one of these resolutions, proclaiming a woman's right to participate in professions, trades, and businesses. Although the call for **suffrage** (the right to vote), which Mott regarded as a minor issue, passed by a narrow margin, all of the other resolutions passed **unanimously**—without a single person voting against it. The 1848 convention at Seneca Falls marked the beginning of the organized women's rights movement.

In 1850, Mott's *Discourse on Woman* examined the question of whether women were inferior to men, a common opinion at that time. Mott argued that the lack of educational and job opportunities, lower pay, and the denial of political rights had created a false image of women's inferiority. In 1852, she was elected president of the Women's Rights Convention in Syracuse, New York, which more than two thousand women attended.

While focusing on women's rights, Mott's commitment to the abolition of slavery remained strong. During the 1850s, the Motts provided refuge to runaway slaves in their home. In 1865, the Thirteenth Amendment to the U.S. Constitution abolished slavery, yet Mott continued her efforts on behalf of freed slaves, joining the Friends Association of Philadelphia for the Aid and Elevation of the Freedmen. The group provided financial assistance to former slaves and established elementary schools for African-American children in the South. In 1866, Mott served as president of the American Equal Rights Association. The association sought to win political, social, and economic equality for both African Americans and women.

Although the American Equal Rights Association was short-lived, it perfectly mirrored the concerns of Lucretia Mott, who saw all social reforms as part of the same struggle for justice.
See STANTON, ELIZABETH CADY

Murphy, Emily

(1868–1933)

ACTIVIST FOR WOMEN'S RIGHTS AND FIRST FEMALE
JUDGE OF CANADA

Writer and judge Emily Gowan Ferguson Murphy promoted the political and legal equality of women. Born in Cookstown, Ontario, Emily Ferguson was educated at the Bishop Strachan School in Toronto. Her 1887 marriage to a missionary led her to a life in small frontier towns. In 1901, she published *The Impressions of Janey Canuck Abroad*, the first of four popular books written under the pen name of "Janey Canuck." Murphy used **satirical** sketches to expose the tragedy of the poor and the cruel conditions of slum life. After moving to Swan River, Manitoba in 1903, Murphy began lecturing and writing to campaign for social reforms that would benefit women and children. She called for women's **suffrage**, property rights for married women, and other legal rights for women. She also encouraged the creation of a women's court to rule on cases involving women.

Murphy in 1907 settled in Edmonton, Alberta. There, she organized public pressure on Alberta lawmakers to pass the Married Women's Relief Act in 1911. The law insured widows at least one-third of their husbands' property in cases without a will or when they were left out of a will. From 1912 to 1916, Murphy helped lead the campaign for women's suffrage in both Alberta and Manitoba. Both provinces allowed women to vote in 1916. A writer of articles and book reviews for Canadian magazines and newspapers, Murphy served as president of the Canadian Women's Press Club from 1913 to 1920.

In 1916, Alberta created the women's court Murphy had long advocated. Murphy herself was named the court's first magistrate (judge). The appointment made her the first female judge not only in Canada, but in the entire British Empire. On her first day in court, lawyers arguing before her challenged her right to serve as a judge. Under British law, a woman was considered a person only when subject to penalties and punishment, but had no legal rights. Murphy noted the lawyers' objections, but ruled and passed sentences in these cases anyway. The Alberta Supreme Court soon upheld women's rights as persons. Having won the fight in the province, Murphy decided to struggle for women's recognition as persons throughout Canada. In 1919, at a conference of the Federated Women's Institute, she won support for a resolution that called on the prime minister to appoint a woman to the Senate. To do so, the prime minister would have to accept women as persons.

As magistrate, Murphy ruled in many cases of prostitution as well as cases involving children charged with crimes. Blaming drug abuse for many of these crimes, she began writing articles for *Maclean's* magazine campaigning against the use of drugs. In 1922, she published *The Black Candle*, which exposed the evils of the drug trade. The book helped prompt harsher drug laws throughout Canada. Two years later, Murphy represented Canada at a League of Nations conference on narcotics (drugs) in Geneva, Switzerland.

In 1927, Murphy led a group of four other **feminists** in petitioning Canada's Supreme Court to decide whether women were persons under the law. The court ruled against the five women—Henrietta Muir Edwards, Alberta legislators Louise McKinney and Nellie McClung, Murphy, and Cabinet Minister Irene Parlby—the following year. Both the Albertan and Canadian governments supported the women in appealing the ruling to the British Privy Council (advisers to the Crown). The privy council reversed the decision of the Canadian Supreme Court in 1929. As "persons," women were now eligible for appointments to government offices, including the Senate. As a result of the "Persons Case," Canada appointed a woman—Cairine

Wilson—to the Senate in 1930. Murphy resigned from the bench the following year. *See* MCCLUNG, NELLIE

Nader, Ralph

(1934–   )

ACTIVIST FOR CONSUMER RIGHTS

Consumer advocate and lawyer, Ralph Nader first fought for the public interest as a student at Princeton University. His attempt to prevent the spraying of campus trees with the poisonous insecticide DDT, however, was unsuccessful. Nader earned a degree in government and economics in 1955. Three years later, shortly before receiving his law degree from Harvard University, Nader published his first article on auto safety, "American Cars: Designed for Death," in the *Harvard Law Record*. After a few years in private practice, Nader moved to Washington, D.C., in 1964 to continue his fight for improved auto safety. Assistant Secretary of Labor Daniel P. Moynihan hired Nader as a consultant on highway safety. In 1965, Nader published *Unsafe at Any Speed: The Designed-in Dangers of the American Automobile*. The book charged the American auto industry with putting style before safety. Nader's bestselling book prompted passage of the National Traffic and Motor Vehicle Safety Act. This 1966 law authorized the government to set safety standards for all cars sold in the country.

Nader used his new fame to focus public attention on other

consumer interests. He called for higher safety standards in the mining and natural-gas industries. He advocated regulation of the meat industry to insure against unhealthy conditions in slaughterhouses and processing plants. In 1969, Nader formed the Center for Study of Responsive Law. The organization investigated federal regulatory agencies such as the Food and Drug Administration, the Federal Trade Commission, and the Interstate Commerce Commission. Nader's group gathered evidence that showed that these agencies were being influenced by the same corporations they were supposed to monitor. Nader received $425,000 from General Motors in 1970 to settle a lawsuit charging them with invasion of privacy. The auto company admitted hiring detectives in 1966 in an attempt to dig up information on him and discredit his book. Nader used the settlement money to found the Corporate Accountability Research Group, which examines how well corporations fulfill their responsibilities to consumers. He also established the Public Interest Research Group, a group of consumer and political activists who fight for reforms on the community level.

Nader founded Public Citizen, Inc. in 1971. Public Citizen lobbies elected government officials on behalf of consumer interests. Nader formed the group to combat the growing influence of corporate lobbyists on the federal government. Public Citizen established a varied network of organizations, including Congress Watch and the Tax Reform Research Group. Nader's efforts helped gain passage in 1974 of the Freedom of Information Act, which gives citizens access to most government files. He also played an important role in the creation of the Occupational Safety and Health Administration, which monitors and regulates job safety.

Throughout the 1970s, "Nader's Raiders"—the group of consumer advocates working with Nader—continued to expose unsafe products, workplace hazards, and the failure to enforce consumer safety laws. In 1978, Nader urged Congress to create a federal Consumer Protection Agency, but the bill failed to pass by several votes. In 1980, Nader resigned as president of Public Citizen, Inc. Organizing at a neighborhood level, he helped create low-cost home-heating oil co-operatives and community organizations that monitor public utilities. During the 1980s, Nader saw many of his greatest successes taken apart by the administration of President Ronald Reagan. Reagan saw the programs sponsored by Nader as putting too many constraints on industry. Yet Nader has refused to give up his attack on the power of giant corporations, as well as the abuses of consumers and the public interest by the nuclear-power industry, the U.S. Postal Service, and the insurance industry. Forced in 1986 to curtail his exhaustive schedule due to illness, Nader nonetheless led the campaign two years later to force apple growers to stop spraying their crops with the pesticide alar, which was linked to high cancer rates among children. In 1989, he urged members of Congress to vote against a raise in their own salaries, linking the measure to the nation's minimum wage, which had remained at $3.25 an hour for nearly a decade. Nader has remained a consumer and public-interest activist in the 1990s. In 1991, he condemned the government for its financial support of mining and logging operations. He also criticized the government for financing corporate research and development. If tax dollars pay for developing a product and consumers then need to spend money to buy that product, Nader insisted, they are in essence paying for the same product twice.

Newton, Huey

(1942–1989)

ACTIVIST FOR BLACK LIBERATION,
AND FOUNDER OF THE BLACK
PANTHERS

> I suggested that we use the panther as our symbol and call our political vehicle the Black Panther Party. The panther is a fierce animal, but he will not attack until he is backed into a corner; then he will strike out.

—Newton, *Revolutionary Suicide*, (1973)

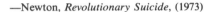

Political activist Huey Percy Newton, in and out of jail throughout his adult life, co-founded the Black Panther Party. Under his leadership, the Black Panthers evolved from an armed band of **vigilantes** defending itself against urban racism to an organization dedicated to improving life in African-American ghettos. Through the Panthers, Newton hoped to restore pride among African Americans.

The youngest of seven children, Huey Newton was born in New Orleans, Louisiana. His father, a Baptist preacher and poor tenant farmer, moved the family to Oakland, California in 1943. There, his father worked seven days a week, holding two or three jobs at a time. From his father's example, Huey learned that hard work does not always lead to success in the American economy. In his adult life, Newton refused to own anything in order to avoid repeating his father's constant run-ins with bill collectors. Newton was not a model student. Although he just barely managed to graduate from Oakland Technical High School, he had still not learned how to read. After leaving school, he taught himself how to read and became eager to read almost anything. In the early 1960s, he earned a degree from a two-year college in Oakland and took courses at San Francisco Law School for two semesters.

During this period, Newton also began a series of clashes with the police. Although he successfully defended himself against a charge of stealing books, he was found guilty and sentenced to one year's probation for battering a police officer in 1962. In 1964, he served six months of a three-year sentence for assault with a deadly weapon (a kitchen knife).

In 1966, Newton and a friend from law school named Bobby Seale founded the Black Panther Party for Self-Defense in an Oakland ghetto. Seale became chair of the Black Panthers, while Newton served as minister of defense. The Black Panthers demanded power in the African-American community to determine their own destiny. The Panthers called upon all African Americans to arm themselves. They demanded the release of all African Americans from jail and the exemption of blacks from the military draft.

The first priority of the Panthers was the creation of "black defense groups" to fight against police brutality and racism. Newton formed small, armed units that patrolled the streets of the Oakland ghetto. The defense groups operated under strict rules of discipline, including staying off drugs. On their nightly patrols, the units observed the behavior of police in their contacts with ghetto residents. Newton and Seale often carried their law books with them on the streets. When a police officer objected to the presence of the Panther patrols, Newton or Seale would point out that California law allowed the carrying of firearms as long as the weapons were not concealed.

The following year, thirty Panthers carried shotguns and rifles into the California State Assembly. The Panthers protested against a state gun control bill apparently introduced at the request of the Oakland police. Newton, still on probation, did not take part in this protest. The Oakland police reacted to this protest by stepping up police action against the Panthers. Every day, more Panthers were stopped, questioned, or arrested by the police. Newton's car was one of those stopped by the police. In the struggle that followed, one police officer died, one was wounded, and Newton was shot through stomach. The police charged Newton with murder and assault.

They added an accusation of kidnapping, charging him with forcing a motorist to drive him to a hospital.

The 1968 trial gave Newton and the Black Panthers nationwide publicity. The Black Panthers became a national organization, with branches forming in thirty cities, including New York, Los Angeles, San Diego, and Detroit. The radical Peace and Freedom Party chose Newton to run for Congress. College students and radicals demonstrated on his behalf, shouting "Free Huey." A crowd of 2,500 protesters circled the Oakland Court House on the opening day of Newton's trial. Under oath, Newton insisted that he did not know what had happened after the officer had punched him in the face and shot him in the stomach. Other witnesses proved that the officer had been killed with his own gun, and that no one, including the other officer on the scene, saw Newton with a gun at any time. Newton was convicted of manslaughter and sentenced to two-to-fifteen years in prison.

While in prison, Newton often ended up in solitary confinement. The experience gave him a new self-discipline. He exercised often in his confinement cell to show the guards that they had not broken his spirit. In 1970, Newton was released when an appeals court overturned his conviction due to errors by the trial judge. He resumed leadership of the Panthers, which had lost half its members during the time he was in prison. Newton established a new direction for the Black Panthers. In a split with Eldridge Cleaver, then exiled in Algeria, Newton abandoned the tactics of violence and militarism. Instead, he called for nonviolent organization of African-American communities. To reflect this shift, Newton changed his title from minister of defense to supreme servant of the people.

The new Black Panthers introduced free social services to help the poor living in the Oakland ghetto. Within two years, the Panthers had established a free health clinic and free psychological services. They founded a free breakfast program for poor children and an elementary school. The organization also operated an agency to help those on welfare and buses that took residents to prison to visit with family members. The Panthers also provided such practical services as plumbing and shoe and clothing outlets. Newton saw these services as tools to help advance a revolution toward a more democratic, **socialist** society free of racism.

In 1971, Newton announced that the Black Panthers would establish a headquarters in Atlanta, Georgia. This would allow the organization to join with African-American churches in promoting **civil rights** in the rural South. That year, Newton headed a six-month campaign of pickets and **boycotts** against a group of African-American liquor-store owners in California. As a result of this action, the store owners agreed to contribute money to the United Black Fund, which provided social services to poor African Americans. Newton continued to use boycotts and pickets to win further support for social services benefitting African Americans. He also helped increase voter registration in the Oakland ghetto. *To Die for the People*, a collection of Newton's speeches, interviews, and writings, was published in 1972.

Again accused of murder in 1974, Newton fled the country, living in Cuba for three years. He returned for trial in 1977, but two juries were unable to reach a verdict. In 1980, he earned a doctorate in social philosophy from the University of California at Santa Cruz. His dissertation was entitled *War Against the Panthers: A Study of Repression in America*. Two years later, the Black Panther Party disbanded. In 1989, Newton did not contest charges that he had misused public funds intended for the elementary school founded by the Panthers. Five months later, he was shot to death outside an Oakland crack house. *See* CLEAVER, ELDRIDGE

Osborne, Thomas

(1859–1926)

ACTIVIST FOR PRISON REFORM

Thomas Mott Osborne grew up in Auburn, New York, the site of one of the state's prisons. After earning an undergraduate degree from Harvard University in 1884, Osborne returned to

Auburn to run the agricultural machinery business he inherited from his father two years later. In the late 1890s, he headed the board of governors of the George Junior Republic, an industrial reform school near Ithaca, New York. Osborne found that by encouraging group harmony and fostering self-government, he could help rebellious boys begin to develop a sense of personal responsibility.

Osborne sold his business in 1903 and served as Auburn's mayor from 1903 to 1905. He founded a newspaper, *The Auburn Citizen*, in 1905. Osborne was appointed chair of the New York State Commission on Prison Reform in 1913. To learn more about prison conditions, Osborne spent a week as "Tom Brown," a prisoner in the Auburn prison. Osborne soon introduced an experiment that he called a Mutual Welfare League at the Auburn prison. The Mutual Welfare League allowed prisoners to govern themselves according to the rules of democracy and prison regulations. Prisoners formed committees, organized their own entertainment, and established a prisoner's court that judged violations of rules. Despite the fears of prison staff members that these policies would result in chaos, the program was a success.

In 1914, Osborne wrote *Within Prison Walls*, which detailed his experience and his findings. He called for the creation of prisons that not only punish criminals, but change them for the better. Osborne sought to prepare prisoners for their reentry into society. From 1914 to 1916, Osborne served as warden of Sing Sing, the largest prison in the state of New York. The Mutual Welfare League at Sing Sing repeated Osborne's success at Auburn. Prisoners began educating themselves and created a self-help program for released convicts. Osborne's innovative and humane programs, however, met with a great deal of resistance. Pressured by his conservative superiors and the governor of New York, Osborne resigned in 1916. *Society and Prisons*, Osborne's second book, was published that same year. From 1917 to 1920, Osborne was commander of the Portsmouth Naval Prison in New Hampshire. Once again, his Mutual Welfare League helped improve prison conditions and prisoner morale. Once again, he was forced to resign by his superiors. Osborne spent the rest of his life writing and lecturing on prison reform. He founded the Welfare League Association, which offered financial assistance to released convicts, and the National Society of Penal Information, which collected statistics on America's prisons.

Packard, Elizabeth

(1816–1897)

ACTIVIST FOR THE RIGHTS OF WOMEN AND THE MENTALLY ILL

Three years in a mental hospital transformed Elizabeth Parsons Ware Packard into a crusader for the rights of married women and for laws to protect the mentally ill. Elizabeth Ware, whose mother had a history of mental illness, was first committed to a mental hospital in Worcester, Massachusetts in 1837, due to emotional problems. After just two months at the state hospital, she was discharged. Two years later, she married Presbyterian pastor Theophilus Packard. By 1857, Elizabeth Packard had developed the conviction that she had divinity within her. She believed that the Holy Ghost—complement of God the Father—was female, and that it was embodied in her. Her new religious views upset her husband, especially when, in 1860, she began expressing them in Bible classes at his church. Her husband publicly condemned the heresy of her beliefs and had Packard committed to the state mental hospital in Jacksonville, Illinois. At that time, the law required a husband only to obtain the consent of a hospital administrator in order to commit his wife. Packard had no legal right to contest the commitment.

In 1863, Packard was judged incurable, and discharged into the care of her husband. Theophilus Packard intended to return to Massachusetts and have his wife committed permanently. With the support of friends, Elizabeth Packard won the right to a jury trial to determine her sanity in 1864. Hearing that her husband had committed Packard solely on the basis of religious differences, the jury quickly judged her as mentally competent. When she returned home, she found that her husband had sold their possessions and taken their children. Since Illinois law granted no property rights to married women, Packard was left in poverty.

The injustices she suffered sparked Packard to crusade for the rights of married women and the reform of insanity laws. From 1864 to 1868, Packard wrote four books calling for freedom for what she called the "slaves" of marriage and exposing the abuses of insane asylums. She also began to urge lawmakers in Illinois, Massachusetts, Iowa, and Maine to reform laws protecting the rights of the mentally ill and the rights of women. Packard's campaign helped lead to new laws in each of these states. In Illinois, an 1869 law provided married women with the right to control their own property. That same year, she forced her husband to return their children to her custody. By 1873, Elizabeth Packard's books—with such titles as *Marital Power Exemplified in Mrs. Packard's Trial; or, Three Years' Imprisonment for Religious Belief* (1866) and *The Prisoner's Hidden Life* (1868)—had sold more than 28,000 copies.

Paine, Thomas

(1737–1809)

RADICAL PAMPHLETEER OF THE
AMERICAN REVOLUTION

> These are the times that try men's souls. The summer soldier and the sunshine patriot will, in this crisis, shrink from the service of their country; but he that stands it *now*, deserves the love and thanks of men and women.
>
> —From Paine, *The Crisis*, (1776)

So Thomas Paine wrote at the dawn of the American Revolution. One of the originators of **radicalism** in both America and

Great Britain, Paine took part in both the American and French revolutions. The greatest writer of political pamphlets in the revolutionary period, Paine helped spark the independence movement with his *Common Sense*. In grasping and giving voice to the revolutionary spirit of the times, Paine sent a message that ordinary men and women had the power to topple or transform governments.

Born in Thetford, England, Thomas Paine grew up in a Quaker family. The practices of the Quakers, who allowed anyone to "preach" at their meetings, probably helped nurture in Thomas a suspicion of authority in both church and state. The reformist Quakers also fostered his later support of social change. Thomas attended grammar school for only seven years, from 1743 to 1750. At the age of thirteen, he served as an **apprentice** to his father, a corsetmaker. For the next twenty-four years, Paine worked at a variety of jobs—corsetmaker, teacher, tax collector—none of which lifted him out of poverty. His work collecting taxes on tobacco and liquor sales, however, raised his awareness of the difficulties of people in the lower class. In 1773, Paine organized a petition asking the government for higher salaries for employees of the tax service, and was quickly fired.

Paine left for America in 1774, hoping to make his fortune. Letters of recommendation from Benjamin Franklin led to Paine's being hired as an editor of *The Pennsylvania Magazine* in Philadelphia. Paine contributed poetry and articles under various pseudonyms. One article, which attacked the slave trade, was written under the name "Justice and Humanity." Paine soon became active in the movement to resist British rule in the colonies. Serving as a spokesperson for the movement, Paine called not just for tax revolt, but for full independence. He also joined Philadelphia craftspeople in calling for a political system that included everyone, not just the wealthy.

In 1776, Paine issued the first of his great pamphlets, *Common Sense*. The pamphlet attacked the rights of kings and queens to rule Great Britain and the colonies. He also criticized Britain's House of Lords as representing only the interests of the wealthy. Paine then urged the creation of a republican government: a type of government that features the elections of representatives to serve the interests of the people and a constitution that guards personal rights. *Common Sense* closed by arguing in favor of American independence. The book, which sold hundreds of thousands of copies, helped transform political debate in the colonies. *Common Sense* paved the way for the Declaration of Independence, signed later that year, and thus helped initiate the American Revolution.

During the Revolutionary War, Paine volunteered as an aide-de-camp (a military aide) to General Nathanael Greene. He continued to support the spirit of revolution, writing sixteen "Crisis" papers issued between 1776 and 1783. These pamphlets portrayed the colonists' struggle for independence as a battle between good and evil. General George Washington found *The American Crisis. Number I* so inspiring that he read it to his troops at Valley Forge, Pennsylvania on Christmas Eve, 1776. That year, Paine also helped draft the Pennsylvania Constitution. The document advocated equal rights in politics and society for all men.

From 1777 to 1779, he served as secretary of the Continental Congress' Committee for Foreign Affairs. As clerk of the Pennsylvania General Assembly in 1779, Paine observed a sinking of troop morale due to the lack of pay and the scarcity of supplies. Using $500 of his own, he started a fund for the relief of soldiers. In 1781, Paine continued his relief efforts. He traveled to France to secure donations of money, clothing, and ammunition for the relief of revolutionary soldiers. Throughout the American Revolution, Paine urged the separate states to work together toward the common good of the nation.

Despite selling hundreds of thousands of pamphlets, Paine remained in poverty when the Revolutionary War ended in 1783. He had refused to take a profit in order to make the inexpensive pamphlets accessible to as many readers as possible. In 1787, Paine returned to Europe, where he would remain for fifteen years. In 1789, he published an unsigned pamphlet warning the people of Great Britain against a war with France over the control of Holland. War, he insisted had "but one thing certain and that is increase of taxes." The following year he joined the growing English reform movement. Paine called for limits on the king's power over lawmakers in Parliament and for an extension of voting rights to the working class.

In 1791 and 1792, Paine published *The Rights of Man* in two parts. What started as a defense of the French Revolution turned into an attack on the British government's neglect of poverty, unemployment, and **illiteracy** (the inability to read or write) among the British working class. In *The Rights of Man*, Paine called for massive social and political reforms. He advocated government-created jobs and relief for the poor and unemployed. He urged the establishment of pension programs that would allow workers to retire at the age of sixty. He called on the state to provide education to all children—rich and poor. He also demanded tax reform so that the wealthy would pay a greater share of taxes than the poor. *The Rights of Man*, which sold two-hundred-thousand copies by the end of 1793, established a new direction for British radicalism. By bringing together the concerns of middle-class reformers and those of poor laborers, the book provided the foundation for the British working-class movement.

Paine escaped arrest for seeking to overthrow the government by leaving for France in 1792. A British court later found him guilty of treason, declared him an outlaw, and banned his book. As a member of the French National Convention, Paine opposed the execution of King Louis XVI, overthrown in the French Revolution. The stance alienated him from the ruling party, who jailed him for ten months. In 1794, the new American minister to France, James Monroe, claimed Paine as an American citizen. Released from prison, Paine remained in France for eight more years.

In 1794 and 1796, he published *The Age of Reason* in two parts. The pamphlet explored the place of religion in society. Its attacks on organized churches and Christian beliefs outraged most readers. Although Paine clearly stated his belief in God, he was labeled an infidel—someone who does not believe in God. Paine wrote one more important work: *Agrarian Justice*, published in 1797. The pamphlet called for massive land reform. It accused wealthy landowners of depriving the poor of their "natural right" to share in the land. Paine returned to the U.S. in 1802. Shunned as an infidel, Paine lived in poverty, drank heavily, and was forgotten as a hero of the American Revolution.

Papineau, Louis-Joseph

(1786–1871)

LAWYER, POLITICIAN, AND REBEL LEADER

Louis-Joseph Papineau was born in Montreal, Quebec. The son of a liberal member of the Assembly of Lower Canada (Quebec), Louis-Joseph Papineau was educated at the Quebec Seminary. In 1808, Papineau was also elected to the House of Assembly of Lower Canada. He became a lawyer in 1810 and practiced law on and off throughout his life. During the war of 1812, Papineau served as a militia officer, helping to defend British interests and defeat invaders from the United States. Returned to the Assembly after the war, Papineau was elected speaker of the Assembly from 1815 to 1822.

Most French Canadians at this time were poor, uneducated tenant farmers called *habitants*. The *habitants* worked the land of landowners called *seigneurs*. Although Papineau himself was a *seigneur*, he won the support of *habitants* in forming the French nationalist *Parti Patriote*. Papineau became a stalwart defender of the French-Canadian heritage of Lower Canada. He fought for preservation of the French language and cultural identity as well as French control of Lower Canada's governing bodies. In 1822, British-Canadian merchants seeking to end French rule of Lower Canada asked Britain to unite Upper Canada (Ontario) and Lower Canada. Papineau went to England the following year to lobby against this proposed Act of Union. He recognized that if Lower Canada joined with the English-dominated Upper Canada, the French Canadians would lose language rights and the little power they had to govern themselves. Papineau's victory in England increased his efforts to oppose British colonial rule of Lower Canada and to reform the government.

Reelected speaker of the Assembly in 1825 and 1826, Papineau urged the Assembly to refuse to pay government officials in order to block government programs favorable to British merchants. The merchants responded to this threat by bringing waves of English-speaking immigrants to Lower Canada in an attempt to sway the political balance away from the French. The British governor of the colony suspended the Assembly in 1827 rather than accept Papineau as Speaker. After Britain recalled the governor in 1828, however, Papineau once again became speaker, a post he would hold until 1837. Papineau became increasingly radical in his demands for government reforms. He called for "responsible government," which he defined as representatives elected through a democratic process. He attacked the ruling council appointed by the colonial governor. Ultimately, he advocated independence, challenging British authority over Lower Canada.

Under Papineau's direction, the Assembly passed Ninety-Two Resolutions, listing their grievances and their demands for responsible government in 1834. These demands included the election of members to the ruling council, which would make these officials more responsible to the people they were supposed to serve. The Assembly refused to collect taxes from Lower Canadians until their demands were met. This refusal would hold up government salaries as well as the building of roads and bridges. In 1837, the British Parliament rejected these calls for reform. It passed resolutions giving the Assembly less power and encouraging increased immigration of British to Lower Canada. The colonial governor immediately dismissed the Assembly.

An economic crisis hit Lower Canada that same year. Crops had failed during the previous year. A depression caused drops in prices and failed businesses. In a district gripped by poverty, starvation, and panic, Papineau lost control of the reform movement. Although he discouraged violence, the movement became revolutionary. The *Patriotes* declared the independence of French Canada and their commitment to defend their new freedom with arms. Although he was named supreme commander of forces, Papineau wanted no part in the violence.

He fled to the United States before the first major defeat of the rebels at Saint-Denis, north of Montreal.

After the defeat of the *Patriotes*, Papineau spent eight years in exile in the U.S. and France. In 1838, he was sentenced to death if he attempted to return to Lower Canada. In 1841, the Act of Union was passed by the British Parliament, creating the united Province of Canada. The Canadian government pardoned the rebels in 1844, and Papineau returned to Montreal the following year. He served in Canada's Legislative Assembly from 1848 to 1854 before retiring from politics. Although the rebellion he sparked had been defeated, Papineau had won the victory of "responsible government." Canada became self-governing in all areas but defense and foreign affairs.

Parks, Rosa

(1913–   )

CIVIL RIGHTS ACTIVIST

> We didn't have any civil rights. It was just a matter of survival . . . of existing from one day to the next. I remember going to sleep as a girl hearing the Klan ride at night and hearing a lynching and being afraid the house would burn down.
>
> —Parks, from a *Chicago Tribune*
> interview, recalling her childhood (1988)

On 1 December 1955, Rosa Louise McCauley Parks, an African-American seamstress, refused to give up her seat on a bus to a white man. Her arrest in Montgomery, Alabama touched off the modern **civil rights movement**: activism aimed at winning equal treatment of all Americans regardless of race or color. For more than a year, African Americans in Montgomery refused to ride the city buses. They protested Parks' arrest and the policy of **segregation** (separate and unequal treatment of people due to their race) that she had been charged with violating. The nonviolent protest became a model for future civil rights activists.

Rosa McCauley was born in Tuskegee, Alabama. At age two, Rosa, her younger brother, and her mother, a teacher, moved to her grandparents' farm in Pine Level, Alabama. In 1924, Rosa began attending the Montgomery Industrial School for Girls. The girls' school, founded by northern liberals, stressed the building of self-respect. The **lynching** and other acts of racism she experienced during her childhood would remain powerful memories throughout her life.

In 1932, Rosa McCauley married Raymond Parks, a barber who helped increase the number of African Americans registered to vote and worked on other civil rights causes. The couple settled in Montgomery, where Rosa took classes at Alabama State College. She also did volunteer work with the Youth Council of the National Association for the Advancement of Colored People (NAACP), among other civic groups.

Parks worked as a housekeeper, a seamstress, and briefly, a life insurance agent. Every day she rode the Montgomery buses to and from work. The Montgomery buses—like most restaurants, hotels, schools, public bathrooms, and other public areas in the South at this time—were segregated. The law did not allow African Americans to sit in the same area as white people. Whether or not the bus had any white passengers, the first ten rows of seats were reserved for whites only. African Americans had to pay for their tickets at the front of the bus, go back outside, and reenter the bus from a rear entrance before the bus pulled away from the curb. If the white seating section was full, African Americans had to give up their seats to allow whites to sit. The bus drivers, all white men, had the legal power to enforce these unfair seating practices. Using shouts and threats of violence, they would force African Americans to stand or sit in the back of the bus.

Rosa Parks had her first run-in with the city's segregation policy in 1943, the same year that the Montgomery branch of the NAACP elected her secretary. When she attempted to board a bus through the front door, the bus driver kicked her off the bus. In 1955, twelve years later, she had a more famous encounter with the very same bus driver. On that day, Parks and three other African Americans were sitting in the first row of their section of the bus. Because white passengers had filled their section, the driver told all four African Americans to stand so that one white man could sit. After hesitating for a moment, the other three stood up. Parks, however, tired from her day's work as a seamstress in a department store, refused to stand. The driver called two police officers onto the bus to arrest her. Rosa Parks was jailed and fined $14 for breaking the segregation law.

E.D. Nixon, the former president of the Alabama and Montgomery branches of the NAACP, asked Parks to appeal the case. Despite the objections of her mother and husband, who feared for her life, Parks agreed to challenge the segregation law. The Women's Political Council, an African-American women's group, organized a protest against Parks' arrest and trial. The group handed out thousands of leaflets calling for a one-day **boycott** (the refusal to ride city buses) on the day of her trial. African-American church leaders, led by Martin Luther King, Jr., supported the boycott. Although normally about 70 percent of city bus passengers were African Americans, very few rode the buses that day. That night, church leaders and the community formed the Montgomery Improvement Association (MIA), with King as its president. The group decided to continue the boycott until the bus company met their demands. At first, the MIA did not demand an end to segregation, only an end to the policy that forced African Americans to give up their seats. The group proposed that whites take seats starting from the front of the bus, and that African Americans take seats beginning at the back. The seats would fill up on a first-come, first-served basis, regardless of color. The MIA also demanded more courteous drivers, and the assignment of African-American drivers on bus routes where most passengers were African Americans.

The Montgomery bus boycott lasted for more than a year, hurting the bus companies financially. In 1956, city police began harassing drivers of carpools: pulling them over, delaying them, and sometimes issuing bogus tickets. Some African Americans who walked to work suffered from beatings or attacks from white passengers in passing cars, who threw bricks and rotten food at them. Parks, like many of the protesters, lost her job. She also received threatening calls that she took seriously after King's house was bombed. In February 1956, Parks's lawyer filed a federal suit challenging the legality of the segregation law. Later that year, the Supreme Court, the highest court of the land, declared that the segregation law violated the U.S. Constitution's guarantee of equal rights for all. In December, a Supreme Court order ended the practice of segregated seating on Montgomery buses. Heading the boycott made Martin Luther King, Jr., a national civil rights leader. And the boycott that Rosa Parks had sparked set the standard for all civil rights protests to come.

The following year, Parks moved to Detroit, Michigan with her husband and mother. A celebrity, Parks made many appearances over the next three decades to raise funds for the NAACP. She also joined King's Southern Christian Leadership Conference (SCLC), working to foster social change through nonviolent protests like the Birmingham boycott. But life in Detroit was not easy for Parks. In 1959, the couple lost their apartment after both she and her husband were hospitalized. By taking in sewing while her husband worked as a caretaker, Parks saved enough money to move into another apartment in 1961.

In 1965, John Conyers, Jr., a member of Congress from Michigan, hired Parks to run his office—a job she would hold for over twenty-five years. She continued to make about two dozen public appearances a year, speaking on the civil rights movement on behalf of the NAACP or SCLC. In 1987, she founded the Rosa and Raymond Parks Institute for Self-Development. The institute offers guidance and career and leadership training to young African Americans. *See* KING, MARTIN LUTHER, JR.

Pertschuk, Michael

(1933–   )

CONSUMER ADVOCATE

Michael Pertschuk, born in London, England, moved to the United States in 1938. Pertschuk earned an undergraduate degree in English and a law degree from Yale University. In 1962, he became legislative assistant to Maurine B. Neuberger, a Democratic senator from Oregon. Two years later, he was promoted to consumer counsel (lawyer) for the Senate Commerce Committee. In this position, Pertschuk was in charge of developing and winning support for laws to protect American consumers. In 1965, Pertschuk framed the landmark law that banned cigarette advertising on television and required all packs of cigarettes to feature labels warning of health risks. He also developed the 1966 law that set national safety standards for all cars and trucks in the United States.

From 1968 to 1977, Pertschuk served as chief counsel and staff director of the Commerce Committee. Under his direction, the committee outlawed the use of flammable fabrics in infants' sleepwear, developed no-fault insurance, and established safeguards against radiation hazards.

President Jimmy Carter appointed Pertschuk head of the Federal Trade Commission (FTC) in 1977. The FTC is responsible for exposing and preventing unfair business practices and protecting consumers. With Pertschuk as chair, the FTC prohibited manufacturers from setting minimum prices for their products and required manufacturers to replace defective products without court process. Pertschuk was especially critical of television advertising aimed at children under eight years old. Advertisers took advantage of young children, he insisted, encouraging them to pressure their parents to buy junk food and popular toys. Pertschuk's attempts to regulate advertising for children, however, were defeated by pressure brought by lobbyists who represented advertisers and cereal companies.

Pertschuk remained on the FTC, filling out his seven-year term, after the election of Ronald Reagan as president in 1980. Pertschuk's proposals to protect consumers were consistently voted down by the newly conservative FTC. The committee adopted only two major resolutions proposed by Pertschuk from 1981 to 1984. In 1982, it required funeral directors to provide customers with itemized price lists. A year later, the FTC called on drug manufacturers to prove their advertising claims.

After leaving the FTC in 1984, Pertschuk co-founded the Advocacy Institute. The institute runs public relations campaigns and trains lobbyists for consumer groups and other organizations created to further the public interest. Pertschuk's institute thereby helps public-interest groups exercise a greater influence among lawmakers.

Pesotta, Rose

(1896–1965)

LABOR ACTIVIST

Born Rose Peisoty in the Russian Ukraine, Rose Pesotta would become a prominent labor organizer after emigrating to the United States in 1913. Pesotta worked in a shirt-waist factory and joined the International Ladies' Garment Workers' Union (ILGWU) that year. In 1915, she helped establish the ILGWU's first program to educate workers. Her efforts on behalf of the union resulted in her election to the executive board of her local branch in 1920. After attending the Bryn Mawr School for Women Workers in 1922, Pesotta studied at the Brookwood Labor College from 1924 to 1926.

In 1933, Pesotta quit her factory job to join the ILGWU as a paid staff member. Her success in organizing dressmakers in Los Angeles led to her election as vice president of the ILGWU in 1934, the only woman on the union's governing board, until 1944. In her labor-organizing activities, Pesotta emphasized training workers to take care of themselves, rather than depending on the union to take care of them. She organized garment workers for the ILGWU in San Francisco, Seattle, and Boston, as well as in San Juan, Puerto Rico and Montreal, Canada. In the late 1930s, the ILGWU lent her services to help organize auto workers in Flint, Michigan, and rubber workers in Akron, Ohio. In 1944, Pesotta announced that she would not run for reelection as vice president of the union. In a speech before the ILGWU convention, she sharply criticized the union for having just one woman board member, while women accounted for 85 percent of the union's members. Pesotta's *Bread Upon the Waters*, published in 1944, tells the story of her life as a union organizer.

Pettit, Katherine

(1868–1936)

SOCIAL REFORMER

Katherine Rhoda Pettit began her activism in the early 1890s, when she joined the Women's Christian Temperance Union (WCTU). Traveling through the mountains of Kentucky, she preached **temperance**: giving up alcohol. Pettit also worked for the State Federation of Women's Clubs, providing library services to rural regions of Kentucky. Her experience made Pettit determined to make a difference in the lives of the poor, isolated people of the Kentucky mountains. In 1899, she volunteered to teach cooking, sewing, nutrition, health, and child rearing skills to the women of Hazard, Kentucky, a poor mountain town. A devout Presbyterian, Pettit also included daily Bible readings and temperance talks in her pioneering six-week project. In 1900, she undertook a similar ten-week project in Hindman, Kentucky. The following year, she spent fourteen weeks teaching outside Sassafras, Kentucky.

The success of her summer projects inspired Pettit to create a rural **settlement house**: a center, located in the heart of a poor area, that allows educators, social workers, and others to work directly toward improving the community's living and working conditions. With the help of the WCTU, Pettit founded the Hindman Settlement in 1902. Surviving two fires in the first eight years, the Hindman Settlement taught more than two-hundred students by 1911. The thirteen resident staff members taught not only reading, writing and arithmetic, but also such crafts as sewing, cooking, woodworking and basketry.

In 1913, Pettit left Hindman to open a second settlement, the Pine Mountain Settlement School in Harlan County, Kentucky. In addition to overseeing the building of the school, Pettit tried to obtain government support for the construction of a road through the mountains. She hoped to reduce the isolation of the people who lived in the mountains by opening up access to the railroad and outside markets. Pettit also established rural health clinics in the mountains. Pettit codirected the Pine Mountain Settlement School until her retirement in 1930. During the **Great Depression** of the 1930s, when jobs and money were scarce throughout the world, Pettit continued to work among the poor residents of Harlan County.

Riel, Louis

(1844–1885)

ACTIVIST FOR METIS RIGHTS AND FOUNDER OF
MANITOBA

> We must make Canada respect us.
> —Reil, (c. 1870) from Desmond Morton's
> *Rebellions in Canada*

So proclaimed Louis Riel, leader and spokesperson among the *Metis*: people of mixed French-Canadian and Native-American ancestry. Riel gave his life to safeguard the rights of the Metis hunters and trappers in the face of Canadian westward expansion. In leading the Red River Rebellion in 1870, Riel founded the Canadian province of Manitoba. The less successful North West Rebellion in 1885 led to little more than Riel's death by hanging.

Riel was born in St. Boniface in the Red River Settlement (now Manitoba). His father had led Metis fur traders in breaking up the Hudson's Bay Company's **monopoly** on the Canadian fur trade. His mother, who taught him the Catholic faith, was the daughter of the first European woman in the West. From 1858 to 1865, Louis studied for the priesthood in Montreal, but he quit school before becoming the first Metis priest. He returned to the Red River in 1868. At that time, the government of Canada was seeking to acquire "Rupert's Land"—the Red River and North-West territories from the Hudson's Bay Company (HBC), which had controlled the land for almost two centuries. The HBC had agreed to a price of 300,000 British pounds, a grant of one-twentieth of the land suitable for farming, and the ability to retain its extensive trading posts. In 1869, the Canadian government sent crews to survey the land along the Red River.

The Metis, who had lived on the land for centuries, felt threatened by the approach of the English-speaking newcomers from Ontario. Although they had no legal title, the Metis insisted they had a right to the lands being surveyed. Using

Metis hunting parties as a military model, they drove away the surveyors. The Metis then organized to halt Canada's purchase of the land until the nation agreed to honor their rights. The Metis buffalo hunters and fur trappers named Riel secretary of the "National Committee" to negotiate with Canada. The Metis rebels first prevented the newly appointed lieutenant-governor of the territory from entering Red River. Riel then led four-hundred armed Metis in seizing Fort Garry (later Winnipeg) from the HBC. This gave the Metis control over the largest store of food, clothing, and money in the region.

Riel hoped to serve not just his people, but to unite all the people of the colony, whites and Metis alike. He met with both French- and English-speaking delegates at Fort Garry to prepare a "List of Rights" to present to the Canadian Parliament. The rebels' demands included respect of Metis rights and customs and recognition of their ownership of lands, whether or not they had legal papers to prove it. They also sought an elected legislature and representation in the Canadian Parliament. The federal government postponed the transfer, but a group of Canadians took up arms to oppose Riel's forces. The Metis easily defeated the Canadians and imprisoned them at Fort Garry. Riel then issued a "Declaration of the People of Rupert's Land and the Northwest." The declaration established a provisional (temporary) government at Red River, with Riel as its head.

In early 1870, Riel called a convention of more than one thousand people from Red River at Fort Garry. In the region's first election, the people chose forty representatives: half French and half English. The delegates then debated a new "List of Rights." At Riel's urging, the new list included the demand that the land become a full province of Canada. The convention endorsed Riel's government and named three delegates to carry their Bill of Rights to Ottawa. The convention also decided to free all Canadian prisoners. The released Canadians immediately organized another resistance, led by surveyor Thomas Scott and veteran Major Charles Boulton. The Metis captured the Canadians and again imprisoned them. Riel wanted to kill Boulton, but agreed to spare him when warned it would anger English settlers and split the colony forever.

Scott, however, was quickly tried and executed by a firing squad. A bishop arrived with the news that Canada had agreed to most of the rebel's demands and persuaded the Metis once again to release their Canadian prisoners. The government agreed that the transfer of Manitoba from the HBC would include a land grant setting aside 1,400,000 acres for the Metis. The Manitoba Act, passed that year, included much of the Bill of Rights. It guaranteed the rights of both French- and English-speaking residents and set up schools and other services in both French and English.

Riel's role later led him to be called the Father of Manitoba. At the time, however, opinion was split. In Quebec, he was considered a hero for defending French culture and Roman Catholicism against the English Protestant government, while in Ontario he was condemned as Scott's murderer. Riel fled to the United States to escape a military force of two-thousand arriving from Ontario. Within a month, he had returned to the Red River. When a $5,000 reward was offered for his arrest in 1871, friends encouraged him to return to exile in the U.S., but Riel refused. In 1873, he was elected to the House of Commons from Manitoba. When he attempted to take his seat in the House in 1874, however, he was discovered and quickly expelled. Although re-elected, Riel did not attempt to claim his seat again. Instead he fled once more to the United States.

In 1875, the Canadian government pardoned Riel, on the condition that he remain in exile for five years. When he suffered a nervous breakdown, however, he spent the next three years under false names in Quebec mental hospitals. Released in 1878, Riel became a trader in the Montana territory. By 1883, he had become a U.S. citizen and worked as a poorly paid teacher in a Jesuit mission school in Montana. The following year, a group of Metis, homesteaders, and people of mixed English and Native-American blood came from the Saskatchewan Valley to ask Riel to help them present their grievances to the Canadian government.

Riel eagerly accepted, believing he had been chosen by God to save the Metis. He established a headquarters at Batoche, the center of the Metis settlement in Saskatchewan. With the help of the Catholic clergy, he founded the Union of St. Joseph as a national Metis society. His mission began peacefully. He sent a petition of grievances, including demands for land rights and for a railway to Hudson Bay. The petition also included a personal claim for monetary compensation—between $35,000 and $100,000—for Riel's role in making Manitoba a part of Canada. His apparent personal interest, the old charges against him, and his meeting with Native Americans who posed the threat of war eroded his support, especially among the English-speaking homesteaders.

Getting little response from Ottawa, Riel initiated the North West Rebellion. As he had done in the Red River, he seized control of the territory and formed a provisional government. But Saskatchewan was not nearly as isolated as the Red River had been. The railway to the West was nearly complete and the North West Mounted Police had been formed. After two months of battles, the rebels surrendered in the Battle of Batoche. Riel fled the final engagement, but surrendered a day later. He hoped that his trial would allow him to publicize Metis grievances. He rejected his lawyers' urging to plead insanity, insisting that to do so would cast doubt on his legitimate goals and achievements. A jury found Riel guilty of treason, but recommended mercy. Riel was nonetheless sentenced to execution. When attempted appeals failed and an inquiry into his sanity proved inconclusive, he was hanged. Riel's second rebellion had not achieved the same success as his first. Only whites found a voice in the new government of the Northwest. Metis and Native Americans were ignored.

Riis, Jacob

(1849–1914)

ADVOCATE FOR THE POOR,
JOURNALIST, AND
PHOTOGRAPHER

Real reform of poverty and ignorance must begin with the
children.

—Riis, from *The Children of the Poor* (1892)

Jacob August Riis became a crusader in New York's tenement districts. Riis had known the horrors of slum dwelling himself in his first years in America. Through his newpaper articles, books, and photographs, Riis made other Americans aware of these horrors, too. He used the power of the press to help improve living and working conditions for thousands of immigrants and their children in New York.

Riis grew up in Ribe, Denmark. Of fourteen children in the family, only three survived childhood. His father, a teacher, also wrote editorials for the town newspaper to help make ends meet. Jacob sometimes helped his father prepare copy, paving the way for his later career as a journalist. From 1858 to 1865, Jacob studied at the Ribe Latin School, where his father taught. But Jacob preferred reading and studying on his own to learning at school. From 1865 to 1868, he served as an **apprentice** to a builder in Copenhagen, Denmark's capital city. But when he received his certificate to become a carpenter, he found few jobs available in Ribe.

In 1870, Riis emigrated to America to find work. For seven years, Riis worked here and there as a farmer, ironworker, coal miner, and peddler. But the poor immigrant several times spent a night or two in jail when he found himself with no money and no home. In 1874, the New York News Association hired Riis as a reporter. Later that year, he got a job with *The South*

Brooklyn News, a political newspaper for the Democratic Party. Within a year, Riis had become editor and bought the newspaper. Riis turned the paper into an advocate of social reform. After returning briefly to Denmark to marry in 1875, Riis resettled in Brooklyn. In 1877, he resigned to work as the police reporter for *The New York Tribune*. Riis covered the police and fire departments and the Board of Health until 1888. In this position, he became familiar with the immigrant population who lived in New York's ghetto district. Riis wrote many stories about ghetto residents and their struggle for survival.

As a reporter, Riis also established contact with many charitable groups and reformers. Riis made their causes his own, using his articles to promote reform. After becoming a member of the New York chapter of the Charity Organization Society, he wrote often about its programs. He provided free publicity for its day-care centers, job-training programs, and shelters for the homeless. In 1884, he focused his calls for reform on the improvement of tenement housing. Riis believed that enhancing the environment in which poor immigrants lived would dramatically improve their lives. He began attacking the greed of landlords and the corruption of city officials who allowed landlords to abuse their tenants. That year, he wrote a series of articles on city corruption exposed by an investigation, led by Theodore Roosevelt, of the city's Department of Public Works. These hearings marked the beginning of a long association between Riis and the reform-minded future president.

In 1888, three years after becoming a U.S. citizen, Riis went on a nationwide tour to lecture on life in New York's slums. One of the first photographers to use flash powder to provide light for indoor photography, Riis highlighted his lectures with photographs of dark, dirty tenements. The photographs magnified the power of his words to convey the horrors of slum housing. The following year, Riis began writing articles contrasting the "two Americas": rich and poor. He called for an end to child labor, the improvement of public schools, reformed health laws, and government support of private charities.

In 1890, at Riis's urging, the King's Daughters of New Jersey, a women's club, founded a permanent **settlement house** in

New York's Lower East Side ghetto. The house, later named the Jacob A. Riis Settlement, provided food, nursing, and educational and cultural services to ghetto residents. To advance his plan for improving city neighborhoods, Riis also began promoting the construction of playgrounds at every public school. That year, Riis published *How the Other Half Lives: Studies Among the Tenements of New York*. The book, with illustrations based on his photographs, offered a vivid description of the horrors of tenement life. Shocking the conscience of many Americans, it prompted the passage of laws that attempted to remedy the evils of slum life. From 1890 to 1894, Riis used his writings—as well as speaking tours throughout New England and the Midwest—to promote reform in the slums.

In 1893, Riis served on a city agency investigating new ways to provide shelter for the homeless. Recalling his own experience in jails twenty years earlier, Riis passionately opposed police "lodging houses" for the homeless, which put poor people together with criminals. Riis had published his second book in 1892: *Children of the Poor*. The book detailed the horrors faced by children in city slums. Improving the lives of ghetto children would become the focus of his reform efforts for many years. Over the next few years, Riis advocated the creation of public kindergartens, city parks and playgrounds, programs for truant children, and job training programs.

In 1895, Riis again tackled the problem of corruption by working with the New York Council of Good Government. He also renewed his association with Theodore Roosevelt, then the head of the Board of Police Commissioners. Riis encouraged Roosevelt to close all of the city's police-lodging houses and to condemn over one hundred tenement **sweatshops**. Riis later served as the state's labor adviser on urban affairs when Roosevelt became New York's governor in 1899.

Riis wrote eight more books between 1898 and 1910. The most important, *The Making of an American*, his autobiography, published in 1901, showed that poor immigrants could contribute to the reforming of America. At the same time, however, he urged the government to help immigrants by rebuilding cities and increasing opportunities for the poor.

During the final ten years of his life, Riis concentrated on settlement work and improving children's lives. He became president of the Jacob A. Riis Settlement House, and volunteered at three other New York settlements. He also championed physical fitness and creative play. Riis helped establish several boys' clubs, and the Boy Scouts of America.

Roosevelt, Eleanor

(1884–1962)

SOCIAL REFORMER, FEMINIST, CIVIL RIGHTS ACTIVIST, AND FORMER FIRST LADY

> Too often the great decisions are originated and given form in bodies made up wholly of men, or so completely dominated by them that whatever of special value women have to offer is shunted aside without expression.

—Roosevelt, last speech to the United Nations, 1952, in Joseph P. Lash, *Eleanor: The Years Alone* (1972)

Anna Eleanor Roosevelt was not content to leave the major decisions of her time exclusively in men's hands. A reformer, she worked in **settlement houses**, the labor movement, and supported the **civil rights movement**. A **feminist**, she acted as the equal of men in the political arena and helped increase the involvement of women in politics. A politician, she reformed the role of First Lady, serving as an advocate for the poor and the powerless. A diplomat, she promoted the causes of peace and the protection of human rights throughout the world.

The niece of future President Theodore Roosevelt was born in New York. A serious child, Eleanor regarded her mother as kind but indifferent toward her. However, she adored her father, an alcoholic who often betrayed her trust. Her parents separated in 1891. A year later, her mother died. Eleanor, eight years old, and her two brothers moved into her grandmother's home in New York. In 1893, one of her brothers died and the following year, her father died. Until she was fifteen, Eleanor was schooled primarily by home tutors. From 1899 to 1902, she attended a girls' boarding school outside of London, England. There, she found some happiness in her relationship with the radical head of the school, who nurtured in Eleanor a spirit of reform.

Upon returning to New York, Roosevelt joined many social-reform groups. At age eighteen, she joined the National Consumers League, a group dedicated to improving the health and safety of workers, especially women. Through visits to **sweatshops** and factories, she became familiar with the plight of the poor. She also worked in a New York settlement house, where she taught dancing and exercise. In 1905, she married a distant cousin, Franklin Roosevelt, then a Columbia University law student. From 1906 to 1916, Roosevelt had six children, one of whom died in infancy. Beginning in 1910, Roosevelt supported her husband's political career: first as a member of the New York State Assembly in 1911, then as assistant secretary of the navy in 1913. The U.S. entry into World War I in 1917 allowed her to resume her work for reform. She worked for the Red Cross, visited wounded soldiers in hospitals, and rallied patriotism in public speeches. She also campaigned for the reform of a Washington hospital for the criminally insane.

In 1920 and 1921, Roosevelt served on the board of the New York branch of the League of Women Voters. She helped draft laws to promote equal rights and lobbied state lawmakers. She also joined the Women's Trade Union League, a radical labor organization led by Rose Schneiderman and Maud Swartz. She raised funds, joined picket lines, and worked for laws setting maximum hours and minimum wages. An organizer for the Democratic Party, Roosevelt attended the party's national convention in 1924. There, she led a group of women who called for laws guaranteeing equal pay for equal work as well as a Constitutional amendment to outlaw child labor.

In the mid-1920s, Roosevelt co-founded Val-Kill Furniture Shop in Hyde Park, New York. The nonprofit furniture factory and store provided winter jobs for many young farm workers. From 1927 to 1933 she also taught at a private girls' school that she partially owned in New York. She found a way to merge her concern for social welfare and her political organizing in 1928 and 1932, when she headed the Democratic Party's national women's campaign.

When Franklin Roosevelt became President in 1933, Eleanor Roosevelt helped women achieve a new level of influence in government. As advocate for the poor and the oppressed, she became the most influential woman of her era while encouraging her husband to appoint women and reformers as government officials. Roosevelt used her regular press conferences—the first ever by a First Lady—to promote her reform activities. Her policy of admitting only female reporters also helped increase women's status in the news business. An advocate for children, she supported federal funding for nursery schools, playgrounds, and child-welfare programs. She supported southern textile workers and northern garment workers in their labor struggles. She also encouraged African Americans seeking equal civil rights and championed a law, rejected by her husband, that would have made lynching a federal crime.

Roosevelt scored a major victory for women's rights at the Democratic National Convention in 1936. Due largely to her efforts with the party's women's division, women and men were for the first time equally represented on the convention's platform committee. (The platform committee determines a party's position on political issues.)

In 1936, she began writing a column called "My Day," which appeared in hundreds of newspapers across the country. The following year, she published her first autobiography, *This Is My Story*.

Roosevelt's activism in the civil rights movement increased in the late 1930s and 1940s. In 1939, she spoke before the annual meeting of the National Association for the Advancement of Colored People (NAACP), the country's leading civil rights organization. Several weeks later, she joined the NAACP. That year, Roosevelt also protested **segregation** at the first meeting of the Southern Conference on Human Welfare. She pointedly placed her chair halfway between the white and

African-American seating sections. During World War II (1941–45), she pointed out the irony of fighting Hitler's racism in Europe while tolerating racism at home. She advocated an end to racial **discrimination** in the armed services and defense industries.

During the war, Roosevelt also urged equal employment opportunities for women. As the financing of the war effort caused cutbacks in many social-welfare programs, Roosevelt fought to maintain programs serving children and African Americans. She also served as an advocate for Jews seeking refuge from Nazi persecution.

Her husband's death in 1945 ended Roosevelt's twelve years as First Lady—the longest period any woman has lived in the White House. Yet she remained the most powerful woman in American politics for another seventeen years. Later that year, President Truman named Roosevelt as a delegate to the newly formed United Nations (U.N.). From 1946 to 1951, Roosevelt served as chair of the U.N. Commission on Human Rights. She was the guiding force behind the Universal Declaration of Human Rights, adopted unanimously (with the exception of eight members who declined to vote) in 1948. The unprecedented document emphasized such traditional personal freedoms as speech, religion, and thought, and the rights of those accused of crime. But it also pledged to honor the right to education, the right to work, the right to social security, the right to rest and leisure, and the right to share in the society's culture and scientific advancements.

In 1948, Roosevelt helped found the Americans for Democratic Action, a group dedicated to promoting social reforms at home and an anti-Communist foreign policy. Although the group did not admit Communists as members, Roosevelt opposed the anti-Communist hysteria whipped up by Senator Joseph McCarthy from 1950 to 1954. In 1961, President John Kennedy appointed Roosevelt as chair of his Commission on the Status of Women. The following year, she testified before Congress on behalf of laws guaranteeing equal pay for equal work—laws she had first advocated thirty-eight years earlier.
See SCHNEIDERMAN, ROSE; SWARTZ, MAUD

Said, Edward

(1935–   )

POLITICAL ACTIVIST FOR A PALESTINIAN STATE,
EDUCATOR, AND LITERARY CRITIC

Edward W. Said was born in the city of Jerusalem, a part of
Palestine at the time of his birth. In 1947, however, Great Britain turned control of Palestine over to the United Nations
(U.N.). The U.N. divided Palestine into an Arab state and a
Jewish state. Arabs from the entire region objected to the division of Palestine Forces from Transjordan Clater Jordan,
Egypt, Syria, Lebanon, and Iraq and attacked the new State
of Israel. The Said family had moved to Cairo, Egypt, five
months before the war. Israel won the war; Jordan took control
of the Arab portion of Palestine. No state remained that was
called Palestine.

Sent by his parents to Mount Hermon prep school in Massachusetts in 1951, Said later earned an undergraduate degree
from Princeton University in 1957 and a graduate degree from
Harvard University in 1960. While working as an instructor of
English at Columbia University, Said earned his doctorate in
English literature from Harvard in 1964. By 1970, he had become a full professor at Columbia.

In 1977, Said became a member of the Palestine National
Council—the self-appointed governing body of those Palestinian Arabs fighting for a separate Palestinian State. Since then,
he has written several books critical of American hostility toward Palestine and the Arab world. *Orientalism*, published in
1978, condemns the biases and hatred revealed in American
and European views of Arabs and the Islamic world. In *The
Question of Palestine*, published in 1979, Said advocates the
creation of a self-governing Palestinian nation along the Gaza
Strip and West Bank—areas occupied by Israel since 1967. He
also challenged the viewpoint that connected most terrorist
acts with Arabs, and especially Palestinians. He defended
Arab acts of terrorism as striking back at what they viewed as

the terrorism of the Israeli occupiers of the Palestinian homeland. Said's 1981 book, *Covering Islam: How the Media and the Experts Determine How We See the Rest of the World*, charged reporters with trying to simplify the extremely complex society. In 1988, Said coedited and contributed to *Blaming the Victims: Spurious Scholarship and the Palestinian Question*, a collection of essays on Palestinian history.

At a meeting of the Palestinian National Council in Algiers in 1988, Said helped write a resolution asserting the establishment of a Palestinian state consisting of the Gaza Strip and the West Bank. At the same meeting, the Palestinian Liberation Organization (PLO), a group linked to many terrorist acts, announced its intention to give up terrorism. For the first time, the PLO also publicly recognized the right of Israel to exist. As a result of these shifts, the United States agreed to open talks with the PLO regarding the future of a Palestinian state.

Sanger, Margaret

(1879–1966)

FEMINIST, BIRTH-CONTROL ACTIVIST

> I resolved that women should have knowledge of contraception [methods of birth control]. They have every right to know about their own bodies. . . . I would scream from the house tops. I would tell the world what was going on in the lives of these poor women. . . . *I would be heard.*
>
> —Sanger (1931)

Margaret Louise Higgins Sanger pioneered the birth-control movement in the United States. A **feminist**, Sanger was committed to the cause of enabling women to control their own bodies. She opened the first birth-control clinic in the United States. Sanger also founded and served as president of both the American Birth Control League and the Birth Control Clinical Research Bureau. These two organizations would later merge to form the Planned Parenthood Federation of America.

The sixth of eleven children, Margaret Higgins grew up in poverty in Corning, New York. Her father, owner of a monument shop, supported a variety of reform causes: women's voting rights, tax reform, and **socialism**. He encouraged his children to join in discussing these issues as his equals. Although her father did not believe in God, her mother was a devout Irish Catholic. Margaret blamed her family's poverty on the teachings of the Catholic church. She was angry that the church encouraged couples to have as many children as possible, whether or not they could support them.

After graduating from Claverack College, a private prep school in Hudson, New York, Higgins for a short time taught first grade among immigrants in Little Falls, New Jersey. In 1896, she returned to Corning to care for her mother, who died of **tuberculosis**. Higgins blamed her mother's illness and death on her exhaustion at having to bear and rear eleven children. Although she objected to her father's demand that she take his wife's place, Higgins ran the household for the next three years.

In 1899, she began attending nursing school at a hospital in White Plains, New York. After completing two years of training as a practical nurse, however, she quit to marry William Sanger, a socialist, architect, and artist. Margaret Sanger gave birth to three children betwen 1903 and 1910. But she was not content with her life as a housewife and mother in Hastings-on-Hudson, New York. In 1912, the family moved to Manhattan, where Sanger joined the Socialist Party and organized women workers for the radical labor group, the International Workers of the World (IWW). Sanger helped organize the withdrawal of strikers' children from Lawrence, Massachusetts, where the IWW was leading textile workers in a strike. The dramatic action brought national attention and sympathy to the strikers, ultimately helping them win their strike. Through her organizing activities, Sanger met Emma Goldman and other labor leaders. Goldman helped Sanger develop the idea that in order to free themselves from male control, women had to seize control over childbearing. The right of women to control their own bodies, they insisted, must take priority over the struggle for higher wages and other labor reforms.

In 1912, Sanger also worked as a visiting nurse in a New York slum. The high rate of venereal (sexually transmitted) diseases and poor women's ignorance about childbirth and **abortion** shocked Sanger. One young woman living in the ghetto told Sanger that her doctor had warned her not to have any more children. However, when the woman asked for information on birth control, the doctor brusquely suggested that her husband sleep elsewhere. After getting pregnant again, the woman tried to give herself an abortion and died. Sanger was infuriated that women were being denied information they needed to know. Witnessing the horrors suffered by this poor woman, Sanger became committed to teaching women about sex education, venereal disease, and **contraception**. That year, she wrote "What Every Girl Should Know," a series of articles on female sexuality for *The Call*, a socialist newspaper. When she wrote about a venereal disease, the government—acting on an 1873 law that defined birth control, abortion, and other subjects related to sex as "obscene"—banned the issue containing her article.

In 1913, she traveled to Paris, France, to learn more about contraceptive methods. Returning to the U.S the following year, she began editing and publishing *Woman Rebel*, a radical feminist journal. She urged lawmakers to make "birth control"—a term that she invented—legal. Not only would birth control free women from forced pregnancies, it would relieve the suffering of many poor women. That year, Sanger wrote *Family Limitation*. This pamphlet insisted that women had a right to sexual fulfillment and called for an end to all laws opposed to birth control. It also included information on how to use a variety of contraceptive methods. In 1914, Sanger fled the country to escape charges of sending obscene materials through the mail. But even in exile, she continued to promote sex education at home. She sent instructions to send thousands of secretly stored copies of her pamphlet to labor leaders across the nation.

When, in 1915, her husband was arrested and jailed for thirty days for handing out *Family Limitation*, Sanger returned to the U.S. The following year, the government dropped the charges against her. Later in 1916, Sanger and one of her sisters opened the nation's first birth control clinic in Brooklyn. In just ten days, they provided information on birth control to nearly five-hundred women before a vice squad raid closed the clinic. Her sister, sentenced to thirty days, went on a hunger strike and almost died in jail. Sanger won a pardon for her sister from the governor. Also in 1916, Sanger established the New York Birth Control League to work for the reform of state laws and to encourage the creation of birth-control clinics. She also founded *The Birth Control Review*, which she edited and published for the next twelve years.

Like her sister, Sanger was sentenced to thirty days in jail during a 1917 trial. She challenged the law in an appeal to a higher court, arguing that the law forced women to risk death in pregnancy. The Court of Appeals upheld her conviction and sentence, but Sanger also achieved an important victory. The judge ruled that doctors had the right to provide married patients with birth-control information in order to cure or prevent venereal disease.

Sanger's 1920 book, *Woman and the New Race*, took the birth-control movement in an ugly direction. She argued that the knowledge and use of contraceptive techniques could help insure the survival of the white race, a very racist idea. The following year, Sanger founded and served as the first president of the American Birth Control League, which promoted the reform of national birth-control laws. Two years later, with funds provided by her new husband, a wealthy oil executive, Sanger opened the Birth Control Clinical Research Bureau in New York. The nation's first birth-control clinic with a staff of medical doctors offered women access to reliable advice about contraceptives. The research bureau also kept records, allowing it to compare the effectiveness and safety of various contraceptive methods. The clinic also offered doctors an education in contraceptive techniques that medical schools were not yet providing. The success of the Clinical Research Bureau served as a model for the three-hundred more birth-control clinics that Sanger would open during the next fifteen years.

In 1926, Sanger organized the first World Population Conference, held in Geneva, Switzerland. The conference addressed the problem of overpopulation, which was just then recognized as a threat to the future of the world. In a dispute with its board of directors, Sanger resigned from both the presidency of the American Birth Control League and her position as editor of *The Birth Control Review* in 1928. The next year, following a police raid of the Clinical Research Bureau, the court ruled that the bureau's work prevented disease and promoted the health of mothers and infants. A 1936 court ruling allowed contraceptive materials to be imported into the United States in order to save lives and promote patients' well-being. This ruling marked the greatest victory of Sanger's birth-control movement: birth control was no longer regarded as obscene. The following year, the American Medical Association accepted birth control as a medical service and recommended teaching contraceptive methods in medical schools.

In 1938, the American Birth Control League and the Birth Control Clinical Research Bureau merged. Sanger was named honorary chair of the new Birth Control Federation of America. As the birth-control movement began to shift its emphasis to the concept of family planning, this organization became the Planned Parenthood Federation of America in 1942. Ten years later, in Bombay, India, Sanger helped found the International Planned Parenthood Federation, serving as the organization's president for the next six years. Also in 1952, Sanger helped obtain funds for research to develop the birth-control pill, which first appeared on the market in 1960. *See* GOLDMAN, EMMA

Schlafly, Phyllis

(1924–   )

CONSERVATIVE SOCIAL ACTIVIST

Educated in Catholic schools in St. Louis, Missouri, Phyllis Stewart tested ammunition in a weapons factory while attending Washington University in St. Louis during World War II. After graduating in 1944, she earned a graduate degree in political science from Radcliffe College in 1945. Stewart spent a year in Washington, D.C., working as a congressional researcher. She then returned home to St. Louis, where she worked as a librarian and researcher for a local bank.

In 1949, Stewart married John Schlafly, Jr., a lawyer and fellow conservative. Phyllis Stewart Schlafly served as a community volunteer, working with the YWCA and directing the local chapter of the National Conference of Christians and Jews. During the early 1950s, she conducted research for Senator Joseph McCarthy, who would gain notoriety for hounding suspected communists in the government, army, and entertainment industries. After an unsuccessful run for Congress in 1952, Schlafly published a pamphlet, *Reading List for Americans*, which recommended conservative books. After a second unsuccessful campaign for Congress in 1960, Schlafly served for four years as president of the Illinois Federation of Republican Women.

In 1962, she began to air her views on a weekly radio program sponsored by "American Wake Up," an organization that her husband had helped found. She also began devoting herself to full-time writing in support of conservative causes. Elected vice president of the National Federation of Republican

Women in 1964, she self-published *A Choice Not an Echo*, which supported the presidential candidacy of Republican Barry Goldwater. Schlafly sold an astounding three million copies of the book. *The Gravediggers*, which she cowrote in 1964, attacked the defense policies of Presidents John Kennedy and Lyndon Johnson. *Strike from Space*, cowritten by Schlafly in 1965, warned against nuclear disarmament and predicted a surprise nuclear attack by the Soviet Union. *Safe—Not Sorry*, published in 1967, accused communists of inciting that year's riots in urban ghettos. In the late 1960s, Schlafly founded The Eagles Are Flying, a group of conservative women drawn from the National Federation of Republican Women. She began publishing the *Phyllis Schlafly Report*, a monthly newsletter intended to inform and direct members of the Eagles. She also established the Eagles Trust Fund to help finance conservative candidates for public office. In 1970, she ran a third time, again without success, for Congress.

When Congress passed the Equal Rights Amendment (ERA) in 1972, Phyllis Schlafly found the cause that would make her famous. The ERA would have prohibited **discrimination** (unequal treatment) based on a person's sex. Schlafly vigorously opposed the measure. She traveled the country speaking out against the ERA and organizing local chapters of Stop ERA and the Eagle Forum, groups she had founded. Schlafly believed that the ERA not only threatened American family life, but would harm women as well. She rallied opposition to the amendment by raising such issues as women in combat, the drafting of mothers for military service, and unisex public toilets. Supporters of the ERA insisted that mothers—like fathers—could be declared exempt from the draft and that only women fit for combat would be sent into battle. Yet due to Schlafly's efforts, by 1977 only thirty-five states had approved the amendment—falling three short of the number needed to make the amendment law. *The Power of the Positive Woman*, published in 1977, summarized Schlafly's opposition to the women's liberation movement. Schlafly and her Eagle Forum gained greater political influence in the 1980s. Led by Ronald Reagan, who won election to the Presidency in 1980, the Republican Party embraced the conservative values that Schlafly and the Forum had advocated for more than a decade. The Reagan Administration (and later the administration of George Bush) echoed Schlafly's support for prayer in school and her opposition to abortion, homosexual rights, homosexualty itself, and what she viewed as the destruction of the family by feminism. When, during the late 1980s, the deadly disease AIDS (Acquired Immune Deficiency Syndrome)—which can be transmitted through sexual activity—became widespread, Schlafly led the opposition to sex education in public schools. Although her son publicly revealed his homosexuality in 1992, Schlafly continued to support the Republican party's condemnation of gay civil rights.

Schneiderman, Rose

(1882–1972)

LABOR AND WOMEN'S RIGHTS ACTIVIST

Born Rachel Schneiderman in Russian Poland, Rose Schneiderman emigrated to the United States with her family in 1890. At age thirteen, Rose began working in a department store, earning just over two dollars for her sixty-four-hour work week. After becoming a capmaker in 1898, Schneiderman cofounded and served as secretary of the first female local of the United Cloth Hat and Cap Makers' Union in 1903. The rapid growth of the local led to Schneiderman's election to the union's executive board in 1904. At that time, this was the highest position in the American labor movement held by a woman. After organizing a successful thirteen-week strike in 1905, she joined the Women's Trade Union League (WTUL). The WTUL helped to create unions for women workers, to promote laws protecting women workers, and to educate women workers. After serving as vice president of the New York branch of the WTUL, Schneiderman quit her factory job in 1907 to become a full-time WTUL organizer. Schneiderman helped organize strikes of waist-makers and women garment workers, which led to the creation of the International Ladies' Garment Workers' Union (ILGWU). She also delivered an inspiring memorial speech for 146 workers at the Triangle Waist Company in 1911. The workers, locked into the factory, had died in a tragic fire.

Schneiderman also used her organizing work as a platform for the cause of women's **suffrage**. Although she opposed the Equal Rights Amendment, which she feared would erode laws protecting women workers, she supported a women's suffrage amendment. In addition to serving on WTUL's suffrage committee, she helped the National American Woman Suffrage Association campaign for the vote in Ohio in 1913. From 1915 to 1916, Schneiderman served as national organizer for the ILGWU. One of only a few women representing the union, which was almost entirely made up of women workers, Schneider grew to resent male domination of women's unions.

In 1918, she was elected president of the New York branch of the WTUL—a post she would hold until 1949. As a delegate to the New York State Federation of Labor convention, she helped build support for a bill limiting the workday of women to eight hours. Elected vice president of the national WTUL in 1919, she attended the Paris Peace Conference, where she helped organize the International Congress of Working Women. To improve the education of women workers, Schneiderman helped organize the Bryn Mawr Summer School for Women Workers in 1921.

From 1926 to 1950, Schneiderman served as president of both the National Women's Trade Union League and its New York branch. Under her direction, the WTUL shifted its emphasis to the education of women workers and the promotion of laws that would protect women workers. Her friendship with Eleanor Roosevelt in the 1920s has been credited with helping to shape the labor policies of President Franklin Roosevelt. Roosevelt appointed Schneiderman to the Labor Advisory Board of the National Recovery Administration in 1933. During the Depression, the WTUL sponsored a minimum-wage bill for minors. Schneiderman helped win support for New York State laws on minimum wage and an eight-hour workday. From 1937 to 1943, Schneiderman also served as secretary of the New York State Department of Labor. Although she retired as president of the New York WTUL in 1949, she remained active in the league until it disbanded in 1955. *See* ROOSEVELT, ELEANOR

Schoff, Hannah Kent

(1853–1940)

CHILD-WELFARE ADVOCATE

In 1897 Hannah Kent Schoff, the mother of seven children, represented the New Century Club, a Philadelphia women's group, at the first National Congress of Mothers in Washington, D.C. Within a year, she had become vice president of the Mothers' Congress, an organization committed to education and child welfare. In 1899, Schoff founded and served as president of the organization's second state branch in Pennsylvania.

That same year, Schoff came to the aid of an eight-year-old girl imprisoned for arson in Philadelphia. While working toward the girl's release from prison and placement in a foster home, Schoff discovered that more than five-hundred children were imprisoned with adult criminals in Pennsylvania. Recognizing a system badly in need of reform, Schoff wrote a bill to change the state's methods of dealing with juvenile lawbreakers. The bill, made law in 1901, created a separate juvenile court system—only the second in the nation. The law also established separate detention homes and a probation system for juveniles. For the next twenty-two years, Schoff served as president of the Philadelphia Juvenile Court and Probation Association. Her growing expertise led other states—Idaho, Louisiana, Connecticut—as well as Canada to seek her help in establishing juvenile court systems.

In 1902, Schoff became president of the National Congress of Mothers. Under her direction, the congress grew to more than 190,000 members in thirty-seven state branches. The Mothers' congress supported child-labor and child-welfare laws and federal funding for kindergarten and elementary schools. In 1905, Schoff also established the congress's Committee on Juvenile Court and Probation Work. In addition to serving as its president, Schoff edited *The Child Welfare*, the organization's magazine, from 1906 to 1920. The National Congress of Mothers devoted much of its energies to creating an alliance between parents and school teachers. This emphasis was reflected in 1908, when the group changed its name to the National Congress of Mothers and Parent-Teacher Associations. (In 1924, the group changed its name again, becoming the National Congress of Parents and Teachers.)

In 1908, Schoff organized the first International Conference on Child Welfare in Washington, D.C. The next year, the U.S. Bureau of Education named Schoff to head the American Committee on the Causes of Crime in Normal Children. The committee explored the origins of criminal behavior among children. Schoff also served as a consultant to the bureau's Home Education Division from 1913 to 1919. *The Wayward Child*, published in 1915, urged continued reforms of the nation's juvenile legal systems.

Schroeder, Pat

(1940 –   )

U.S. REPRESENTATIVE AND WOMEN'S RIGHTS ACTIVIST

Patricia Scott Schroeder received an undergraduate degree from the University of Minnesota in 1961 and a law degree from Harvard University in 1964. For the next two years, she worked as an attorney for the National Labor Relations Board, covering the area of Colorado, Wyoming, and Utah. Establishing a private practice in Denver in 1969, she also taught law at the University of Denver, the Community College of Denver, and Regis College. In 1971, she served as legal counsel for the Colorado chapter of Planned Parenthood.

With her husband as campaign manager, Schroeder ran for

the House of Representatives in 1972. In running for the House, Schroeder argued that education, child care, health services, and protection of the natural environment should be among the nation's highest priorities. She also spoke out against the Vietnam War. Although given little chance of defeating her popular Republican opponent, Schroeder won the election. Schroeder, one of the few female members of Congress, became the first woman elected as Representative in Colorado. In her first term in Congress, Schroeder won a seat on the House Armed Services Committee. Contending that the defense of women and children means more than building military bases, Schroeder immediately called for huge cuts in the military budget. She fought to eliminate wasteful and unnecessary military spending and to put the money saved toward social welfare programs.

In her first term, Schroeder sponsored a child-abuse bill that provided federal aid for treatment centers and educational programs. She cosponsored a bill to expand Head Start, an early-education program for poor and minority children. In 1975, Schroeder helped develop an alternative defense budget to replace the one submitted by the Pentagon. The alternative budget cut hundreds of millions of dollars from the Pentagon requests. She also opposed the creation of expensive new weapons systems that she regarded as unnecessary. A supporter of a woman's right to choose to have an abortion, Schroeder chaired a National Task Force on Equal Rights for Women in 1975. She later cosponsored a bill requiring all congressional committee and agency meetings to be open to the press and public.

Schroeder's first term set the tone for her more than twenty years as a member of Congress. She has continued to focus on eliminating nuclear weaponry and wasteful military spending in order to increase funding for programs that benefit women and children. In 1987, she briefly explored the possibility of running for the Democratic nomination for Presidency, but instead opted to remain in Congress.

In the late 1980s, Schroeder became one of the most influential advocates of "defense burden sharing": cutting the U.S. military budget by insisting that other nations pay more to finance their own defense. Following the U.S. invasion of Panama in 1989, Schroeder introduced a bill to allow women to participate in all military activities, including combat. Although the bill was defeated, she introduced a less ambitious—but equally unsuccessful—bill, which would have allowed women to fly warplanes, after the Persian Gulf War in 1991. In addition to sponsoring laws promoting education, Schroeder has introduced many other laws supporting American families. In 1990, she wrote the Family and Medical Leave Act, which requires employers to provide temporary leave to workers in case of childbirth or family illness. That same year, she introduced the Women's Health Equity Act intended to promote medical research of women's health issues and greater gender equality in receiving medical services. In 1992, she sponsored a law to end the ban on homosexuals in the military services. With more than two decades in the House of Representatives, Schroeder has served as a member of Congress longer than any other woman today.

Seeger, Pete

(1 9 1 9 –   )

ENVIRONMENTALIST, FOLKSINGER, AND SONGWRITER

Seeger performing at an opening of a labor canteen (1944).

Pete Seeger was first exposed to folk music at a festival in Asheville, North Carolina in 1935. He studied **sociology** for two years at Harvard University, but left college to ride freight trains and hitchhike across the country in 1938. He supported himself by painting rural landscapes and singing folk songs. During the last years of the **Great Depression**, Seeger performed on street corners, in churches, saloons, camps for migrant workers, and trainyards where hoboes lived. In 1939, he worked as an assistant in the Archive of American Folk Song in Washington, D.C., and took advantange of the opportunity to listen to the archive's vast collection of folk recordings.

In 1940, Seeger and renowned folk singer Woody Guthrie toured union halls and farm meetings together, singing work songs and union songs as members of the Almanac Singers. Drafted into the Army in 1942, Seeger entertained the troops with the Army's Special Services Unit. After his discharge in 1945, Seeger co-founded and directed People's Songs, a songwriters' union and research center on folk songs. From 1949 to 1952, Seeger toured with a folk group called the Weavers.

Seeger's liberal and labor activism created controversy in the 1950s. Seeger was committed to the organized labor movement, which he saw as closely tied to the folk-music revival. But in the anticommunist hysteria of the 1950s, Seeger—and the Weavers—found themselves **blacklisted** by the entertainment industry. Television networks would not let them appear on the air and concert bookings became difficult. In 1955, he was called before the House Un-American Activities Committee. The committee was investigating "anti-American" influences—and especially communists—in the entertainment industry. Seeger, citing the U.S. Constitution's guarantees of freedom of speech and association, refused to answer the committee's questions. His silence led to ten counts of contempt of Congress. In 1961, Seeger was found guilty of all ten contempt charges and sentenced to one year in prison. An Appeals Court reversed the conviction one year later.

Despite his blacklisting, the songs Seeger wrote in the early 1960s—including "Where Have All the Flowers Gone?", "If I Had a Hammer," and "Turn, Turn, Turn"—reflect his continued commitment to social justice. In the early 1960s, he performed a benefit concert for the Freedom Riders, civil rights activists protesting against **segregation** (separation of the races) in interstate bus terminals. *The Incompleat Folksinger*, published in 1972, offered a collection of Seeger's writings on civil rights and the history of folk songs.

In the 1970s and 1980s, Seeger became a commited **environmentalist**: an activist concerned with repairing the damage done to the earth. He focused on local organizing efforts, particularly to try to clean up the polluted Hudson River. Seeger helped build the "Clearwater," a Hudson River sailing ship that offers programs on the life of the river and the ruinous effects brought on by pollution. In addition to promoting the Clearwater, Seeger has joined in many environmental protests in the Northeast—especially those opposing nuclear power.

Smeal, Eleanor

(1939–)

WOMEN'S RIGHTS ACTIVIST AND PRESIDENT OF THE NATIONAL ORGANIZATION OF WOMEN

A Roman Catholic, Eleanor Marie Cutri attended public schools as a child because her mother wanted to broaden her perspective. As a student at North Carolina's Duke University, where she received an undergraduate degree in 1961, Eleanor Cutri supported the opening of the university to African-American students. A month after getting married in 1963, Eleanor Smeal earned a graduate degree in political science and public administration from the University of Florida.

Moving to Upper St. Clair, Pennsylvania, Smeal served on the board of the local chapter of the League of Women Voters from 1968 to 1972. In 1969, a back problem forced Smeal to remain in bed for a year. Unable to find day-care services for her two children, Smeal became convinced that wives and mothers needed disability insurance. The experience transformed Smeal and her husband into radical **feminists**, and joined the National Organization of Women (NOW) in 1970. As the first president of a NOW chapter she formed in South

Hills, Pennsylvania, Smeal first set out to organize a nursery school for the community. As president of the Pennsylvania NOW from 1972 to 1975, Smeal forced the state to guarantee equal opportunity for girls in school physical education and sports programs.

Elected to NOW's national board of directors in 1973, Smeal became the board's chairperson in 1975. Two years later, she was elected NOW's president. Smeal became the first nonprofessional woman to lead NOW and the first to receive a salary, which she had advocated in order to open up leadership of the organization to all women, rich or poor. As president, Smeal helped develop NOW's strategy to seek passage of the Equal Rights Amendment to the U.S. Constitution. Smeal led one-hundred thousand demonstrators in a march through Washington, D.C., spoke before Congress, and organized a **boycott** of states that had not approved the amendment. Due to these efforts, Congress extended the seven-year time limit for state approval of the amendment to ten years. But the extra time did not yield results. The ERA fell three states short of approval.

Under Smeal's leadership, NOW expanded the range of issues it addressed. It focused attention on the problems of families and the economic security of homemakers. NOW condemned economic discrimination against women—with women earning 59 cents for every dollar a man earned. Smeal also supported the rights of homosexuals and a woman's right to choose an abortion. By 1979, Smeal had doubled NOW's membership to more than one-hundred thousand, making it the largest feminist organization in the world. Succeeded by Molly Yard as president of NOW in 1987, Smeal has continued to promote women's issues—especially the increased participation of women in seeking elected office. In 1991, she founded and headed the Fund for the Feminist Majority, which seeks to develop new ideas and strategies to advance the cause of feminism. At that time, she also announced her intention to form a national feminist party in order to overcome the scarcity of women in politics.

Smith, Abby

(1797–1878) and

Smith, Julia

(1792–1886)

ACTIVISTS FOR WOMEN'S RIGHTS AND TEMPERANCE

For more than seventy years, the Smith sisters, Abby Hadassah and Julia Evelina, lived quiet lives in rural Glastonbury, Connecticut. Although they never attended church, they had received a religious upbringing. (Their father had left the ministry because he felt it was wrong to take money for preaching God's word.) They had taken part in an occasional **temperance** meeting and had provided charity to the sick and needy in their community. They had played a small part in the movement to ban slavery. But the Smiths had devoted most of their lives to maintaining their farm and home.

In 1869, the sisters attended a meeting for women's **suffrage** (the right to vote) in Hartford. This introduction to the notion of women's rights inspired the Smiths. In 1873, Abby Smith attended the first meeting of the Association for the Advancement of Women, cofounded by Julia Ward Howe, in New York. Later that year, she spoke at a town meeting (traditionally, an all-male gathering) to protest against property taxes levied against women who had no right to vote. Echoing the revolutionary founders of the United States, Abby Smith spoke out against "taxation without representation." If the town intended to tax women, the Smiths insisted, then they deserved a voice in the government.

Several months later, the sisters again tried to speak before the town meeting, but were refused the right to speak. In a speech given from an oxcart outside the town hall, Abby Smith announced that the sisters would refuse to pay property taxes until they had the right to vote. To cover unpaid taxes, the town seized seven of the Smiths' cows and sold them back to the sisters. The town later seized fifteen acres of the Smiths' land and auctioned it off. The Smiths quickly sued the tax collector. (They could do this because town law prohibited seizing land to pay for delinquent taxes unless all other property had already been sold.)

Two years later, Abby and Julia Smith had won their lawsuit and had become nationally known for their fight against the injustice of denying women the right to vote. "The Glastonbury Cows"—seized and sold back twice more—became famous. Souvenirs made of their tail hairs were sold as far away as Chicago. In 1876, the sisters began speaking before the National Woman Suffrage Association convention and other gatherings of suffragists. In 1878, Julia Smith spoke before a U.S. Senate committee, while Abby Smith addressed state lawmakers in Hartford. In 1879, a year after Abby Smith's death at age 81, Julia Smith married for the first time at age 87. She gave her last speech on women's rights before the Connecticut Woman Suffrage Association in 1884. *See* HOWE, JULIA WARD

Solomon, Hannah

(1 8 5 8 – 1 9 4 2)

SOCIAL REFORMER

Hannah Greenebaume actively participated in Jewish social and cultural clubs in her youth. In 1877, she and her sister became the first Jews to join the Chicago Woman's Club. By 1884, Hannah Greenebaume Solomon had become president of the club. From 1890 to 1893, Solomon organized a nationwide Jewish Women's Congress, bringing together prominent Jewish women from all over the country. At the first meeting of the congress, organized for Chicago's World's Columbian Exposition in 1893, the group voted to become a permanent association. The National Council of Jewish Women named Solomon as its president, an office she would retain until 1905. The council set as its goal the promotion of religious and community obligations among Jewish women. The group encouraged the study of Judaism and sponsored various social-service programs. In 1896, Solomon surveyed Chicago's community of Jewish immigrants from Russia and assessed the social-service agencies and schools in the community. The following year, she established the Bureau of Personal Service, funded by the Chicago branch of the National Council of Jewish Women. The bureau offered legal advice and practical guidance to the city's Russian Jewish immigrants.

Solomon was also involved in nonreligious women's organizations. In 1896, she helped found the Illinois Federation of Women's Clubs. She also joined Jane Addams in her efforts to establish the nation's first juvenile court in Cook County, Illinois in 1899. With Susan B. Anthony, Solomon represented the Council of Women of the United States at the International Council of Women convention in Berlin in 1904. A year later, the National Council of Jewish Women named Solomon honorary president for life. From 1906 to 1909, she served as president of the board of the Illinois Industrial School for Girls (renamed the Park Ridge School for Girls when it moved in 1907). In 1910, Solomon was a founding member of a civic reform group, the Women's City Club, and headed a committee that investigated the city's system of waste disposal. *See* ADDAMS, JANE, ANTHONY, SUSAN B.

Spock, Benjamin

(1903–   )

A LEADER OF THE PEACE
MOVEMENT, PEDIATRICIAN, AND
AUTHOR

> What is the use of physicians
> like myself trying to help par-
> ents to bring up children
> healthy and happy, to have
> them killed in such numbers for
> a cause that is ignoble?
>
> —From Spock's trial testimony (1968)

The world's most well-known pediatrician, Benjamin McLane
Spock, became a leader of the peace movement in the 1960s.
The author of *Baby and Child Care,* which has sold more cop-
ies than any other original book produced in the United States,
Spock offered advice on child rearing to two generations of
parents.

Spock, born in New Haven, Connecticut, learned from his
strict parents a commitment to high moral principles that
would later inform his activism. Benjamin was educated in
private schools in Hamden, Connecticut and Andover, Massachusetts. When he enrolled at Yale University in 1921, Spock
planned on a career as an architect. A summer job as a coun-
selor at a camp run by the Newington Crippled Children's
Home, however, changed the direction of Spock's life. He decided to become a doctor.

Graduating from Yale University in 1925, he studied medicine at Yale Medical School and at the Columbia University
College of Physicians and Surgeons. After receiving his medical degree from Columbia in 1929, Spock worked as an intern
and a resident (in pediatrics and in psychiatry) at several New
York hospitals over the next four years. He also received six
years of training in **psychoanalysis.** From 1933 to 1944, Spock

had a private practice as a pediatrician (a children's doctor). Near the end of World War II, he served as a **psychiatrist** in New York and California naval hospitals run by the U.S. Naval Reserve Medical Corps.

The Common Sense Book of Baby and Child Care (in later editions, simply called *Baby and Child Care*) first appeared in 1946. This comprehensive, supportive guide for parents stood apart from other books on child care. Rather than simply telling readers what to do, Spock focused on explaining child development. While setting out general guidelines, Spock stressed that every baby was unique. He called on parents to remain flexible and supportive of their child's individual talents and abilities. Spock advocated feeding infants on demand: whenever the baby wants to eat, feed her or him. He encouraged parents not to worry about spoiling the baby. This advice marked a departure from the strict child rearing practices recommended in the past. The book, in its original and revised versions, has sold well over forty-million copies and has been translated into more than thirty languages.

For the next twenty years, Spock taught **psychiatry** and child development at universities in Minneapolis, Minnesota, Pittsburgh, Pennsylvania, and Cleveland, Ohio. From 1955 to 1967, he also served as supervising pediatrician at Western Reserve University's Family Clinic in Cleveland. He also continued to advise parents on child rearing. Beginning in 1954, he wrote a regular column on the problems of parenting for *Ladies Home Journal* and then *Redbook*. He cowrote *A Baby's First Year* in 1954 and *Feeding Your Baby and Child* in 1955. Two collections of his magazine columns—*Dr. Spock Talks with Mothers* and *Problems of Parents*—were published in 1961 and 1962.

Spock increased his political activism in the 1960s. He endorsed Presidential candidate John Kennedy's proposal for Medicare—a federal program providing medical care to the aged—in 1960. Two years later, President Kennedy announced that the U.S. would resume above-ground testing of nuclear weapons. Spock quickly joined the growing peace movement, committing himself to the cause of world peace. He criticized the nuclear arms race between the United States and the Soviet Union as a futile and never-ending attempt to catch up or stay ahead of each other. That year, he joined the board of the National Committee for a Sane Nuclear Policy (SANE). His first public statement on the nuclear arms race appeared in a paid advertisement in the *New York Times* later that year. Spock warned that nuclear testing contaminates milk and other food. He then described how radioactive contamination affects a child's growing body. In 1963, he was elected co-chair of SANE.

When President Lyndon Johnson massively increased U.S. military involvement in Vietnam in 1965, Spock wrote a series of letters urging the President to reverse his policies on the war. His letters ignored, the angry pediatrician joined in antiwar demonstrations. By 1967, Spock had retired from Western Reserve's clinic in order to devote all of his time and energy to ending the war. He attended antiwar rallies in Washington and New York. Later that year, he was elected co-chair of the National Conference for a New Politics. The conference brought together militant African Americans, **pacifists** (peace activists), and other radicals. When the more conservative SANE board members objected to his growing association with radicals, Spock resigned as co-chair, but remained a SANE member.

Spock also actively opposed the military draft. In 1967, he joined poet Allen Ginsberg and others in collecting nearly one-thousand draft cards from young men who refused to serve with the armed forces in Vietnam. He then turned them over to the Justice Department. Later that year, he was arrested for crossing a police line during a protest in front of a New York draft board. At Johnson's urging, the Justice Department began to take action against draft resisters and those who promoted resistance. With four others, including Yale University chaplain William Sloane Coffin, Jr., Spock was charged with conspiring to aid and abet illegal resistance of the draft.

Four of the five men were found guilty and sentenced to two years in prison in 1968. Spock and Coffin were also fined $5,000 each. Yet at a news conference after he had been sentenced, Spock vowed to continue to work against a war he considered illegal. Later that year, he coauthored *Dr. Spock on Vietnam,* detailing his opposition to the war. In 1969, an appeals court overturned the four convictions. The court ruled that the trial judge had denied the defendants' right to a fair trial by issuing improper instructions to the jury. Spock continued to speak out against the war until American involvement ended in 1974. He ran for president in 1972 as the candidate of the pacifist People's Party. In 1974, tying together his concern for child care and his opposition to U.S. policies, he published *Raising Children in a Difficult Time. Spock has continued to provide comforting advice to parents as a columnist for Redbook*, and as a contributing editor of *Parenting* magazine beginning in 1992. Because he sees pediatrics as a concern for public health and social welfare in the broadest sense, Spock has also remained active on behalf of family issues. He has supported movements to overcome the lack of quality daycare facilities and to improve the government's financial support of schools, especially those serving poor communities. In the 1980s, he was arrested several times for taking part in peaceful demonstrations to protest cuts in the government's housing budget and to support more aid to the homeless. His autobiography, *Spock on Spock: A Memoir of Growing Up with the Century*, was published in 1989. See COFFIN, WILLIAM SLOAN, JR., GINSBERG, ALLEN

Stanton, Elizabeth Cady

(1815–1902)

ACTIVIST FOR WOMEN'S RIGHTS

Born on November 12, 1815, Elizabeth Cady was exposed early to the legal limitations on women by her father, a lawyer

and judge. In those days, women were not allowed to vote or serve on juries. Nor could they practice law or medicine. Very few colleges would accept them as students. If a woman was married, she could not sign a will or contract without her husband's consent, and her husband had control over her money and property. Many women came to Mr. Cady seeking legal aid, but because of the laws, he was unable to help them.

In her own life, Elizabeth seemed determined at and early age to prove that women were equal to men. She refused to confine herself to activities like embroidery, music and art—instead, she studied Latin Greek, and mathematics, subjects then usually studied by boys. But she still was not allowed to attend Union College in Schenectady, where her brother had gone. Instead, she attended Troy Female Seminary, now called the Emma Willard School.

When she graduated in 1832, Elizabeth became interested in the **abolitionist movement**, which opposed slavery. She began attending meetings and was deeply affected by the words of one of the speakers, Harry B. Stanton. When they married in 1840, Elizabeth insisted that the woman's promise to "obey" her husband be dropped from the vows. She also insisted on being called Elizabeth Cady Stanton, not Mrs. Henry B. Stanton, because she wanted to remain an independent person, not just an extension of her husband.

The Stantons settled in the town of Seneca Falls, New York. Elizabeth was busy caring for her home and raising her seven children. In July 1848, her friends James and Lucretia Mott came to visit, and the two women invited other women to meet and discuss women's rights. They placed an ad in various newspapers announcing a public meeting on July 19 and 20 to continue the discussion. Nearly three hundred women and forty men appeared at the meeting. Elizabeth wrote a statement for the convention called *Declaration of Sentiments*, a document which resembled Thomas Jefferson's *Declaration of Independence*. Where Jefferson had written "all men are created equal," Stanton substituted "all men and women are created equal." The document called for equal opportunities in education, jobs for women, fairer laws about marriage and divorce, and the right to vote for women.

The Seneca Convention, as it came to be called, attracted much attention, some of it angry, much of it satirical: only one newspaper, the *New York Tribune*, had a positive reaction. But Stanton continued her work, becoming friends with other important feminists, including Amelia Bloomer and Susan B. Anthony. She and Anthony worked closely together, making use of their differences to further their cause. While Stanton was outgoing and enjoyed public speaking, Anthony was more reserved with an ability to organize conferences and arrange speeches.

During the years of the Civil War (1861–65), Stanton and Anthony set aside their concerns for women's rights to help the cause of African Americans. They believed that when the war ended, women would get the vote. But that did not happen. New laws were passed that gave black men the right to vote; nothing at all was said about women of either race. The two women were angry, and when they learned that the state of Kansas had declared and election to settle the issue of votes for blacks and women, they set off at once to begin campaigning. But their efforts did not pay off: women did not get the vote in Kansas.

Stanton and Anthony did not give up, and started a weekly newspaper in New York called the *The Revolution*. They printed articles supporting women's rights and other social causes, such as an eight-hour work day for workers, instead of the customary twelve or fourteen hours. Gradually, the friendship between Stanton and Anthony began to dissolve. Their newspaper also faltered, and within three years of its first issue was forced to fold.

In 1887, Henry B. Stanton, Elizabeth's husband, died. After that she divided her time between New York and England, where her daughter Harriet lived. Harriet later became and important leader in the women's rights movement. Elizabeth Cady Stanton died in 1902. *See* ANTHONY, SUSAN B.; BLOOMER, AMELIA

Steinem, Gloria

(1 9 3 4 –   )

FEMINIST WRITER AND POLITICAL
ORGANIZER

> We are human beings first. . . .
> We share the dreams, capabili-
> ties, and weaknesses of all hu-
> man beings, but our occasional
> pregnancies and other visible
> differences have been used . . .
> to mark us for an elaborate di-
> vision of labor that may once
> have been practical but has
> since become cruel and false.
> The division is continued for
> clear reason, consciously or
> not: the economic and social
> profit of men as a group.
> —From Steinem's "Sisterhood" (1972)

Gloria Steinem has long fought against the second-class treatment of women in the American society and economy. Her *Ms.* magazine, founded in 1971, became the most important and widely read journal of the U.S. **feminist** (women's rights) movement. Through *Ms.*, Steinem has campaigned for the Equal Rights Amendment (ERA) to the U.S. Constitution, equal pay for equal work, a woman's access to safe and legal abortions, and shared parental responsibility. In promoting these measures to further equal treatment of women, Steinem has stressed that their adoption would advance the personal growth of both women and men.

Born in Toledo, Ohio, Gloria Steinem had an erratic childhood. Her mother, a college graduate and former journalist, had given up her career for marriage. Plagued by attacks of anxiety and depression, she suffered her first nervous breakdown just before Gloria was born. Her father, a dreamer, plunged the family into debt while pursuing various money-making schemes. Gloria spent much of her preteen years roaming the country in a trailer home while her father tried to make money. Around 1946, her parents divorced. Gloria lived with her mother in a rat-infested basement apartment in a slum in East Toledo, Ohio. For the first time in her life, she began attending school regularly. She found it difficult to concentrate on her studies, however. Gloria needed to care for her mother, who was unable to work due to her mental instability. With dreams of becoming a dancer, Gloria entered and sometimes won various local amateur contests.

After living with her sister (ten years older than Gloria) in Washington, D.C. for a year, Gloria Steinem enrolled at Smith College. No longer distracted by concern for her family, Steinem was an excellent student. She earned an undergraduate degree in government in 1956.

Steinem then spent two years of study in India, where she wrote articles for Indian newspapers and a guidebook printed by the government. Steinem was unable to find a job as a reporter in New York after returning to the United States in 1958. She moved to Cambridge, Massachusetts, where she enlisted students to go to communist youth festivals in Europe for a liberal group called the National Student Association. (It was later uncovered that the Central Intelligence Agency, the chief spy network of the U.S. government, had funded the association and its programs.)

In 1960, Steinem landed her first U.S. publishing job. She wrote photo captions and met with celebrities who would appear on the cover of *Help!*, a political satire magazine. "The Moral Disarmament of Betty Coed," her first article written for an American publication, was published in *Esquire* magazine two years later. The article was about the feminist revolution and warned of the future conflict between women's changing roles and the failure of men to change their attitudes toward women. For the next six years, she wrote articles for many popular magazines: *Vogue, Glamour, McCall's*, and *Cosmopolitan*, among others. For one of these articles, Steinem exposed sexism by working undercover as a Playboy "bunny" in a New York club.

In 1968, she began writing a weekly column on politics for the newly established *New York* magazine. She advocated a variety of social reforms. She joined labor activist Cesar Chavez when he led a march of poor people to the California state capital in Sacramento. She raised funds for the legal defense of African-American activist Angela Davis. That year, New York lawmakers debated the future of the state's abortion laws. The Redstockings, a radical women's group, called a meeting and asked women to share their experience of illegal abortions. Steinem, who had had an abortion shortly after college, was moved by the dozens of women sharing their feelings of shame. She believed that the shame had been created by a society that forced women to remain silent about their abortions. Her next column for *New York*, "After Black Power, Women's Liberation," began her career as a feminist writer.

In addition to writing on behalf of women's rights, Steinem became a political organizer. In 1971, she joined Betty Friedan and members of Congress Shirley Chisholm and Bella Abzug to form the National Women's Political Caucus. This group supported women who ran for public office. She also helped found the Women's Action Alliance. The alliance worked to organize nonwhite women and men to fight against social and economic **discrimination**: unequal treatment based on race or sex. At the end of the year, *New York* magazine printed an insert: a short sample issue of *Ms.*, a woman's magazine designed to mirror the concerns of the feminist movement.

The first full issue of *Ms.*, published in 1972, sold out its three-hundred-thousand copies in just eight days. The magazine, entirely owned and edited by women, featured a petition calling for safe and legal abortions in its first issue. By reflecting the concerns of a generation of feminists, *Ms.* attracted half-a-million regular readers by the mid-1970s. A supporter of the ERA throughout the 1970s, Steinem served on President Jimmy Carter's committee to observe International Women's Year in 1977. She also helped found such political groups as Voters for Choice (a group promoting safe and legal abortions) and Women Against Pornography.

In the 1980s, Steinem promoted feminism as a source of personal growth for women *and* men. She insisted that to become complete as human beings, women needed to adopt traditionally masculine traits such as ambition, assertiveness, and the ability to deal with conflict. Likewise, men needed to absorb what were usually considered feminine traits like empathy, compassion, and comfort working within the home and family life. Like Friedan, Steinem foresaw the home as the future battleground for feminism. She attacked the myth of the "Superwoman": the modern woman expected to excel in a professional career, motherhood, home care, and marital life. Instead, she urged men to relieve the burden by assuming equal responsibility in the home, especially in child rearing.

As other women's magazines began to join *Ms.* in addressing feminist concerns, the magazine began losing readers in the 1980s. After selling the magazine in 1987, Steinem remained a consultant with *Ms.* while taking a job as an editor at Random House. She continued to write articles on women and their images as presented in advertising, the movies, politics, and business. In *Revolution from Within: A Book of Self-Esteem*, published in 1992, Steinem attempted to relate the personal growth she had achieved through feminism. *See* CHAVEZ, CESAR; CHISOLM, SHIRLEY; DAVIS, ANGELA; FRIEDAN, BETTY

Stevens, Alzina

(1849–1900)

LABOR ACTIVIST

> It [is] the worst kind of snobbishness to assume that you must not have the same standards of honor for working people as you have for the well-to-do.
> —said when presented with the defense
> of a notoriously corrupt labor leader

At age thirteen, the poverty of her family forced Alzina Ann Parsons to go to work in a textile factory in Maine. The loss of a finger in a factory accident helped motivate her later work to reform working conditions and child-labor laws. After a brief marriage, Alzina Parsons Stevens learned the printing trade, working as a proofreader and typesetter in Toledo, Ohio from 1867 to 1872. After moving to Chicago, she joined a printer's union and in 1877 organized a Working Woman's Union. She served as president of the union, which sought to improve working conditions for women, until 1882. Stevens in 1881 became one of the first women to join the Knights of Labor, a labor group dedicated to **socialism**. She moved to Toledo, Ohio in 1882, becoming a proofreader for the *Toledo Bee.*

Though she had received little formal education, Stevens worked as a writer and editor of the *Bee* from 1885 to 1891. For the Knights of Labor, she founded a women's local, the Joan of Arc Assembly, and served as its first leader. In 1888, she joined Leonora Barry on the Knights' committee on women's work. Stevens turned down an offer to succeed Barry as director of women's work in order to focus on local organization of workers. Elected district leader of the Knights in 1890, she represented twenty-two local assemblies of workers. In 1892, she moved to Chicago, where she co-owned and edited a short-lived labor reform newspaper, the *Vanguard.*

In Chicago, Stevens became a resident of Hull House, the **settlement house** founded by Jane Addams. Stevens served as an invaluable link between the labor movement and settlement workers who were dedicated to improving life in the community. She also organized new unions for the American Federation of Labor, a collection of skilled trade and crafts unions. From 1893 to 1897, Stevens served as assistant factory inspector for the state of Illinois, where she gathered data and urged state lawmakers to enact new laws to protect workers.

For the last five years of her life, Alzina Stevens focused on the welfare of children. In 1895, she cowrote a study of child labor for *Hull-House Maps and Papers.* Stevens urged that children be required to remain in school and not be allowed to work until age sixteen. She also called on the state to create agencies to enforce these recommended child-labor laws. Responding to Stevens' appeals, the state passed an improved child-labor law in 1897 and a law requiring children to attend school in 1899. Stevens also joined in the Hull House campaign for the creation of the nation's first juvenile court in Cook County. In 1899, she served as the new court's first probation officer. *See* ADDAMS, JANE; BARRY, LEONORA

Stokes, Rose

(1879–1933)

SOCIAL REFORMER AND CO-FOUNDER OF THE COMMUNIST PARTY

Born in Poland, Rose Harriet Pastor Stokes moved with her family to a London ghetto as a child. She began working at age four, helping her mother sew bows on women's slippers. Her formal education consisted of two years of study at a Jewish school for the poor in London. In 1890, the Pastors moved to Cleveland, Ohio, where Rose worked in a cigar factory throughout her teens. She began writing poetry for Jewish newspapers, publishing her first collection of poems in 1893. A regular contributor to the *Jewish Daily News and Jewish Gazette* in New York, Pastor became the paper's assistant editor in 1903. At this time she also began contributing articles to the *International Socialist Review.* For the next sixteen years, she actively promoted **socialism.**

While continuing her writing, Rose Pastor Stokes lectured at colleges on behalf of the Socialist Party from 1907 to 1915. Her own factory background made her an effective spokesperson for the Socialist Party among working women. She joined striking garment workers in 1909 and was active in a strike of New York's hotel and restaurant workers three years later. Her 1916 play, *The Woman Who Wouldn't*, promoted both socialism and **feminism.** In the play, a woman who is denied an **abortion** later becomes a single mother and a famous labor leader. In 1917, Stokes resigned from the Socialist Party to protest its opposition to the United States entry into World War I. Less than a year later, however, she returned to the Socialist Party.

In 1918, she wrote a letter to the *Kansas City Star* accusing the U.S. government of serving the industries making a profit from the war. "I am for the people," she wrote, "while the government is for the profiteers." Stokes was arrested and charged with lowering troop morale and interfering with military recruitment. Found guilty, Stokes was sentenced to ten years in prison. Although an appeals court reversed the decision in 1920, the case became a symbol of the fragility of freedom of speech during wartime.

Stokes again left the Socialist Party in 1919. She co-founded the American Communist Party, which advocated a workers' revolution. In 1922, Stokes served as an American delegate to the Fourth Congress of the Communist International in Moscow, Russia. Although Stokes wanted to maintain the American Communist Party as an illegal underground organization, the Soviet leaders rejected this proposal. Stokes was elected to the central committee of the new Workers' Party, which in 1929 would become the Communist Party U.S.A. Throughout the decade, Stokes wrote articles for *Pravda*, a Soviet newspaper, and the *Daily Worker*. She also continued to join striking workers on picket lines. In 1929 she was arrested for joining the picket line of the Needle Trades' Industrial Union, a union of factory seamstresses. She was also clubbed by police in a protest against the occupation of Haiti by U.S. Marines.

Stone, Lucy

(1818–1893)

ACTIVIST FOR WOMEN'S RIGHTS AND ABOLITIONIST

> I was a woman before I was an **abolitionist**. I must speak for the women.

—Stone, Conversation with Reverend Samuel May, c. 1848, quoted in *Morning Star* by Elinor Rice Hays

Although Lucy Stone spoke out for the **abolitionist** cause, her greatest commitment was to the movement for women's rights. Stone also founded and edited the leading newspaper of the women's rights movement in the nineteenth century. Through this paper and her lecture tours, she urged the creation of laws insuring property rights for married women and supported state campaigns to win the vote for women.

Lucy Stone was born on a farm outside West Brookfield, Massachusetts. From an early age, she began resenting the unequal treatment of women in American society. She rejected her parents' view that the husband automatically rules the family. Lucy felt her mother's efforts on the farm went unnoticed and unappreciated by the family. She was also stung by the unfairness of her father, who supported his sons' education, but thought little of educating his daughters. As a child, Lucy sold nuts and berries to earn money to buy books and pay for her own tutor. The local Congregational church also angered Lucy in denying her and other women a vote in its meetings. When she read in the Bible that men have the right to rule women, she became convinced that poor translations from the Greek and Hebrew had corrupted the original meaning of these passages. To correct these mistakes, she decided she would study these languages herself. Her sense of injustice was further aroused in 1834, when she began teaching at a district school—earning half the salary paid to male teachers.

In 1843, Stone began attending Oberlin College in Ohio. The first college in the nation to accept both women and men as students, Oberlin had also become famous for promoting the abolition of slavery. At first, Stone paid for her studies through housework, teaching, and loans. Finally, her father consented to help, as he had more willingly done for her brothers. At Oberlin, Stone joined a group of women who secretly practiced public speaking—an activity closed to women, even at the liberal college. Her graduation in 1847 made Stone the first woman from Massachusetts to receive a college degree.

After graduation, Stone was hired to lecture for the Massachusetts Anti-Slavery Society. When she attempted to speak about women's rights in her lectures, her sponsor objected. So Stone arranged to lecture without a fee on women's rights while working for the antislavery society on weekends. Through her speeches on women's rights, Stone stirred up anger at the unequal treatment of women. Her church soon expelled her for her speeches on **feminism**. In Boston, Stone founded the first national organization for women's rights in 1850. The group's first convention, held in Worcester, attracted more than one-thousand people. Stone used this event to attack the system that regarded married women as the property of their husbands.

For the next seven years, Stone toured America, lecturing in Canada, the South, and in states east of the Mississippi River. She also helped organize annual women's rights conventions throughout the decade. Stone also lectured on behalf of the **temperance movement**. She joined with Susan B. Anthony and Amelia Bloomer in organizing the "Whole World's Temperance Convention" in 1853. Stone and other women had been denied the right to speak at the so-called World's Temperance Convention earlier that year.

In 1855, Stone married abolitionist Henry Blackwell, the brother of pioneer women physicians Elizabeth and Emily Blackwell. Although Stone was reluctant to marry, Blackwell promised her she would remain free in their marriage. Both signed an agreement that protested women's lack of property rights in marriage and laid out their vision of equality in marriage. In a decision almost unheard of in her day, Stone retained her own name. Stone and Blackwell shared in each other's goals, while allowing each other independence.

From 1857 to 1867, Stone stopped her lecture tours to care for her daughter. While in the care of a nursemaid, her daughter had had some minor accidents, raising Stone's concern. Living in Orange, New Jersey, she protested against the practice of taxing women without giving them a voice in their government. Refusing to pay taxes in 1858, she allowed the auction of several household possessions in order to pay her tax bill. In 1863, Stone chaired a meeting at which Elizabeth Cady Stanton and Anthony organized the Women's Loyal National League. The league organized a petition drive demanding freedom for slaves and later urged adoption of the Thirteenth Amendment, which outlawed slavery in 1865.

Following the end of the Civil War, Stone helped organize the American Equal Rights Association in 1866. The group called for the extension of voting rights to both African Americans and women. The following year, she resumed her lecture tours. After working in the unsuccessful drives for women's **suffrage** (the right to vote) in Kansas and New York, Stone became president of the New Jersey Woman Suffrage Association in 1868. That same year, Stone and Julia Ward Howe founded the New England Woman Suffrage Association.

Like other women's rights activists, Stone was outraged that the proposed Fourteenth and Fifteenth Amendments to the U.S. Constitution provided citizenship and voting rights to African Americans, but excluded women. In response, she cofounded the American Woman Suffrage Association (AWSA). Unlike its rival organization, the National Woman Suffrage Association (NWSA) led by Stanton and Anthony, AWSA supported the passage of the Fourteenth and Fifteenth Amendments despite their neglect of women. AWSA also differed from NWSA in focusing solely on the issue of suffrage, and in using a state-by-state approach to win voting rights instead of calling for a national amendment. Stone served on the executive board of AWSA for twenty years.

In 1870, Stone raised funds to create *Woman's Journal*, AWSA's weekly newspaper, which she began editing two years later. The paper became the foremost advocate of women's rights. A weekly column that Stone wrote for the *Journal* was soon published in hundreds of newspapers across country. Her voice failing, Stone began to cut back on her lecturing in 1887. Three years later, when AWSA and NWSA merged to form the National American Woman Suffrage Association, Stone served for two years as chair of its executive committee. A pioneer in death as well as life, Stone became the first person in New England ever cremated (burning the body down to ash) after her death in 1893. *See* ANTHONY, SUSAN B.; BLACKWELL, ELIZABETH; BLACKWELL, EMILY; HOWE, JULIA WARD; STANTON, ELIZABETH CADY

Stowe, Harriet Beecher

(1811–1896)

ABOLITIONIST AND WRITER

Through her novel *Uncle Tom's Cabin*, writer Harriet Elizabeth Beecher Stowe did more to advance the **abolitionist** cause than any of the many lecturers or organizers who urged an end to the brutal practice of slavery. Harriet Beecher's father was a Congregational pastor committed to spreading his faith and winning converts to Christianity. He instilled in his family a sense of high mission, a calling to perform services for their community. After her mother died in 1816, Harriet's father upheld the image of his wife as a woman saved by her selfless love of God. Catherine Beecher, her older sister, brought Harriet up from the time she was four. Catherine's belief that women had the power to inspire and shape the nation's moral standards through their roles as mothers, housewives, teachers, and nurses had a powerful influence on Harriet. Harriet was a student at Catherine's newly opened Hartford Female Seminary from 1824 to 1827, when she began teaching there.

In 1832, the Beechers moved to the frontier town of Cincinnati, Ohio. Harriet Beecher helped her sister found the Western Female Institute and wrote a children's geography text. In Cincinnati, located across the Ohio River from the slave-owning state of Kentucky, she first came into contact with fugitive slaves, escaping to the North through the "Underground Railroad." The Western Female Institute closed in 1836, the same year that Harriet Beecher married, hoping to fulfill the ideals of marriage and motherhood taught by her sister and her father. The success of her stories, collected and published as *The Mayflower* in 1843, steered her in a different course. Although she voiced some reluctance to neglect her duties as a mother to pursue a career as a writer, her husband encouraged her to continue writing.

In 1850, the Stowes moved from Cincinnati to Brunswick, Maine. That year, the passage of the Fugitive Slave Act, which allowed the capture and return of escaped slaves, strengthened Stowe's opposition to slavery. She began writing *Uncle Tom's Cabin; or, Life Among the Lowly*, which in 1851 and 1852 appeared chapter by chapter in *The National Era*, an abolitionist newspaper. Published as a book in 1852, *Uncle Tom's Cabin* quickly sold more than three-hundred-thousand copies and was later translated into fifty-five languages. Approaching the issue of slavery in a novel allowed Stowe to personalize it, giving it a human face. The book told the story of the good and loyal slave Uncle Tom and the evil of slavery, in its extreme represented by the character of the drunk and brutal slave-owner Simon Legree. When Tom is beaten to death for refusing to tell where two escaped slaves have hidden themselves, he became a fictional **martyr** to the abolitionist cause. Stowe used the novel to condemn the church, the law, and the economy for accepting the evil practice of slavery. With the novel, Stowe helped rouse the nation's awareness of the evils of slavery.

Attacked by defenders of slavery for making up the evils she portrayed, Stowe published *A Key to Uncle Tom's Cabin*. This book offered various documents that told of the brutality of the system: It offered evidence of slaves tortured and mutilated by their masters as well as tales of enslaved mothers who killed their own babies to spare them from the horrors of slavery. On a tour of Europe that year, Stowe accepted a document presented to the "Women of the United States" from the "Women of Great Britain and Ireland." The document expressed support for women's efforts to free the slaves.

In 1854, Kansas erupted in a violent civil war as proslavery and antislavery settlers poured into the state. Both sides hoped to provide votes to determine whether the territory would allow slavery. During this five-year battle known as "Bleeding Kansas," Stowe wrote *Dred*. The novel argued that slavery corrupted all of society and predicted a holy war that would settle the issue. When the Civil War began in 1861, Stowe wrote newspaper columns portraying the bloodshed as punishment from God for the nation's immoral support of slavery.

For the next twenty-five years, Stowe wrote almost a book a year. Many of her essays, novels, and advice on homemaking promoted her sister's notion that women were replacing the clergy as shapers of the nation's moral character. She thus brought to a vast popular audience the idea that women, by managing both the home and the education of children, helped civilize the world. The concept that women had a special moral worth was soon adopted by some women's rights activists as an argument in favor of giving women the right to vote.

Swartz, Maud

(1879–1937)

SUFFRAGIST AND LABOR LEADER

Maud O'Farrell Swartz was born in County Kildare, Ireland. After attending convent schools in Germany and in Paris, she worked in Italy as a governess. In 1901, Maud O'Farrell arrived in New York with virtually no money. After a series of jobs, she became a proofreader for a foreign-language printing company, remaining with the company for over twelve years.

In 1912, Maud Swartz began her career as an activist by joining in the New York State drive for women's **suffrage**. She volunteered to deliver speeches supporting the cause among Italian-speaking audiences. Her work attracted the attention of labor leader and suffrage campaigner Rose Schneiderman. Schneiderman asked Swartz to help organize women workers into unions for the National Women's Trade Union League (WTUL). In addition to organizing workers, the WTUL also campaigned to obtain laws protecting women workers and developed programs to educate women workers. Swartz herself did not join a union until 1913, but three years later she spent a year learning how to organize unions at the WTUL training school. From 1917 to 1921, she served as secretary of the New York branch of the WTUL. She represented the national organization at the American Federation of Labor convention in 1919. That year, she was also named secretary of the new International Congress of Working Women (later called the International Federation of Working Women). At the federation's first meeting in Geneva, Switzerland in 1921, Swartz was chosen as its American vice president.

The following year, Swartz began her most significant work. On behalf of the New York WTUL, she offered free aid to women seeking workers' **compensation** following an accident in the workplace. Compensation involves payments that make up for a worker's lost ability to work after an accident. Swartz worked alone in these efforts. She would approach women workers just prior to their compensation hearings and offer to help. Her desire to help the helpless, her command of foreign languages, and her expert knowledge of state labor laws allowed her to provide valuable help to many women workers, especially immigrants.

From 1922 to 1926, Swartz served as president of the national WTUL. While continuing to work with women workers seeking compensation, she became the primary spokesperson for the women's labor movement. She represented the interests of working women in testimony before congressional committees. During this period, she also began speaking out against war and calling for world peace. From 1931 until her death in 1937, Swartz served as secretary of the New York State

Department of Labor. During her tenure, she greatly expanded the labor department's activities on behalf of women workers. *See* SCHNEIDERMAN, ROSE

Swisshelm, Jane

(1815–1884)

JOURNALIST, ABOLITIONIST, WOMEN'S RIGHTS ACTIVIST

Jane Grey Cannon Swisshelm was born in Pittsburgh, Pennsylvania, in 1815. An early reader, Jane began her schooling at age three. After her father died in 1823, her mother tried to support the family by making straw hats. At age ten, Jane began teaching lacemaking to help the family survive. From age fourteen to age twenty, she worked as a schoolteacher. When she married in 1836, she reluctantly gave up painting and reading to devote herself to the customary duties of a wife.

Her opposition to slavery grew out of an 1838 move to Louisville, Kentucky, where she first encountered the brutality of the slave system. From 1839 to 1840, she returned to Pittsburgh to care for her dying mother. Her irate husband threatened to sue her mother's estate for the value of her nursing services. The experience awakened Swisshelm to the legal powerlessness of married women. For the next two years, she headed a girls' school in Butler, Pennsylvania. During this period, she began contributing unsigned articles promoting the rights of married women and opposing the death penalty for the local paper. In 1842, Swisshelm returned to her husband, who had resettled on his family's farm in Pittsburgh. With her husband's support, she wrote stories, poems, and articles opposing slavery and favoring women's property rights for newspapers in Philadelphia and Pittsburgh and for *The Spirit of Liberty*, a Pittsburgh antislavery journal. She founded *The Pittsburgh Saturday Visiter*, a reform newspaper, in 1848. Swisshelm used the paper to promote various reform movements, including the **abolition** of slavery and **temperance**: giving up of alcohol. *The Visiter* also advocated the recognition and protection of the rights of women—especially property rights for married women and **suffrage** (the right to vote).

After nine years editing *The Visiter*, Swisshelm sold the newspaper, left her husband, and moved with her six-year-old daughter to St. Cloud, Minnesota. There, in 1858, she revived a dying newspaper and renamed it *The St. Cloud Visiter*. Her editorials opposing slavery resulted in the destruction of her press and type, and a libel suit soon forced the closing of the paper. She immediately founded *The St. Cloud Democrat* and began lecturing throughout the state in support of reform movements. Although she supported Abraham Lincoln in the presidential race of 1860, she criticized him for not zealously pursuing reforms.

In 1863, Swisshelm sold her newspaper and moved to Washington, D.C. While serving as a nurse in military hospitals in the Washington area, she wrote many angry dispatches about hospital conditions for *The St. Cloud Democrat* and *The New York Tribune*. While working as a clerk in the War Department in 1865, she founded *The Reconstructionist*, a paper promoting the views of radical Republicans. Her criticism of President Andrew Johnson's policies cost Swisshelm her job. After the newspaper folded in 1867, Swisshelm retired from journalism. Having won a lawsuit claiming part of her dead ex-husband's estate, she returned to the farm in Pittsburgh.

Szold, Henrietta

(1 8 6 0 – 1 9 4 5)

ZIONIST LEADER

Henrietta Szold was born in Baltimore, Maryland. Her father, a Hungarian rabbi, had emigrated to the United States after taking part in a failed revolution in Austria in 1848. The Szolds spoke German in their home, but Henrietta's father also taught her Hebrew and French. After graduating from a girls' high school in 1877, Szold began teaching classes for both children and adults in her father's religious school. She also began writing articles for *The Jewish Messenger* in New York.

In 1889, Szold established a night school to teach newly arrived Jewish immigrants from Eastern Europe the English language as well as American history and customs. In its nine years, the school helped more than five-thousand immigrants—Jews and Christians alike. In 1893, Szold joined Baltimore's Hebras Zion—perhaps the first U.S. organization that promoted **Zionism**: the creation of a Jewish national state in Palestine, the ancient homeland of the Jews. From 1893 to 1916, she worked for the Jewish Publication Society, which published Jewish literature in English. In 1899, she began working on the *American Jewish Year Book*, an annual that offered information on the American and world Jewish communities. She became sole editor of the annual from 1904 to 1908. A 1909 trip to Palestine, where she was horrified by the sight of poor people without medical care or proper standards of hygiene, solidified her commitment to Zionism. In 1912, Szold became the founding president of the Hadassah Chapter of Daughters of Zion, a group intended to promote health work in Palestine. Hadassah would soon grow to become the Women's Zionist Organization of America.

Szold's first priority, accomplished in 1913, was to establish the Hadassah Medical Unit, which sent two nurses to work in Jerusalem. During World War I, she organized new chapters of Hadassah throughout the United States and wrote articles for the *Maccabean*, a Zionist journal. In 1918, Szold helped organized the American Zionist Medical Unit, which sent doctors, nurses, dentists, nutritionists, and medical equipment to Palestine, which came under British control during the war. That year, she was also named director of the Department of Education for the new Zionist Organization of America. Szold supervised the creation of educational materials, the training of adult and youth group leaders, and the creation of programs in Zionism for Jewish summer camps. In 1920, Szold journeyed to Palestine once more, serving briefly as director of the medical unit in 1922, and directing the training of nurses and oversaw the introduction of health programs in Jewish schools.

Returning to the United States in 1923, Szold resumed presidency of Hadassah until 1926, when she was named honorary president. The following year, she was elected to the executive committee of the World Zionist Organization. She spent three more years in Palestine in charge of the group's health and education department. After spending 1930 in the United States, Szold returned again to Palestine the following year. On this trip, she established social services, expanded her program to promote more sanitary practices, and founded job-training centers. Unlike many Zionists, Szold called for a future Palestine in which Jews and Arabs each had their own nation. Although she devoutly believed in Judaism, she was tolerant of different faiths and extended her help to everyone in Palestine: Jews, Moslems, and Christians.

In 1933, she began working with Youth Aliyah, a program that brought Jews from Adolf Hitler's Germany to Palestine to finish their education, and would bring almost thirty-thousand teenagers to Palestine over the next fifteen years. Many of these teenagers became the sole survivors of their families, who were wiped out by Hitler's systematic murder of Jews.

On her eightieth birthday, in 1940, Szold founded an institute to study the problems of children and to promote children's welfare in Palestine. The institute was renamed Mosad Szold (the Szold Foundation) after her death in 1945.

Troup, Augusta

(c. 1848–1920)

WOMEN'S LABOR ORGANIZER AND JOURNALIST

Augusta Lewis Troup was born in New York. Orphaned in infancy, Augusta was taken into the home of a New York broker. After several years of teaching by private tutors, she studied at a girls' school in Brooklyn Heights. She graduated from a convent school, Sacred Heart, in Manhattanville.

Around 1866, Augusta Lewis began working as a reporter

for *The New York Sun*. She served as an apprentice typesetter for *The New York Era*, and was then hired by *The New York World*. In 1867, the International Typographical Union (ITU), a union of male typesetters, went on strike. Women, however, not welcomed as union members, continued working throughout the strike. When the strike ended in 1868, most of the women were fired. Lewis took jobs with small printing companies and reform periodicals. One of these was *The Revolution*, the woman's rights paper founded by Susan B. Anthony and Elizabeth Cady Stanton. With Anthony and Stanton, Augusta Lewis founded the New York Working Women's Association in 1868. The association had the same goals as men's unions: to improve wages and working conditions. Lewis saw the aim of economic equality as the first priority of the association. Although she personally favored **suffrage** (the right to vote) for women, she feared the issue might divide the membership. This stand created tension between Lewis and Anthony, who wanted the women's union to endorse the cause of suffrage.

That year, Lewis also helped organize and served as first president of the Women's Typographical Union (WTU). Although the WTU gained the support of the men's ITU, women typesetters still faced job **discrimination**. Although WTU members supported the ITU by refusing to replace striking male workers, male union members did not accept them. Since employers still paid women less than men, male typesetters saw women as a threat to the pay scale won by their union.

The struggle between Lewis and Anthony became clear in 1869. During a New York printers' strike, Lewis urged women to show their loyalty to all unions by not replacing strikers. Anthony wanted women to take advantage of any and all employment opportunities, so she encouraged employers to hire women typesetters to replace strikers. The print shop that published *The Revolution* then fired Lewis due to her union activities. Lewis, the first woman member of the ITU, was elected corresponding secretary in 1870. Her efforts brought many women workers into the union.

Lewis married Alexander Troup, secretary-treasurer of the ITU and an early backer of the WTU, in 1874. The couple settled in New Haven, where Troup wrote articles for her husband's *The New Haven Union* and reported on the women's suffrage movement. She also did charitable work, especially among the city's Italian community. In 1878, the WTU disbanded and the ITU voted not to accept any other women's unions. Yet through the efforts of Augusta Lewis Troup, women were now admitted into printers' unions. *See* AN-THONY, SUSAN B.; STANTON, ELIZABETH CADY

Truth, Sojourner

(c . 1 7 9 7 – 1 8 8 3)

ACTIVIST FOR WOMEN'S AND
CIVIL RIGHTS

> That man over there says that women need to be helped into carriages, and lifted over ditches, and to have the best place everywhere. Nobody ever helps me into carriages, or over mud puddles, or gives me any best place, and ain't I a woman? . . . I could work as much and eat as much as a man (when I could get it), and bear the lash as well—and ain't I a woman? I have borne five children and seen them most all sold off into slavery, and when I cried out with a mother's grief, none but Jesus heard—and ain't I a woman?
>
> —Truth, from a speech (1851)

Born a slave, Sojourner Truth grew up to become a traveling street preacher. She told everyone who would listen to trust in God's love and to live in harmony with one another. Her personal experience—thirty years as a slave—provided an emotional dimension to Truth's speeches against slavery. Her experience of oppression also led her to become an outspoken advocate of women's rights.

The child of slaves, Sojourner Truth was born to the home of a wealthy landowner in Hurley, New York. All but one of her brothers and sisters were sold away from the family. Her master named her Isabella, and she was often called Bell. Isabella and the other slaves lived in the dank cellar of the slaveowner's house. After his death, Isabella was sold in an auction for $100 to an abusive shopkeeper. In 1810, her third owner sold her to John Dumont, a wealthy landowner in New Paltz, New York, for $300. Isabella married Thomas, an older slave, and over the next seventeen years, she gave birth to at least five children, some of whom may have been fathered by her master. Dumont sold three of Isabella's four surviving children to other slaveowners.

In 1817, the State of New York freed all slaves over age forty and passed a law calling for freedom for all others by 1828. Dumont had promised Isabella that he would free her in 1827. When he failed to keep his promise, Isabella fled with her only unsold child, a baby girl. A couple named Van Wagener gave her refuge in their home and purchased her freedom for $20. In gratitude, Isabella took their last name as her own. While working as a servant in the New Paltz area, she learned that her son had been illegally sold to a slaveowner out of the State of New York. With the help of some Quaker friends, Isabella Van Wagener won a lawsuit to have her son returned from Alabama. The lawsuit was one of the first successful suits filed by an African-American woman against a white man.

Around 1829, Isabella Van Wagener brought her two children to New York, where she found work as a household servant. Through one of her employers, she met Sarah and Elijah Pierson, street preachers on a mission to save the souls of prostitutes. Isabella Van Wagener joined the Piersons in preaching in the dangerous streets of a New York slum. Soon, she had moved into their home, where she worked as both servant and missionary. In 1833, she and the Piersons turned over all of their savings and possessions to join Zion Hill, a religious community in Sing Sing, New York. Two years later, Pierson died under mysterious circumstances. The leader of

Zion Hill, Robert Matthews, was charged with murder, tried, and found not guilty. Before the trial, a member of Zion Hill accused Van Wagener of taking part in the murder. She later won $125 in damages as a result of a lawsuit filed against her accuser.

For the next eight years, she lived in New York, working as a cook, a maid, and a laundress. Isabella Van Wagener had always had religious visions and heard voices that she was convinced belonged to God. In 1843, the voices told her to take the name Sojourner Truth and spread the word of God. Truth traveled by foot throughout Long Island and Connecticut that year, preaching the word of God.

That winter, Truth stopped in Northampton, Massachusetts. There she joined a **utopian** communal farm and silk factory. The founder was the brother-in-law of William Lloyd Garrison, a famed **abolitionist**: an activist working to end slavery. Truth remained in Northampton until 1846, when the community disbanded. She began to tour New England, lecturing against slavery and describing, quietly but forcefully, her past life as a slave. Since she could not write, she dictated her autobiography, *Narrative of Sojourner Truth: A Northern Slave*, to a friend named Olive Gilbert in 1850. Truth sold her book to support herself while on tour. That year, she attended the first national women's rights convention in Worcester, Massachusetts. Soon, her lectures addressed the cause of women's rights as well as the abolition of slavery. Also in 1850, she toured the Midwest, lecturing in Ohio, Indiana, Missouri, and Kansas. On this tour, she met many other abolitionist leaders, such as Frederick Douglass. Proslavery mobs often tried to disrupt her speeches, and she was beaten with a club in Kansas. She attended the National Woman's Suffrage Convention in Akron, Ohio in 1851. There, Truth delivered a famous speech in which she attacked the notion that women needed men to protect them and therefore did not deserve equal rights.

After more than ten years of lecturing, Sojourner Truth settled in Harmonia, a spiritualistic community outside of Battle Creek, Michigan in 1857. During the Civil War (1861–65), Truth nursed northern soldiers and gathered gifts of food and clothing for African-American volunteer regiments. In 1864, she met with President Abraham Lincoln at the White House. She remained in Washington for the next two years at the request of the National Freedmen's Relief Association. The group asked Truth to advise freed slaves held in refugee camps in Arlington Heights, Virginia. Truth helped former slaves find new homes and unsuccessfully appealed to the government to found vocational and industrial schools to educate them. While in Washington, Truth also conducted some of the first **sit-in** protests in the United States. The demonstrations helped end the illegal **segregation** of the city's streetcars.

In the decade after the Civil War ended, Truth continued to lecture on religion, equal rights for African Americans, women's rights (especially women's **suffrage**), and the evils of alcohol. She worked with the American Equal Rights Association, founded in 1867 to promote voting rights for African Americans and women. In 1870, she presented President Ulysses Grant with a petition to form a "Negro State." Truth proposed setting aside unoccupied public land in the West for African Americans to make their home. Although the government rejected the proposal, it may have helped inspire large numbers of African Americans to move to Kansas and Missouri during that decade. Truth herself moved back to Battle Creek in 1875, and remained there until her death eight years later. *See* DOUGLASS, FREDERICK

Tubman, Harriet

(1820–1913)

ANTI-SLAVERY ACTIVIST, LEADER OF THE
UNDERGROUND RAILROAD

Born in 1820 in Dorchester County, Maryland, Harriet Tubman began her life in slavery. She was not considered a person, but rather as a piece of property. She lived in the plantation's slave quarters, and at the age of six was set out work. Along with the other slaves, young Harriet worked in the fields from dawn to dusk, watched by an overseer, whose job it was to make sure that they wasted no time while they worked.

After the owner of the plantation died, there was a rumor that all the slaves would be sold to another plantation. Sometime earlier, she had married a man named John Tubman, but she was not happy in her marriage. She decided she would escape from the plantation, and told no one of her decision, not even her husband. Instead, she slipped quietly out of their cabin one night, and found shelter in the home of a Quaker woman. Quakers were a religious group who opposed slavery. This woman directed Harriet to other stations, or safe houses where she would be given shelter.

She was trying to make her way to the Northern states where slavery was illegal. The secret system for helping slaves escape to the North, which included the stations, was called the **Underground Railroad**. All along the way North, Harriet was hidden by free blacks and sympathetic whites in their houses and barns. She travelled by night, using the North Star to guide her, and in the day, she slept in the woods. Once, a farmer drove her part of the way, hidden under blankets in his wagon.

Finally, she arrived in Philadelphia, Pennsylvania, where she was able to find work. But the thought of her family, still enslaved in the South and waiting to be sold would not leave her. She made plans to become a conductor on the Underground Railroad: she would return to the South and lead other blacks to freedom. If she was caught, the penalty was death. All along the routes of the Underground Railroad were spies and slave catchers, hoping to reap the rewards offered for capturing fugitive slaves.

Over the next several years, and 19 trips back to Maryland, she led more than 300 slaves to freedom. Many times she was nearly caught, but Harriet Tubman was cunning and managed to evade the captors. Her most dangerous mission was bringing her parents—by then quite old—out of slavery. Tubman became something of a legend in her own time. She was called Moses, after the character in the Old Testament, because she, like the Biblical figure, led her people out of bondage into freedom. A reward of $60,000 was set for her capture, but it was never collected.

When the Civil War broke out between the North and the South, Tubman served with the Northern (or Union) Army. She traveled in a government ship to Beaufor, on one of the Sea Islands off the coast of South Carolina. There she cared for sick and homeless slaves who had taken refuge with the Union Army. She also acted as a Union scout and spy. In 1863, she led a group of black soldiers under Colonel James Montgomery on a raid into enemy territory. Nearly eight hundred slaves were freed as a result of that mission.

After the war ended, Harriet Tubman returned to her home in Auburn, New York, where she lived with her second husband. She took care of her parents until their deaths, and continued to give support and shelter to many people.

Washington, Booker T.

(1856–1915)

AFRICAN-AMERICAN LEADER AND EDUCATIONAL REFORMER

Booker Taliaferro Washington was born a slave on a plantation in Virginia. His mother was a cook on the plantation and his father was white, possibly a member of the slaveowner's family. Booker showed an early interest in education and an intense longing to read. In 1865, when the end of the Civil War freed all slaves, his family moved to Malden, West Virginia. While working in a salt furnace and later in coal mines, Booker took classes at night from an African-American teacher in charge of the local day school. Hired as a house servant in 1867, he received further teaching from his employer. In 1872, he began attending the Hampton Normal and Agricultural Institute in Virginia. The principal of the school stressed practical education: industrial skills that would help build character and train African Americans for employment.

After graduating in 1875, Washington returned to Malden.

There, he taught children in day school and adults in night school for two years. For a year, he attended the Wayland Seminary in Washington, D.C., considering a possible career in law. But he returned to the Hampton Institute in 1879 as a teacher, and organized a night school for adults and supervised a training program for Native-American children.

In 1881, Washington was hired as principal of the Tuskegee Institute, a new school for African Americans in Tuskegee, Alabama. For the next thirty-four years, Washington used his job as director of the Tuskegee Institute to promote the economic advancement of African Americans. Drawing from his experience at the Hampton Institute, Washington developed a program that stressed teaching crafts, farming, and industrial skills. This practical education, he believed, would prepare African Americans for skilled manual jobs. Washington felt that the school needed to do more for its students than teach them how to read and write. He insisted on teaching the social and moral values of hard work, patience, and thrift. He believed that by applying their new skills, working hard, and living according to these moral virtues, African Americans would build wealth, buy land, and gain the social acceptance of whites.

Washington was often criticized by other African-American activists for ignoring the importance of political action aimed at winning equal civil rights for African Americans. Other social activists insisted that his program accepted existing race relations, capitalist use and abuse of African-American labor, and a power structure built on racism. But Washington believed that if African Americans and whites demonstrated mutual interests and a shared culture, the problem of racism would resolve itself. He was convinced that the acquisition of wealth and culture by African Americans would lead to their gradual acceptance and respect by whites. Although Washington hoped for full equality among people of different races, he placed a greater priority on economic security than on civil rights or political power. Washington promoted a path of progressive reforms, rather than revolution.

Washington's work to advance their training, education, and economic standing made him the leading spokesperson for African Americans at the turn of the century. In an 1895 speech

in Atlanta, he urged African Americans to set aside their struggle for political and social equality and concentrate instead on
economic advancement. The speech split African-American
activists into two groups: those who agreed with Washington's
program and those who opposed it. Those who called for political and social equality united and organized, which thus helped
spark the modern **civil rights movement**.

Wattleton, Faye

(1 9 4 3 –   )

ABORTION-RIGHTS ACTIVIST AND
HEAD OF PLANNED PARENTHOOD

Alyce Faye Wattleton was born in St. Louis. Her mother, a
seamstress and minister, instilled in her only daughter a sense
of her duty to help the less fortunate. In 1959, at age sixteen,
she began studying at Ohio State University. After receiving
an undergraduate degree in nursing in 1964, Wattleton taught
at a Dayton, Ohio, nursing school for two years. She won a
full scholarship to the Columbia University program in maternal and infant health care in 1966. While training as a midwife
at Harlem Hospital in New York, she first encountered the
suffering of women who tried to terminate their pregnancies illegally.

After earning her graduate degree in 1967, Wattleton worked
for two years as assistant public health director in Montgomery
County, Ohio. In 1970, she was appointed executive director
of the Dayton Planned Parenthood board. When, in 1977, the
Supreme Court ruled that states did not have to fund abortions
for poor women, two-thirds of the states cut off Medicaid fund-

ing of **abortions**. This action denied poor women the same access to safe, legal abortions that wealthier women had. Less than a year later, Wattleton was named president of the Planned Parenthood Federation of America. The first African American, first woman, and youngest person ever to head Planned Parenthood, Wattleton made the campaign to restore Medicaid funding of abortions her first priority.

This campaign initiated Wattleton's crusade to protect a woman's right to have a safe and legal abortion. The stand on a volatile political issue changed the image of Planned Parenthood, the nation's oldest and largest family planning agency. But Wattleton insisted that the right to choose abortion was fundamental to family planning. By definition, unwanted pregnancies are contrary to the concept of family planning. Wattleton repeatedly stressed that Planned Parenthood was not pro-abortion, but rather pro-choice.

As head of Planned Parenthood, Wattleton made countless public and television appearances to raise awareness of family planning issues. She saw family planning as part of the solution to such social ills as teenage pregnancy, sexually transmitted diseases, child abuse, poverty, and hunger. In addition to fighting for abortion rights, Wattleton increased funding for **contraceptive** (birth-control) research, community education programs, and programs to reduce the number of teen pregnancies. She also introduced a program to test for AIDS (Acquired Immune Deficiency Syndrome).

In the 1980s, the Reagan administration attempted to restrict a woman's right to an abortion. Planned Parenthood led the opposition to these efforts in court. When President Reagan cut back federal funds to family-planning clinics, Wattleton argued that the reduction would lead to more unwanted pregnancies and a greater demand for abortions. In 1982, Planned Parenthood refused to comply with a new regulation that required clinics that receive federal funds to notify parents when a minor asked for birth control and defeated this regulation in court.

When the Supreme Court in 1989 upheld a Missouri law that restricted abortions, many states began introducing new limits on abortion rights. The ruling sparked a revival of the pro-choice movement. Wattleton established the Planned Parenthood Action Fund to lobby state and federal lawmakers against abortion restrictions. She also proposed an amendment to the Constitution that would insure a woman's right to choose when and if she would have a child. Two years later, the Supreme Court upheld a regulation that prohibited family planning clinics that receive federal funding from providing information on abortions. Wattleton announced that Planned Parenthood would continue to defy the regulation even if it cost them their federal funding. After fourteen years as president of Planned Parenthood, Wattleton resigned in 1992 to develop a television talk show.

Woodsworth, James Shaver

(1874–1942)

SOCIAL REFORMER, MINISTER, AND POLITICIAN

James Shaver Woodsworth was born in Etobicoke, Ontario. The son of a Methodist missionary, James grew up in Brandon, Manitoba. Educated at Wesley College in Winnipeg, Woodsworth became a Methodist minister in 1896. While furthering his studies at Victoria College in Toronto and England's Oxford University from 1898 to 1900, he became aware of the human costs of capitalism and industrial labor in both Canada and Britain. He began preaching a reform-minded "social gospel," calling for changes in society that would establish the Kingdom of God on Earth. From 1904 to 1913, Woodsworth worked with poor immigrants in the slums of Winnipeg through that city's All People's Mission. In 1909, he wrote *Strangers Within Our Gates; or, Coming Canadians*, calling for social justice for the poor immigrants unable to make a living in Canada. Two years later, in *My Neighbor*, he called on the Christian church to work to improve society.

In 1913, Woodsworth resigned from the city mission to work for the newly formed Canadian Welfare League. By this time,

Woodsworth had become a supporter of the labor movement and an advocate of democratic **socialism**, which sought to eliminate the "evil" profit motive with collective control of industry and markets. He had also become a **pacifist**, viewing war as a competition for profits and power. In 1916, he was appointed director of the Bureau of Social Research in the three prairie provinces. He was fired a year later for making pacifist speeches and opposing the military draft during World War I. Woodsworth resigned from the ministry in 1918 to protest the church's support of the war. He worked on the docks in Vancouver and joined the dockworkers' union, becoming increasingly committed to the cause of labor reform.

In 1919, Winnipeg metal workers and construction workers went on strike, calling for recognition of their union. To support the strikers, 22,000 workers, including most city and government employees, joined in the Winnipeg General Strike. On what came to be known as "Bloody Saturday," police and soldiers broke up a nonviolent protest march. The troops fired into the crowd, killing two strikers and injuring twenty others.

Woodsworth wrote an editorial accusing the government of trampling on the rights of workers. He was arrested and charged with "seditious libel"—advocating the use of force to change society—which had been declared illegal during the war. The government later dropped its case, but never formally withdrew the charges.

Campaigning with a slogan of "Human Needs Before Property Rights," Woodsworth was elected to the House of Commons in 1921. In every one of his twenty-one years in the House, Woodsworth introduced a resolution to replace **capitalism** and its profit motive with **socialism**. But recognizing the slim chances that this resolution would pass, he also worked for more immediate social reforms. He attacked laws that favored banks and large corporations and pushed for social-security laws. In 1926, he traded his vote on another issue for a promise from the Prime Minister to enact an old-age **pension plan**. This plan, passed in 1927, became the foundation of the nation's social-security program.

In 1932, Woodsworth united groups of workers, farmers, socialists, and a group of radicals who had broken off from the

Progressive Party to found a federal socialist party. The party, called the Co-operative Commonwealth Federation (CCF) in 1933, pledged to serve human needs rather than making profits. To fight social injustice, the CCF proposed such welfare measures as unemployment insurance and universal socialized medicine, which were later adopted and enacted by other parties. Woodsworth served as president of the CCF until 1940, when he was named honorary president until his death.

As World War II approached, Woodsworth renewed his call for pacifism. In vain, he attempted to persuade the government to declare Canada's right to neutrality. Even the National Council of the CCF gave limited support to Canada's declaration of war in 1939. In his last major act in parliament, Woodsworth alone spoke out against the war.

Wright, Frances

(1795–1852)

SOCIAL REFORMER AND WRITER

Frances Wright was born in Dundee, Scotland. Although orphaned at two years old, her parents had left her a large inheritance. "Fanny" and her sister Camilla grew up with an aunt in England. At age twenty-one, the Wrights lived with a great-uncle who taught at Glasgow College in Scotland. Allowed to use the college library, Wright studied the culture and history of the United States. After a year in Glasgow, the Wrights set out for New York in 1818. The sisters spent almost two years traveling throughout the Northeast before returning to Great Britain. Wright's travel diary, *Views of Society and Manners in America*, published in 1821, presented a rosy view of the U.S.

The Wrights came to America again in 1824. Frances Wright was horrified by the abuse African Americans suffered in the slave trade. In 1825, she published a pamphlet that suggested a plan to end slavery without harming the whites of the South.

Wright wanted the government to set aside public land for slave labor. While working in the fields, the slaves would take advantage of schools and workshops that would "prepare" them for freedom. The profits of their work would then be used to purchase their freedom. To put her plan to the test, Wright bought 640 acres near Chicasaw Bluffs (later Memphis), Tennessee. She bought slaves and promised them freedom after five years of work at her settlement, which she called Nashoba. In ill health, Wright returned to Europe in 1827. When she returned a year later, poor crops and scandals had nearly destroyed Nashoba. Wright immediately wrote an article defending Nashoba. The article also attacked the institution of marriage, taboos against sex between whites and African Americans, and religion.

That year, Wright became part owner and editor of *The New-Harmony Gazette*, a newspaper linked with the **utopian** community of New Harmony, Indiana. She used the newspaper to promote such reforms as equal rights for women, birth control, and public education for all Americans (including women). In 1829, following a lecture tour of the East and Midwest, Wright moved the paper, now called *The Free Enquirer*, to New York. She continued to urge reforms: legal rights for married women, less rigid divorce laws, and an end to the death penalty. She helped spark a working-class movement that aimed at organizing workers and pushing for free public education. She also briefly returned to Tennessee to close Nashoba and personally found homes and jobs for around thirty freed slaves whom she resettled in Haiti. Wright achieved very few of the reforms she sought during her lifetime. But she identified the issues and raised questions about social justice that would inspire reformers for the next hundred years.

Yard, Molly

(c. 1912–   )

SOCIAL ACTIVIST, FEMINIST, AND PRESIDENT OF NATIONAL
ORGANIZATION OF WOMEN

Molly Yard worked to advance the cause of social justice for
more than fifty years. Molly was born and grew up in China,
the daughter of a Methodist missionary. Around 1925, her father was forced out of his job after urging the church to turn
control of missions over to the Chinese. He was later fired as
religious director of Northwestern University in Illinois for
actively supporting the labor, peace, and social justice movements. Taught social activism by her parents, Yard began
working toward social justice at Swarthmore College in Pennsylvania. When a sorority rejected a friend of Yard's because
she was Jewish, Yard organized a successful movement to abolish sororities and fraternities from campus.

Yard earned a degree in political science in 1933. She worked
for a brief time as a social worker, then became an organizer
and later chairperson for the American Student Union (ASU).
The ASU called for expanded programs of social welfare and
dramatic social change during the Depression. Because few
college graduates were finding jobs, Yard and the ASU sharply
criticized the "New Deal" programs of President Franklin
Roosevelt. Yard met with First Lady Eleanor Roosevelt to discuss the ASU's complaints. The two women became friends
and worked together for many years.

In 1938, Yard married but retained her own name. She
soon discovered that she could not open a joint bank account
with her husband unless they shared the same last name.
Yard became a political organizer for Democratic Party of-
fice-seekers in the 1940s and 1950s. During one campaign in
the late 1940s, an opponent accused her of being a Communist. Backed by supporting testimony from Eleanor Roosevelt, Yard won $1,500 and a front-page apology in a lawsuit.
While working as chair of the Pittsburgh Young Women's

Christian Association in the 1960s, she became active in the **civil rights movement**. In addition to working locally to end racism in housing, employment, and education, Yard worked for the passage of national civil-rights laws. She organized support in western Pennsylvania for the historic March on Washington in 1963, when Martin Luther King, Jr., called for a national civil rights act. The following year, she led a march on the Pittsburgh Post Office, where she delivered thousands of letters to Congress supporting the 1964 Civil Rights Act.

In the 1970s and 1980s, Yard turned to **feminism**, and joined the Pittsburgh chapter of the National Organization for Women (NOW), the nation's largest feminist group. In 1978, Yard headed a campaign to extend the deadline for state approval of the Equal Rights Amendment (ERA) to the U.S. Constitution. The amendment, which would have prohibited unequal treatment of men and women in jobs, housing, and other areas, failed to win approval in 1982. As the political director of NOW, Yard gained the support of more than 350 organizations as cosponsors of the 1986 National March for Women's Lives, a massive feminist rally in Washington, D.C. She also helped win several statewide votes affirming the right of women to obtain a safe, legal abortion. In 1987, Yard was elected president of NOW. The first grandmother in this post, Yard worked to reintroduce the ERA. She also sought to broaden the range of issues addressed by NOW. She attacked wasteful spending on U.S. defense programs and urged the cleanup of toxic waste dumps. In 1987, she organized a protest against the Catholic Church for betraying the cause of women's rights. Yard was arrested while demonstrating outside the Vatican Embassy during an American tour by the Pope. The following year, Yard presented a petition with one-hundred-thousand signatures to Congress. The petition urged Congress to pass the ERA once again, renewing the fight for a legal guarantee of women's equal rights. In 1990, a year after the U.S. invasion of Panama, Yard supported a bill introduced in Congress by Representative Pat Schroeder that would allow women to take part in military combat. Yard encourage NOW to address more fully the concerns of its lesbian members in 1991. Later that year, Yard was succeeded by Patricia Ireland as president of NOW, which had now grown to include 250,000 members—by far the largest feminist organization in the world. *See* KING, MARTIN LUTHER, JR., ROOSEVELT, ELEANOR; SCHROEDER, PAT

Glossary

abolitionist movement   a nineteenth-century social reform movement aimed at banning the practice of slavery. An activist committed to the cause was known as an abolitionist.

abortion   the termination of a pregnancy before birth.

affirmative action   job, promotion, housing, and education programs that offer favorable treatment to past victims of racism or sexism. Affirmative action policies take into account not only an applicant's present ability, but also the negative effects of past discrimination.

agism   prejudice and discrimination (unequal treatment) based on a person's age.

agitator   one who arouses public feeling, especially over controversial issues.

agnostic   a person who believes that one cannot know anything, especially about God, beyond one's experience.

anarchist   a person opposed to all forms of government or authority. A society with no government or authority is called anarchy.

annexation   the act of taking territory that was previously outside of a state's realm.

anthropology   the study of human beings. Anthropology is presently divided into three field: biological, cultural and social.

apartheid   the system of racial segregation that exist in the Republic of South Africa.

apprentice   one who is learning a trade through practical experience.

beat generation   a literary and artistic movement of the 1950's. Artists associated with the movement, such as Jack Kerouac, rejected traditional middle-class values and experimented with artistic forms.

blacklist   the unjust attempt to punish someone for their past or present political beliefs by refusing to hire their services.

boycott   a method of social protest in which a group refuses to buy certain goods or services. Boycotts aim to pressure the provider(s) of these goods or services to change policies that the protest group opposes.

braille   a system of writing designed for the blind, in which characters are represented by raised dots.

capitalism   an economic system in which companies, factories and land are privately owned and where goods are distributed in a competitive market, their prices determined by supply and demand.

civil disobedience   a strategy of social protest in which a group refuses to obey laws they regard as unjust. The ultimate goal of civil disobedience is to change the laws to provide greater social justice.

civil rights movement   a twentieth-century social reform movement aimed at winning equality for the nation's African Americans and other racial minorities.

commission   the assignment of a responsibility, or task.

commonlaw marriage   one in which the partners consider themselves married even though no official ceremony has taken place.

compensation   something that counterbalances or offsets a loss, such as payment given to an unemployed worker.

conservative   political outlook that is generally averse to change in existing institutions and policies.

contraception   method of preventing conception (impregnation).

countercultural movement   a social protest movement, led primarily by young adults and teenagers, in the 1960s. The young rebelled against the society created by their parents and grandparents. Although some protesters turned to drugs or left society to join communes, others demonstrated for peace and love and protested against war and social injustice.

cremated   when a dead body is reduced to ashes.

discrimination   unequal treatment based on some arbitrary difference: e.g., race, sex, religion, or ethnic background.

divinity   the state of being divine, godly.

draft   the method used by the army to select people for mandatory military service.

emancipation   freedom from slavery.

entomology   the study of insects.

environmental movement   a twentieth-century reform movement aimed at repairing, as much as possible, the damage done to the earth and its environment by human technology. The movement aims at maintaining the world's ability to support life. Environmental concerns include clean air, clean water, the richness of soil, and preventing the extinction of entire plant and animal species. Activists in the environmental movement are called environmentalists.

esophagus   the muscular tube that connects the mouth with the stomach.

evangelism   preaching of the gospel.

excommunicated   when an individual is excluded from membership of a particular community, usually that of a church, for behavior, beliefs or practices the community objects to.

fascist   one who believes in the doctrines of Fascism. Fascism places the state above the individual and often stresses allegiance to a dictatorial leader.

feminist movement   a social reform movement of the nineteenth and twentieth centuries, also called the women's rights movement. The goal of the movement is equal rights for women in the voting booth, in marriage, in the workplace, and under the law. An activist for women's rights is known as a feminist.

food chain   the hierarchical arrangement of organisms, where each organism preys on the one below it in the chain.

gender   the sex role that identifies a person as male or female.

Great Depression   a severe economic crisis in American history, that brought about large-scale poverty and unemployment, thought to have been partly caused by the stock-market crash of 1929.

illiteracy   the state of being unable to read or write.

internment   the confinement of a person (such as a prisoner of war) to a certain area.

irrigation   the method of supplying water, usually to land.

kibbutz   cooperative farming settlement in Israel. All farm activities are shared by the members of the kibbutz.

liberal   political outlook in favor of democratic reform and individual liberty.

martyr   a person who willingly or unwillingly dies for an activist cause.

monopoly   to have exclusive control of an aspect of the economy.

obstetrics   the science of childbirth.

occupational therapy   a method of therapy that prescribes creative activity as a means of cure.

organic farming   the production of food grown with natural, instead of chemical, fertilizers.

overseer   a supervisor, often of plantations.

pacifism   the opposition to war or violence as a means of settling disputes. A person who holds such a belief is called a pacifist.

paralyzed   to be rendered powerless, to lose control of motor or sensory functions because of injury, disease or birth defects.

pension plan   plan that insures that workers will receive periodic payments from their employers, or the government, after their retirement.

physiology   the science of how the different parts of living things work together to perform the functions necessary for life.

plantation   a large farming estate. Before abolition, plantations often used slave labor.

psychiatry   a branch of medicine that studies and treats mental disorders. A doctor who practices psychiatry is called a psychiatrist.

psychoanalysis   a treatment for some mental illnesses. In psychoanalysis, doctors ask patients questions about their lives. The doctors then search the patient's answers for clues to the causes of their problems.

prohibition   a law banning the sale of alcohol. Prohibition laws were enacted in many states and Canadian provinces in the late 1800s and early 1900s. The United States enacted a national prohibition law through an amendment to the Constitution in 1920. The amendment was repealed in 1933.

pseudonym   a false name, or pen name.

radicalism   a political doctrine in favor of extreme change.

sanctuary   a place of refuge, often offering immunity from the law, e.g. a church.

satirical   given to the use of irony and ridicule, usually for the purpose of exposing vice or hypocrisy.

segregation   separation of people based on race. Segregation often leads to inferior treatment or services provided to people of a particular race.

settlement house   a means of reforming poor neighborhoods from within. Settlement houses bring together social workers, educators, lawyers, artists, and other reformers to live and work in a city slum or other poor neighborhood. Through their work, residents of settlement houses improve living and working conditions within the neighborhood.

socialism   a system of government that outlaws private property and attempts to distribute goods and services on an equal basis to all individuals. The system is aimed at correcting the gap between the quality of life of the rich and that of the poor.

sociology   the science of human society.

suffrage movement   nineteenth- and twentieth-century activism directed at winning the right to vote (also called suffrage) for women, African Americans, and other non-whites. Those active in the movement were known as suffragists.

sweatshop   a workplace where long hours, low pay and unhealthy conditions are the norm.

temperance movement   a social reform movement of the late nineteenth and early twentieth centuries. The temperance movement opposed the drinking of alcohol. Temperance activists encouraged people to give up alcohol and also promoted prohibition laws that banned the sale of alcohol.

theology   the study of religion.

tuberculosis   a highly contagious infectious disease that usually affects the lungs.

unanimously   to decide on something with the agreement of all concerned.

underground   a secret movement or group that is usually against the established order. To go underground means to go into hiding.

Underground Railroad   a system used in the nineteenth century to help slaves escape from the South. "Station" was the name given to a home where slaves could be sheltered. People who helped the slaves on their journey were called "conductors."

utopia   a community of people united by shared ideals. Many social reformers of the nineteenth century attempted to form utopian communities. Community residents were expected to share, support one another, and pursue common interests.

valedictorian a person who delivers the farewell address at commencement, usually the highest ranking member of the graduating class.

vigilante a member of a self-appointed group organized to maintain order.

withdrawal the process of giving up addictive drugs.

Zionism a movement established in the nineteenth-century with the purpose of setting up a Jewish state in Palestine.

Sources and Further Reading

ABBOTT
James, Edward T., ed. *Notable American Women, 1607–1950*. Cambridge, MA: The Belknap Press of Harvard University Press, 1971.
The New Encyclopaedia Britannica, Fifteenth Edition. Chicago: Encyclopaedia Britannica, 1989.
Whitman, Alden, ed. *American Reformers*. New York: H.W. Wilson, 1985.

ABERNATHY
Abernathy, Ralph. *And the Walls Came Tumbling Down*. NY: Harper & Row, 1989.
1991 Britannica Book of the Year. Chicago: Encyclopaedia Britannica, 1991.
Current Biography. New York: H.W. Wilson, July, 1968.
Current Biography. New York: H.W. Wilson, June, 1990.
Severo, Richard. "Ralph David Abernathy, Rights Pioneer, Is Dead at 64." *The New York Times*, April 18, 1990.

ADDAMS
Brin, Ruth F. *Contributions of Women: Social Reform*. Minneapolis: Dillon Press, 1977.
Jacobs, William Jay. *Great Lives: Human Rights*. New York: Charles Scribner's Sons, 1990.
James, Edward T., ed. *Notable American Women, 1607–1950*. Cambridge, MA: The Belknap Press of Harvard University Press, 1971.
Kittredge, Mary. *Jane Addams*. New York: Chelsea House, 1988.
The New Encyclopaedia Britannica, Fifteenth Edition. Chicago: Encyclopaedia Britannica, 1989.
Peavy, Linda and Ursula Smith. *Dreams Into Deeds*. New York: Charles Scribner's Sons, 1985.
Wheeler, Leslie A. *Jane Addams*. Englewood Cliffs, NJ: Silver Burdett Press, 1990.
Whitman, Alden, ed. *American Reformers*. New York: H.W. Wilson, 1985.

ALINSKY
Current Biography. New York: H.W. Wilson, November, 1968.
Current Biography. New York: H.W. Wilson, July, 1972.
The New Encyclopaedia Britannica, Fifteenth Edition. Chicago: Encyclopaedia Britannica, 1989.
Whitman, Alden, ed. *American Reformers*. New York: H.W. Wilson, 1985.

ANDREWS (FANNIE FERN PHILLIPS)
James, Edward T., ed. *Notable American Women, 1607–1950*. Cambridge, MA: The Belknap Press of Harvard University Press, 1971.
Whitman, Alden, ed. *American Reformers*. New York: H.W. Wilson, 1985.

ANTHONY
Archer, Jules. *Breaking Barriers*. New York: Viking Press, 1991.
Cooper, Ilene. *Susan B. Anthony*. New York: Franklin Watts, 1984.
Jacobs, William Jay. *Great Lives: Human Rights*. New York: Charles Scribner's Sons, 1990.
James, Edward T., ed. *Notable American Women, 1607–1950*. Cambridge, MA: The Belknap Press of Harvard University Press, 1971.

The New Encyclopaedia Britannica, Fifteenth Edition. Chicago: Encyclopaedia Britannica, 1989.

Weisberg, Barbara. *Susan B. Anthony*. New York: Chelsea House, 1988.

Whitman, Alden, ed. *American Reformers*. New York: H.W. Wilson, 1985.

BAKER

James, Edward T., ed. *Notable American Women, 1607–1950*. Cambridge, MA: The Belknap Press of Harvard University Press, 1971.

Peavy, Linda and Ursula Smith. *Women Who Changed Things: Nine Lives That Made a Difference*. New York: Charles Scribner's Sons, 1983.

Whitman, Alden, ed. *American Reformers*. New York: H.W. Wilson, 1985.

BALCH

James, Edward T., ed. *Notable American Women, 1607–1950*. Cambridge, MA: The Belknap Press of Harvard University Press, 1971.

Whitman, Alden, ed. *American Reformers*. New York: H.W. Wilson, 1985.

BARRETT

James, Edward T., ed. *Notable American Women, 1607–1950*. Cambridge, MA: The Belknap Press of Harvard University Press, 1971.

The New Encyclopaedia Britannica, Fifteenth Edition. Chicago: Encyclopaedia Britannica, 1989.

BARTON

Dolin, Arnold. *Great American Heroines*. New York: Hart Publishing, 1960.

Jacobs, William Jay. *Great Lives: Human Rights*. New York: Charles Scribner's Sons, 1990.

BELLANCA

James, Edward T., ed. *Notable American Women, 1607–1950*. Cambridge, MA: The Belknap Press of Harvard University Press, 1971.

Whitman, Alden, ed. *American Reformers*. New York: H.W. Wilson, 1985.

BERRIGAN (DANIEL)

Current Biography. New York: H.W. Wilson, September, 1970.

BERRIGAN (PHILIP)

Current Biography. New York: H.W. Wilson, February, 1976.

BIRNEY

The New Encyclopaedia Britannica, Fifteenth Edition. Chicago: Encyclopaedia Britannica, 1989.

Whitman, Alden, ed. *American Reformers*. New York: H.W. Wilson, 1985.

BLACKWELLS (ELIZABETH AND EMILY)

Baker, Rachel. *The First Woman Doctor*. New York: Scholastic Books, 1961.

Brown, Jordan. *Elizabeth Blackwell*. New York: Chelsea House, 1989.

Hays, Elinor Rice. *Those Extraordinary Blackwells*. New York: Harcourt Brace Jovanovich, 1967.

James, Edward T., ed. *Notable American Women, 1607–1950*. Cambridge, MA: The Belknap Press of Harvard University Press, 1971.

The New Encyclopaedia Britannica, Fifteenth Edition. Chicago: Encyclopaedia Britannica, 1989.

Sabin, Francene. *Elizabeth Blackwell: The First Woman Doctor*. Mahwah, NJ: Troll Associates, 1982.

Schleichert, Elizabeth. *The Life of Elizabeth Blackwell*. Frederick, MD: Twenty-First Century Books, 1992.

Whitman, Alden, ed. *American Reformers*. New York: H.W. Wilson, 1985.

BLOOMER

Archer, Jules. *The Unpopular Ones*. New York: Crowell-Collier Press, 1968.
James, Edward T., ed. *Notable American Women, 1607–1950*. Cambridge, MA: The Belknap Press of Harvard University Press, 1971.
The New Encyclopaedia Britannica, Fifteenth Edition. Chicago: Encyclopaedia Britannica, 1989.
Whitman, Alden, ed. *American Reformers*. New York: H.W. Wilson, 1985.

BONNEY

James, Edward T., ed. *Notable American Women, 1607–1950*. Cambridge, MA: The Belknap Press of Harvard University Press, 1971.
Whitman, Alden, ed. *American Reformers*. New York: H.W. Wilson, 1985.

BONNIN

James, Edward T., ed. *Notable American Women, 1607–1950*. Cambridge, MA: The Belknap Press of Harvard University Press, 1971.
Whitman, Alden, ed. *American Reformers*. New York: H.W. Wilson, 1985.

BRADY

Current Biography. New York: H.W. Wilson, October, 1991.

BROWN

Bennett, Lerone Jr. *Pioneers in Protest*. Chicago: Johnson Publishing, 1968.
Collins, James L. *John Brown and the Fight Against Slavery*. Brookfield, CT: The Millbrook Press, 1991.
Kent, Zachary. *The Story of John Brown's Raid on Harpers Ferry*. Chicago: Children's Press, 1988.
The New Encyclopaedia Britannica, Fifteenth Edition. Chicago: Encyclopaedia Britannica, 1989.
Scott, John A. and Robert A. Scott. *John Brown of Harpers Ferry*. New York: Facts on File, 1988.
Whitman, Alden, ed. *American Reformers*. New York: H.W. Wilson, 1985.

BROWNMILLER

Current Biography. New York: H.W. Wilson, January, 1978.

CARMICHAEL

Current Biography. New York: H.W. Wilson, April, 1970.

CARSON

Jezer, Marty. *Rachel Carson*. New York: Chelsea House Publishers, 1988.
Stwertka, Eve. *Rachel Carson*. New York: Franklin Watts, 1991.

CHAVEZ

Jacobs, William Jay. *Great Lives: Human Rights*. New York: Charles Scribner's Sons, 1990.
Roberts, Naurice. *Cesar Chavez and La Causa*. Chicago: Children's Press, 1986.

CHISHOLM

Brownmiller, Susan. *Shirley Chisholm*. Garden City, NY: Doubleday and Co., 1970.
Current Biography. New York: H.W. Wilson, October, 1969.
Haskins, Jim. *One More River to Cross*. New York: Scholastic Books, 1992.
Ross, Pat. *Young and Female: Turning Points in the Lives of Eight American Women*. New York: Random House, 1972.
Scheader, Catherine. *Shirley Chisholm: Teacher and Congresswoman*. Hillsdale, NJ: Enslow Publishers, 1990.

CLEAVER
Current Biography. New York: H.W. Wilson, March, 1970.
The New Encyclopaedia Britannica, Fifteenth Edition. Chicago: Encyclopaedia Britannica, 1989.

COFFIN
Current Biography. New York: H.W. Wilson, April, 1980.
Playboy Magazine, editors. *Voices of Concern.* New York: Harcourt Brace Jovanovich, 1971.

COMMONER
Current Biography. New York: H.W. Wilson, September, 1970.

CONVERSE
James, Edward T., ed. *Notable American Women, 1607–1950.* Cambridge, MA: The Belknap Press of Harvard University Press, 1971.
Whitman, Alden, ed. *American Reformers.* New York: H.W. Wilson, 1985.

DAVIS
Bray, Rosemary L. "A Black Panther's Long Journey." *The New York Times Magazine*, January 31, 1993.
Current Biography. New York: H.W. Wilson, November, 1972.
The New Encyclopaedia Britannica, Fifteenth Edition. Chicago: Encyclopaedia Britannica, 1989.

DAY
Church, Carol Bauer. *Dorothy Day: Friend of the Poor.* Minneapolis, MN: Greenhaven Press, 1976.
Current Biography. New York: H.W. Wilson, April, 1962.
Jacobs, William Jay. *Great Lives: Human Rights.* New York: Charles Scribner's Sons, 1990.
Nies, Judith. *Seven Women: Portraits from the American Radical Tradition.* New York: The Viking Press, 1977.
Ross, Pat. *Young and Female: Turning Points in the Lives of Eight American Women.* New York: Random House, 1972.
Whitman, Alden, ed. *American Reformers.* New York: H.W. Wilson, 1985.

DECTER
Current Biography. New York: H.W. Wilson, April, 1982.

DELLINGER
Current Biography. New York: H.W. Wilson, August, 1976.

DIX
Daugherty, Sonia. *Ten Brave Women.* New York: J.B. Lippincott, 1953.
Jacobs, William Jay. *Great Lives: Human Rights.* New York: Charles Scribner's Sons, 1990.
James, Edward T., ed. *Notable American Women, 1607–1950.* Cambridge, MA: The Belknap Press of Harvard University Press, 1971.
The New Encyclopaedia Britannica, Fifteenth Edition. Chicago: Encyclopaedia Britannica, 1989.
Whitman, Alden, ed. *American Reformers.* New York: H.W. Wilson, 1985.

DOUGLASS
Douglass, Frederick, adapted by Barbara Ritchie. *Life and Times of Frederick Douglass.* New York: Thomas Y. Crowell, 1966.
Jacobs, William Jay. *Great Lives: Human Rights.* New York: Charles Scribner's Sons, 1990.

Rollins, Charlemae Hill. *They Showed the Way: Forty American Negro Leaders*. New York: Thomas Y. Crowell, 1964.

Young, Margaret B. *Black American Leaders*. New York: Franklin Watts, 1969.

DUMONT

The Canadian Encyclopedia, Second Edition. Edmonton, Alberta: Hurtig Publishers, 1988.

Colombo, John Robert. *Colombo's Canadian References*. Toronto: Oxford University Press, 1976.

Morton, Desmond. *Rebellions in Canada*. Toronto: Grolier Limited, 1979.

Story, Norah. *The Oxford Companion to Canadian History and Literature*. Toronto: Oxford University Press, 1967.

EASTMAN

James, Edward T., ed. *Notable American Women, 1607–1950*. Cambridge, MA: The Belknap Press of Harvard University Press, 1971.

Whitman, Alden, ed. *American Reformers*. New York: H.W. Wilson, 1985.

EVANS

James, Edward T., ed. *Notable American Women, 1607–1950*. Cambridge, MA: The Belknap Press of Harvard University Press, 1971.

The New Encyclopaedia Britannica, Fifteenth Edition. Chicago: Encyclopaedia Britannica, 1989.

Whitman, Alden, ed. *American Reformers*. New York: H.W. Wilson, 1985.

FAUNTROY

Current Biography. New York: H.W. Wilson, February, 1979.

FLETCHER

James, Edward T., ed. *Notable American Women, 1607–1950*. Cambridge, MA: The Belknap Press of Harvard University Press, 1971.

The New Encyclopaedia Britannica, Fifteenth Edition. Chicago: Encyclopaedia Britannica, 1989.

Whitman, Alden, ed. *American Reformers*. New York: H.W. Wilson, 1985.

FOX

Current Biography. New York: H.W. Wilson, May, 1970.

Current Biography. New York: H.W. Wilson, June, 1984.

FRIEDAN

Archer, Jules. *Breaking Barriers*. New York: The Viking Press, 1991.

Blau, Justine. *Betty Friedan*. New York: Chelsea House, 1989.

Current Biography. New York: H.W. Wilson, March, 1989.

Meltzer, Milton. *Betty Friedan: A Voice for Women's Rights*. New York: Viking Kestrel, 1985.

The New Encyclopaedia Britannica, Fifteenth Edition. Chicago: Encyclopaedia Britannica, 1989.

Taylor-Boyd, Susan. *Betty Friedan*. Milwaukee: Gareth Stevens Children's Books, 1990.

GLASSER

Current Biography. New York: H.W. Wilson, January, 1986.

GOLDMAN

James, Edward T., ed. *Notable American Women, 1607–1950*. Cambridge, MA: The Belknap Press of Harvard University Press, 1971.

The New Encyclopaedia Britannica, Fifteenth Edition. Chicago: Encyclopaedia Britannica, 1989.

Waldstreicher, David. *Emma Goldman*. New York: Chelsea House, 1990.

Whitman, Alden, ed. *American Reformers*. New York: H.W. Wilson, 1985.

GREELEY

Archer, Jules. *Fighting Journalist: Horace Greeley*. New York: Julian Messner, 1966.

Archer, Jules. *The Unpopular Ones*. New York: Crowell-Collier Press, 1968.

The New Encyclopaedia Britannica, Fifteenth Edition. Chicago: Encyclopaedia Britannica, 1989.

Whitman, Alden, ed. *American Reformers*. New York: H.W. Wilson, 1985.

GREEN

Current Biography. New York: H.W. Wilson, February, 1988.

HALE

1993 Britannica Book of the Year. Chicago: Encyclopaedia Britannica, 1993.

Current Biography. New York: H.W. Wilson, July, 1985.

Hale, Lorraine. *The House That Love Built*. New York: Hale House, 1991.

HARRINGTON

1990 Britannica Book of the Year. Chicago: Encyclopaedia Britannica, 1990.

Current Biography. New York: H.W. Wilson, October, 1988.

Current Biography. New York: H.W. Wilson, September, 1989.

HAYDEN

Current Biography. New York: H.W. Wilson, April, 1976.

HAYES

Current Biography. New York: H.W. Wilson, April, 1989.

HILL (JOE)

Koustrup, Susan. *Shattered Dreams: Joe Hill*. Translated by J.R. Christianson and Birgitte Christianson. Mankato, MN: Creative Education, 1982.

The New Encyclopaedia Britannica, Fifteenth Edition. Chicago: Encyclopaedia Britannica, 1989.

Stavis, Barrie. *The Man Who Never Died*. South Brunswick, NJ: A. S. Barnes, 1972.

Whitman, Alden, ed. *American Reformers*. New York: H.W. Wilson, 1985.

HOFFMAN

1990 Britannica Book of the Year. Chicago: Encyclopaedia Britannica, 1990.

Current Biography. New York: H.W. Wilson, April, 1981.

Current Biography. New York: H.W. Wilson, June, 1989.

Jezer, Marty. *Abbie Hoffman: American Rebel*. New Brunswick, NJ: Rutgers University Press, 1992.

Simon, Dan, ed. *The Best of Abbie Hoffman*. New York: Four Walls Eight Windows, 1989.

HOWE

James, Edward T., ed. *Notable American Women, 1607–1950*. Cambridge, MA: The Belknap Press of Harvard University Press, 1971.

Bolton, Sarah Knowles. *Famous Leaders Among Women*. Freeport, New York: Books for Libraries Press, 1972.

The New Encyclopaedia Britannica, Fifteenth Edition. Chicago: Encyclopaedia Britannica, 1989.

Pollard, Michael. *People Who Care*. Ada, OK: Garrett Educational Corporation, 1992.

Whitman, Alden, ed. *American Reformers*. New York: H.W. Wilson, 1985.

JACKSON
1989 Britannica Book of the Year. Chicago: Encyclopaedia Britannica, 1989.
Celsi, Teresa. *Jesse Jackson and Political Power.* Brookfield, CT: The Millbrook Press, 1991.
Current Biography. New York: H.W. Wilson, January, 1986.
Kosof, Anna. *Jesse Jackson.* New York: Franklin Watts, 1987.
McKissack, Patricia. *Jesse Jackson: Keep Hope Alive.* New York: Scholastic Books, 1989.
Otfinoski, Steven. *Jesse Jackson.* New York: Fawcett Columbine, 1989.
Wilkinson, Brenda. *Jesse Jackson: Still Fighting for the Dream.* Englewood Cliffs, NJ: Silver Burdett Press, 1990.

JACOB
Current Biography. New York: H.W. Wilson, February, 1986.

JOHNSON
Current Biography. New York: H.W. Wilson, February, 1985.

JONES
Atkinson, Linda. *Mother Jones: The Most Dangerous Woman in America.* New York: Crown Publishers, 1978.
James, Edward T., ed. *Notable American Women, 1607–1950.* Cambridge, MA: The Belknap Press of Harvard University Press, 1971.
Jones, Mary. Edited by Mary Field Parton, *Autobiography of Mother Jones.* New York: Arno, 1969.
Merriam, Eve, ed. *Growing Up Female in America.* Garden City, NY: Doubleday, 1971.
The New Encyclopaedia Britannica, Fifteenth Edition. Chicago: Encyclopaedia Britannica, 1989.
Peavy, Linda and Ursula Smith. *Dreams Into Deeds.* New York: Charles Scribner's Sons, 1985.
Werstein, Irving. *Labor's Defiant Lady: The Story of Mother Jones.* New York: Thomas Y. Crowell, 1969.
Whitman, Alden, ed. *American Reformers.* New York: H.W. Wilson, 1985.

KELLER
Current Biography. New York: H.W. Wilson, December, 1942.
Current Biography. New York: H.W. Wilson, July, 1968.
Graff, Stewart and Polly Anne Graff. *Helen Keller: Toward the Light.* Champaign, IL: Garrard Publishing, 1965.
Keller, Helen. *The Story of My Life.* New York: Doubleday, .
Kudlinski, Kathleen V. *Helen Keller: A Light for the Blind.* New York: Viking Kestrel, 1989.
Lash, Joseph P. *Helen and Teacher: The Story of Helen Keller and Anne Sullivan Macy.* New York: Delacourte, 1980.
The New Encyclopaedia Britannica, Fifteenth Edition. Chicago: Encyclopaedia Britannica, 1989.
Sicherman, Barbara and Carol Hurd Green. *Notable American Women: The Modern Period.* Cambridge, MA: The Belknap Press of Harvard University Press, 1980.
Wepman, Dennis. *Helen Keller.* New York: Chelsea House, 1987.

KENYON
Current Biography. New York: H.W. Wilson, April, 1972.
Sicherman, Barbara and Carol Hurd Green. *Notable American Women: The Modern Period.* Cambridge, MA: The Belknap Press of Harvard University Press, 1980.

KING

deKay, James T. *Meet Martin Luther King, Jr.* New York: Random House, 1969.

Jacobs, William Jay. *Great Lives: Human Rights.* New York: Charles Scribner's Sons, 1990.

Young, Margaret B. *Black American Leaders.* New York: Franklin Watts, 1969.

KOVIC

Current Biography. New York: H.W. Wilson, August, 1990.

KOZOL

Current Biography. New York: H.W. Wilson, January, 1986.

KUHN

Current Biography. New York: H.W. Wilson, July, 1978.

LATHROP

James, Edward T., ed. *Notable American Women, 1607–1950.* Cambridge, MA: The Belknap Press of Harvard University Press, 1971.

The New Encyclopaedia Britannica, Fifteenth Edition. Chicago: Encyclopaedia Britannica, 1989.

Whitman, Alden, ed. *American Reformers.* New York: H.W. Wilson, 1985.

LEWIS

Current Biography. New York: H.W. Wilson, September, 1980.

LOVEJOY

The New Encyclopaedia Britannica, Fifteenth Edition. Chicago: Encyclopaedia Britannica, 1989.

Whitman, Alden, ed. *American Reformers.* New York: H.W. Wilson, 1985.

LOWERY

Current Biography. New York: H.W. Wilson, November, 1982.

MACKENZIE

The Canadian Encyclopedia, Second Edition. Edmonton, Alberta: Hurtig Publishers, 1988.

Colombo, John Robert. *Colombo's Canadian References.* Toronto: Oxford University Press, 1976.

Morton, Desmond. *Rebellions in Canada.* Toronto: Grolier Limited, 1979.

The New Encyclopaedia Britannica, Fifteenth Edition. Chicago: Encyclopaedia Britannica, 1989.

Story, Norah. *The Oxford Companion to Canadian History and Literature.* Toronto: Oxford University Press, 1967.

MALCOLM X

Adoff, Arnold. *Malcolm X.* New York: Thomas Y. Crowell, 1970.

Haskins, James. *Revolutionaries: Agents of Change.* Philadelphia: J.B. Lippincott, 1971.

MANKILLER

Current Biography. New York: H.W. Wilson, November, 1988.

Glassman, Bruce. *Wilma Mankiller: Chief of the Cherokee Nation.* New York: Blackbirch Press, 1992.

Simon, Charnan. *Wilma P. Mankiller: Chief of the Cherokee.* Chicago: Children's Press, 1991.

MARSHALL

Current Biography. New York: H.W. Wilson, September, 1989.

The New Encyclopaedia Britannica, Fifteenth Edition. Chicago: Encyclopaedia Britannica, 1989.

MCCLUNG

The Canadian Encyclopedia, Second Edition. Edmonton, Alberta: Hurtig Publishers, 1988.
Morton, Desmond. *Rebellions in Canada*. Toronto: Grolier Limited, 1979.
Ray, Janet. *Towards Women's Rights*. Toronto: Grolier Limited, 1981.
Story, Norah. *The Oxford Companion to Canadian History and Literature*. Toronto: Oxford University Press, 1967.

MEANS

Current Biography. New York: H.W. Wilson, January, 1978.

MILLETT

Current Biography. New York: H.W. Wilson, January, 1971.

MOTT

James, Edward T., ed. *Notable American Women, 1607–1950*. Cambridge, MA: The Belknap Press of Harvard University Press, 1971.
Levinson, Nancy Smiler. *The First Women Who Spoke Out*. Minneapolis, MN: Dillon Press, 1983.
The New Encyclopaedia Britannica, Fifteenth Edition. Chicago: Encyclopaedia Britannica, 1989.
Whitman, Alden, ed. *American Reformers*. New York: H.W. Wilson, 1985.

MURPHY

The Canadian Encyclopedia, Second Edition. Edmonton, Alberta: Hurtig Publishers, 1988.
Colombo, John Robert. *Colombo's Canadian References*. Toronto: Oxford University Press, 1976.
Morton, Desmond. *Rebellions in Canada*. Toronto: Grolier Limited, 1979.
Ray, Janet. *Towards Women's Rights*. Toronto: Grolier Limited, 1981.
Story, Norah. *The Oxford Companion to Canadian History and Literature*. Toronto: Oxford University Press, 1967.

NADER

Current Biography. New York: H.W. Wilson, April, 1986.
The New Encyclopaedia Britannica, Fifteenth Edition. Chicago: Encyclopaedia Britannica, 1989.

NEWTON

1990 Britannica Book of the Year. Chicago: Encyclopaedia Britannica, 1990.
Current Biography. New York: H.W. Wilson, February, 1973.
Current Biography. New York: H.W. Wilson, October, 1989.
Haskins, James. *Profiles in Black Power*. Garden City, NY: Doubleday, 1972.

OSBORNE

The New Encyclopaedia Britannica, Fifteenth Edition. Chicago: Encyclopaedia Britannica, 1989.
Whitman, Alden, ed. *American Reformers*. New York: H.W. Wilson, 1985.

PACKARD

James, Edward T., ed. *Notable American Women, 1607–1950*. Cambridge, MA: The Belknap Press of Harvard University Press, 1971.
Whitman, Alden, ed. *American Reformers*. New York: H.W. Wilson, 1985.

PAINE

Coolidge, Olivia. *Tom Paine, Revolutionary*. New York: Charles Scribner's Sons, 1969.

Dabney, Virginius, ed. *The Patriots*. New York: Atheneum, 1975.

Jacobs, William Jay. *Great Lives: Human Rights*. New York: Charles Scribner's Sons, 1990.

The New Encyclopaedia Britannica, Fifteenth Edition. Chicago: Encyclopaedia Britannica, 1989.

O'Connor, Richard. *The Common Sense of Tom Paine*. New York: McGraw-Hill, 1969.

Vail, John. *Thomas Paine*. New York: Chelsea House, 1990.

Whitman, Alden, ed. *American Reformers*. New York: H.W. Wilson, 1985.

PAPINEAU

The Canadian Encyclopedia, Second Edition. Edmonton, Alberta: Hurtig Publishers, 1988.

Colombo, John Robert. *Colombo's Canadian References*. Toronto: Oxford University Press, 1976.

Morton, Desmond. *Rebellions in Canada*. Toronto: Grolier Limited, 1979.

The New Encyclopaedia Britannica, Fifteenth Edition. Chicago: Encyclopaedia Britannica, 1989.

Story, Norah. *The Oxford Companion to Canadian History and Literature*. Toronto: Oxford University Press, 1967.

PARKS

Current Biography. New York: H.W. Wilson, May, 1989.

Friese, Kai. *Rosa Parks: The Movement Organizes*. Englewood Cliffs, NJ: Silver Burdett Press, 1990.

Meriwether, Louise. *Don't Ride the Bus on Monday: The Rosa Parks Story*. Englewood Cliffs, NJ: Prentice-Hall, 1973.

The New Encyclopaedia Britannica, Fifteenth Edition. Chicago: Encyclopaedia Britannica, 1989.

Parks, Rosa with Jim Haskins. *Rosa Parks: My Story*. New York: Dial Books, 1992.

Siegel, Beatrice. *The Year They Walked: Rosa Parks and the Montgomery Bus Boycott*. New York: Four Winds Press, 1992.

Sterne, Emma Gelders. *I Have a Dream*. New York: Alfred A. Knopf, 1965.

PERTSCHUK

Current Biography. New York: H.W. Wilson, September, 1986.

PESOTTA

Sicherman, Barbara and Carol Hurd Green. *Notable American Women: The Modern Period*. Cambridge, MA: The Belknap Press of Harvard University Press, 1980.

PETTIT

James, Edward T., ed. *Notable American Women, 1607–1950*. Cambridge, MA: The Belknap Press of Harvard University Press, 1971.

RIEL

The Canadian Encyclopedia, Second Edition. Edmonton, Alberta: Hurtig Publishers, 1988.

Colombo, John Robert. *Colombo's Canadian References*. Toronto: Oxford University Press, 1976.

Flanagan, Thomas and Claude Rocan. *Rebellion in the North-West*. Toronto: Grolier Limited.

Lurie, Nancy Oestreich. *North American Indian Lives*. Milwaukee: Milwaukee Public Museum, 1985.

McNamee, James. *Them Damn Canadians Hanged Louis Riel!* Toronto: Macmillan, 1971.

Morton, Desmond. *Rebellions in Canada*. Toronto: Grolier Limited, 1979.
The New Encyclopaedia Britannica, Fifteenth Edition. Chicago: Encyclopaedia Britannica, 1989.
Story, Norah. *The Oxford Companion to Canadian History and Literature*. Toronto: Oxford University Press, 1967.

RIIS
Jacobs, William Jay. *Great Lives: Human Rights*. New York: Charles Scribner's Sons, 1990.
Meyer, Edith Patterson. *Champions of the Four Freedoms*. Boston: Little, Brown & Co., 1966.
Meyer, Edith Patterson. *"Not Charity, But Justice": The Story of Jacob A. Riis*. New York: The Vanguard Press, 1974.
The New Encyclopaedia Britannica, Fifteenth Edition. Chicago: Encyclopaedia Britannica, 1989.
Ware, Louise. *Jacob A. Riis: Police Reporter, Reformer, Useful Citizen*. Appleton-Century, 1938.
Whitman, Alden, ed. *American Reformers*. New York: H.W. Wilson, 1985.

ROOSEVELT
Current Biography. New York: H.W. Wilson, January, 1949.
Current Biography. New York: H.W. Wilson, January, 1963.
Faber, Doris. *Eleanor Roosevelt: First Lady of the World*. New York: Viking Kestrel, 1985.
Jacobs, William Jay. *Eleanor Roosevelt: A Life of Happiness and Tears*. New York: Coward-McCann, 1983.
James, Edward T., ed. *Notable American Women, 1607–1950*. Cambridge, MA: The Belknap Press of Harvard University Press, 1971.
McAuley, Karen. *Eleanor Roosevelt*. New York: Chelsea House, 1987.
The New Encyclopaedia Britannica, Fifteenth Edition. Chicago: Encyclopaedia Britannica, 1989.
Schaff, Lois. *Eleanor Roosevelt: First Lady of American Liberalism*. Boston: Twayne Publishers, 1987.
Whitman, Alden, ed. *American Reformers*. New York: H.W. Wilson, 1985.
Whitney, Sharon. *Eleanor Roosevelt*. New York: Franklin Watts, 1982.

SAID
Current Biography. New York: H.W. Wilson, November, 1989.

SANGER
Archer, Jules. *Breaking Barriers*. New York: Viking, 1991.
Brin, Ruth F. *Contributions of Women: Social Reform*. Minneapolis: Dillon Press, 1977.
Current Biography. New York: H.W. Wilson, November, 1966.
The New Encyclopaedia Britannica, Fifteenth Edition. Chicago: Encyclopaedia Britannica, 1989.
Ross, Pat. *Young and Female: Turning Points in the Lives of Eight American Women*. New York: Random House, 1972.
Sicherman, Barbara and Carol Hurd Green. *Notable American Women: The Modern Period*. Cambridge, MA: The Belknap Press of Harvard University Press, 1980.
Taylor, Kathryn. *Generations of Denial*. New York: Times Change Press, 1971.
Topalian, Elyse. *Margaret Sanger*. New York: Franklin Watts, 1984.
Whitman, Alden, ed. *American Reformers*. New York: H.W. Wilson, 1985.

SCHLAFLY
Current Biography. New York: H.W. Wilson, June, 1978.

SCHNEIDERMAN
Current Biography. New York: H.W. Wilson, October, 1972.
Sicherman, Barbara and Carol Hurd Green. *Notable American Women: The Modern Period.* Cambridge, MA: The Belknap Press of Harvard University Press, 1980.
Whitman, Alden, ed. *American Reformers.* New York: H.W. Wilson, 1985.

SCHOFF
James, Edward T., ed. *Notable American Women, 1607–1950.* Cambridge, MA: The Belknap Press of Harvard University Press, 1971.
Whitman, Alden, ed. *American Reformers.* New York: H.W. Wilson, 1985.

SCHROEDER
Current Biography. New York: H.W. Wilson, October, 1978.

SEEGER
Current Biography. New York: H.W. Wilson, December, 1963.
The New Encyclopaedia Britannica, Fifteenth Edition. Chicago: Encyclopaedia Britannica, 1989.

SMEAL
Current Biography. New York: H.W. Wilson, March, 1980.

SMITH (ABBY HADASSAH AND JULIA EVELINA)
James, Edward T., ed. *Notable American Women, 1607–1950.* Cambridge, MA: The Belknap Press of Harvard University Press, 1971.
Whitman, Alden, ed. *American Reformers.* New York: H.W. Wilson, 1985.

SOLOMON
James, Edward T., ed. *Notable American Women, 1607-1950.* Cambridge, MA: The Belknap Press of Harvard University Press, 1971.

SPOCK
Current Biography. New York: H.W. Wilson, November, 1969.
LeVert, Suzanne. *The Doubleday Book of Famous Americans.* Garden City, NY: Doubleday, 1989.
The New Encyclopaedia Britannica, Fifteenth Edition. Chicago: Encyclopaedia Britannica, 1989.

STANTON
Beatty, Patricia. *Hail Columbia.* New York: William Morrow, 1970.
Faber, Doris. *Oh Lizzie! The Life of Elizabeth Cady Stanton.* New York: Lothrop, Lee & Shepard, 1972.
Faber, Doris. *Petticoat Politics: How American Women Won the Right to Vote.* New York: Lothrop, Lee & Shepard, 1967.
Jacob, William Jay. *Great Lives: Human Rights.* New York: Charles Scribner's Sons, 1990.
Severn, Bill. *Free But Not Equal: How Women Won the Right to Vote.* New York: Julian Messner, 1967.

STEINEM
Current Biography. New York: H.W. Wilson, March, 1988.
Daffron, Carolyn. *Gloria Steinem.* New York: Chelsea House, 1990.
Henry, Sondra and Emily Taitz. *One Woman's Power: A Biography of Gloria Steinem.* Minneapolis: Dillon Press, 1987.
Hoff, Mark. *Gloria Steinem: The Women's Movement.* Brookfield, CT: Millbrook Press, 1991.

STEVENS (ALZINA)
James, Edward T., ed. *Notable American Women, 1607–1950*. Cambridge, MA: The Belknap Press of Harvard University Press, 1971.
The New Encyclopaedia Britannica, Fifteenth Edition. Chicago: Encyclopaedia Britannica, 1989.
Whitman, Alden, ed. *American Reformers*. New York: H.W. Wilson, 1985.

STOKES
James, Edward T., ed. *Notable American Women, 1607–1950*. Cambridge, MA: The Belknap Press of Harvard University Press, 1971.
Whitman, Alden, ed. *American Reformers*. New York: H.W. Wilson, 1985.

STONE
Bolton, Sarah Knowles. *Famous Leaders Among Women*. Freeport, New York: Books for Libraries Press, 1972.
Burnett, Constance Buel. *Five for Freedom*. New York: Greenwood Press, 1968.
James, Edward T., ed. *Notable American Women, 1607–1950*. Cambridge, MA: The Belknap Press of Harvard University Press, 1971.
Levinson, Nancy Smiler. *The First Women Who Spoke Out*. Minneapolis: Dillon Press, 1983.
McPherson, Stephanie Sammartino. *I Speak for the Women: A Story about Lucy Stone*. Minneapolis: Carolrhoda Books, 1992.
The New Encyclopaedia Britannica, Fifteenth Edition. Chicago: Encyclopaedia Britannica, 1989.
Whitman, Alden, ed. *American Reformers*. New York: H.W. Wilson, 1985.

STOWE
James, Edward T., ed. *Notable American Women, 1607–1950*. Cambridge, MA: The Belknap Press of Harvard University Press, 1971.
The New Encyclopaedia Britannica, Fifteenth Edition. Chicago: Encyclopaedia Britannica, 1989.
Whitman, Alden, ed. *American Reformers*. New York: H.W. Wilson, 1985.

SWARTZ
James, Edward T., ed. *Notable American Women, 1607–1950*. Cambridge, MA: The Belknap Press of Harvard University Press, 1971.

SWISSHELM
James, Edward T., ed. *Notable American Women, 1607–1950*. Cambridge, MA: The Belknap Press of Harvard University Press, 1971.
Whitman, Alden, ed. *American Reformers*. New York: H.W. Wilson, 1985.

SZOLD
James, Edward T., ed. *Notable American Women, 1607–1950*. Cambridge, MA: The Belknap Press of Harvard University Press, 1971.

TROUP
James, Edward T., ed. *Notable American Women, 1607–1950*. Cambridge, MA: The Belknap Press of Harvard University Press, 1971.
Whitman, Alden, ed. *American Reformers*. New York: H.W. Wilson, 1985.

TRUTH
James, Edward T., ed. *Notable American Women, 1607–1950*. Cambridge, MA: The Belknap Press of Harvard University Press, 1971.
Lindstrom, Aletha Jane. *Sojourner Truth: Slave, Abolitionist, Fighter for Women's Rights*. New York: Julian Messner, 1980.
Macht, Norman L. *Sojourner Truth*. New York: Chelsea House, 1992.

McKissack, Patricia and Frederick McKissack. *Sojourner Truth: Ain't I a Woman?* New York: Scholastic Books, 1992.

The New Encyclopaedia Britannica, Fifteenth Edition. Chicago: Encyclopaedia Britannica, 1989.

Ortiz, Victoria. *Sojourner Truth, A Self-Made Woman.* New York: J.B. Lippincott, 1974.

Taylor-Boyd, Susan. *Sojourner Truth.* Milwaukee: Gareth Stevens Children's Books, 1990.

Whitman, Alden, ed. *American Reformers.* New York: H.W. Wilson, 1985.

TUBMAN

Petry, Ann. *Harriet Tubman, Conductor on the Underground Railroad.* New York: Thomas Y. Crowell, 1955.

Rollins, Charlemae. *They Showed the Way: Forty American Negro Leaders.* New York: Thomas Y. Crowell, 1964.

Young, Margaret B. *Black American Leaders.* New York: Franklin Watts, 1969.

WASHINGTON

The New Encyclopaedia Britannica, Fifteenth Edition. Chicago: Encyclopaedia Britannica, 1989.

Whitman, Alden, ed. *American Reformers.* New York: H.W. Wilson, 1985.

WATTLETON

1992 Britannica Book of the Year. Chicago: Encyclopaedia Britannica, 1992.

Current Biography. New York: H.W. Wilson, January, 1990.

WOODSWORTH

The Canadian Encyclopedia, Second Edition. Edmonton, Alberta: Hurtig Publishers, 1988.

Colombo, John Robert. *Colombo's Canadian References.* Toronto: Oxford University Press, 1976.

The New Encyclopaedia Britannica, Fifteenth Edition. Chicago: Encyclopaedia Britannica, 1989.

Story, Norah. *The Oxford Companion to Canadian History and Literature.* Toronto: Oxford University Press, 1967.

WRIGHT

James, Edward T., ed. *Notable American Women, 1607–1950.* Cambridge, MA: The Belknap Press of Harvard University Press, 1971.

The New Encyclopaedia Britannica, Fifteenth Edition. Chicago: Encyclopaedia Britannica, 1989.

Whitman, Alden, ed. *American Reformers.* New York: H.W. Wilson, 1985.

YARD

Current Biography. New York: H.W. Wilson, November, 1988.

Index